ALTERNATIVE ENFORCEMENT TECHNIQUES IN EC COMPETITION LAW

—

Settlements, commitments and other novel instruments

ALTERNATIVE ENFORCEMENT TECHNIQUES IN EC COMPETITION LAW

—

Settlements, commitments and other novel instruments

Edited by

CHARLES GHEUR AND NICOLAS PETIT

Foreword by JEAN-FRANÇOIS BELLIS

BRUYLANT
BRUXELLES
2009

ISBN 978-2-8027-2688-3

D / 2009 / 0023 / 55

IMPRIMÉ EN BELGIQUE

INTRODUCTION

The enforcement of European Community competition law is witnessing yet another velvet revolution. In recent years, the European Commission has gradually introduced a range of novel procedural and institutional instruments, most of which have their roots in the Anglo-Saxon legal systems : private actions for damages, settlements and leniency applications for cartel members, negotiated commitments, sector-wide market inquiries, informal regulation via guidelines, guidance letters, and so on.

To date, legal scholars have addressed these reforms in a fragmented, piecemeal fashion. In our view, they now need to be addressed more systematically, as when viewed together it is clear that a new world of competition law enforcement – characterised by negotiation, privatisation and informal regulation – is taking shape. The myriad of changes triggered by these new legal instruments will definitely require a learning process just as painstaking as the incorporation of antitrust economics into EC competition law a decade ago.

To assist legal practitioners, academics, officials as well as firms and their legal advisers understand some of these issues, the Federation of Enterprises in Belgium (FEB) and the University of Liège's LL.M. programme in Competition and IP Law organised a conference in Brussels on 5 May 2008 entitled *Alternative Enforcement Techniques under EC Competition Law – A New Paradigm of European Competition Law*. The conference's proceedings are presented in this book. It is divided into three parts. Part I deals with private enforcement of EC competition law. Part II reviews the issue of settlements and spans both the EC settlement mechanism recently introduced by the Commission and the commitment decisions provided in Article 9 of Regulation 1/2003. Finally, Part III considers a number of transversal issues (judicial review, etc.).

The editors are grateful to Ms Daisy Marits, Ms Caroline Langevin and Julie Mestré for their invaluable support in organising the conference. We also thank all the speakers who made the publication of this book possible.

Charles GHEUR and Nicolas PETIT
Brussels, September 2008

FOREWORD

BY

JEAN-FRANÇOIS BELLIS

VAN BAEL & BELLIS
PROFESSOR AT THE INSTITUTE OF EUROPEAN STUDIES
OF THE UNIVERSITY OF BRUSSELS (ULB)

The organizers of this conference have chosen to focus the discussion on alternative enforcement techniques of European Competition law. This is a commendable initiative. Much attention has in the past been given to the use of the traditional instruments by which European Competition law is applied, namely, the formal infringement decisions adopted by the European Commission and the judgments rendered by the Community Courts. In contrast, other enforcement instruments and techniques have tended to be overlooked. The organizers have boldly raised the question of whether alternative enforcement techniques constitute a new paradigm of European Competition law. It is not clear whether the various speakers who participated in this most interesting conference have been able to provide an answer to this question but, at the very least, the discussion has shown that, as is to be expected, alternative enforcement instruments are not problem-free and should by no means be regarded as a panacea.

The first alternative enforcement technique discussed during the conference was that of private enforcement. This subject was all the more topical in view of the recent publication by the Commission of its White Paper on Damages Actions for breach of the EC Antitrust Rules. This Paper was awaited with some anxiety by the business community, which had feared that the Commission would seek to import into Europe the widely despised US private action model. The Commission had not made any attempt to disguise its interest in the US private enforcement experience but had always stressed that it wished to develop a European private action model that would avoid the "excesses" of the US system. With this in mind, the representatives of the business community present at the conference could not hide the sense of relief which they experienced upon reading the White Paper. The Commission has indeed spurned a number of features of the US private actions system, including discovery, the possibility of opt-out in collective actions, multiple damages, contingency fees and punitive damages. As noted by a number of participants at the conference, however, the fact that the White Paper does not recommend these options does not mean that they will not resurface in one form or the other in Member State legislation adopted under the impetus of the White Paper.

As the discussion has shown, the Commission's attempt to encourage the filing of private actions against undertakings involved in infringements of European Competition law raises several questions. First, one might ask why this initiative was taken in the first place. The implementation of the White Paper will require the development of special procedural mechanisms which will classify breaches of competition law as a special category of torts under Member State law. Yet breaches of competition law are not the only form of business misconduct which can inflict harm and the question may therefore be validly raised as to why they are singled out in this way. Another question raised by the White Paper initiative is whether the purpose of private actions should be only to provide compensation to the victims of breaches of competition law or whether the damages granted as a result of these private actions should also have a punitive character. While the White Paper appears to favour a compensatory approach, it may in practice often be difficult to identify and quantify the extent of the damage actually incurred by the alleged victims of breaches of competition law; any attempt to rely on assumptions or other simplifications to compute the damages awards would inevitably introduce a punitive element to the equation. Finally, it is impossible to consider the issue of private enforcement without considering at the same time that of public enforcement. As we all know, the fines imposed by the Commission for breaches of European Competition law, especially in cartel cases, are increasingly severe. There is therefore a risk of "over-enforcement" if significant damages are awarded on top of already very significant fines. The problem with private enforcement is that, contrary to what is suggested by the title of the conference, it is not necessarily an "alternative" enforcement technique. As the US experience in the field of cartels shows, public enforcement is often accompanied by private enforcement. It is submitted that fines imposed by the Commission cannot remain at the level at which they currently stand if private enforcement takes off in Europe and cartel participants find themselves subject to both Commission fines and, in addition, actions for damages brought by private plaintiffs.

The topic of commitment decisions and settlements was also hotly debated during the conference. In particular, concern was expressed that a new "settlement culture" would develop in competition cases that would marginalize the role of the Community Courts and would subject the parties to undue pressure by Commission officials. I personally do not share this concern.

As regards the settlement procedure recently introduced in EC anti-cartel proceedings, I welcome this development and regard it as a logical final component of the enforcement model brought about by the success of the leniency programme. Today, a large number of cartel cases are essentially uncontested as regards their substance since most participants routinely admit their guilt. The only issue that remains open is that of the fine. I find it increasingly anomalous that this is precisely the only question on which there cannot be any discussion with the Commission in the usual course of proceedings. Indeed, the Statement of Objections usually contains only very vague statements about the level of the fine that the Commission is considering imposing and no meaningful debate can take place on this key issue until after the Commission has adopted the decision imposing the fine. At that point, it may become apparent that mistakes were made in the determination of the fine, in which case the parties will have no choice but to lodge an appeal with the Court of First Instance. Such a scenario could be avoided if a discussion could take place with the Commission services on the level of the fine prior to the adoption of the decision. At the very least, the settlement procedure will make this discussion possible. Of course, the settlement procedure will result in the parties waiving some of the procedural guarantees offered by Regulation 1/2003, such as access to the complete file or the right to a hearing. However, to the extent that settlements would be offered only in uncontested cartel cases, the waiver of these procedural guarantees should not have any material consequences. Experience will tell whether this positive assessment of the settlement procedure is justified.

Commitment decisions under Article 9 of Regulation 1/2003 are another important alternative enforcement technique. Compared to infringement decisions under Article 7 of Regulation 1/2003, commitment decisions present the advantage for the parties concerned that they are not accompanied by fines. One of the benefits for the Commission of the commitment procedure is that it makes it possible to resolve competition concerns through a negotiated process which may produce innovative solutions that could not otherwise be achieved by an Article 7 decision. However, the 2007 *Alrosa* judgment of the Court of First Instance, currently under appeal to the Court of Justice, has cast a shadow on the usability of the commitment procedure as it seems to erase any distinction between Article 7 and Article 9 decisions. It will be interesting to see whether the Court of Justice shares the Court of First Instance's analysis on this point.

The last category of alternative enforcement mechanisms discussed during this conference consisted of a number of tools used (and sometimes not used at all) by the Commission in lieu of, or in addition to, classical enforcement decisions. This category was referred to as "sunshine enforcement instruments" by analogy to a method of intervention developed in the nineteenth century in the United States, pursuant to which unfair practices were revealed to the public through the release of statements that shone a bright light on those practices, hence the concept of "sunshine regulation". One may wonder, however, whether the interesting list of alternative methods of enforcement discussed under this category do in fact constitute alternative enforcement techniques. For instance, oral statements, press releases, or press conferences by the Commissioner for Competition or Commission officials are usually a mere complement to the adoption of classical infringement decisions. Their purpose is to give media visibility to classical enforcement decisions taken by the Commission. By the same token, articles written by Commission officials about recent cases are another form of dissemination of information about the Commission activities, which is not a substitute for actual enforcement decisions.

On the other hand, the case for regarding Commission guidelines, notices and communications as alternative enforcement mechanisms seems more compelling. It is indeed striking to observe that the areas covered by guidelines, such as, for instance, the guidelines on vertical restraints and horizontal cooperation agreements, are characterized by an almost complete absence of Commission decisions. In the field covered by Articles 81 and 82, decisions adopted by the Commission since the entry into force of Regulation 1/2003 are essentially restricted to cartels and abuses of a dominant position. The Commission appears to have lost any interest in adopting decisions concerning vertical cases or non-cartel horizontal cooperation agreements.

Two other instruments discussed under the category of "sunshine regulation", namely, guidance letters and inapplicability decisions, hardly qualify for this label : they shine no light at all for the simple reason that the Commission does not use them. Indeed, since the adoption of Regulation 1/2003, the Commission has not issued a single guidance letter or inapplicability decision. In effect, the Commission has reorganized itself as an authority that performs an essentially repressive function focused on the prosecution of cartels and abuses of a dominant position. The guidance provided by the Commission under Regulation 17/62 through the issuance of negative clearances, exemptions and comfort letters is a thing of the past. I find this evolution regrettable as I consider that an important positive dimension of the Commission's enforcement function has been lost in the process. I do not wish to be misunderstood : I am not advocating a return to the old notification system and its excessive focus on exemptions from the prohibitions but I feel that the pendulum has swung from one extreme to the other. The review of Regulation 1/2003 currently underway provides an opportunity for considering a rehabilitation of the Commission's role as an authority that does not limit itself to punishing undertakings for violating the competition rules but also provides guidance to assist them in achieving compliance with the rules.

To conclude, I wish to congratulate the organizers of this conference for having had the insight and courage to structure a discussion around this fascinating and original theme.

PART I.

Private Enforcement

THE WHITE PAPER ON DAMAGES ACTIONS FOR BREACH OF THE EC ANTITRUST RULES [1]

BY

Rainer BECKER,

Nicolas BESSOT

AND

Eddy DE SMIJTER [2]

1. – Introduction

On 2 April 2008, the European Commission adopted a White Paper on damages actions for breach of the EC antitrust rules (hereinafter "the White Paper"). [3] It presents a set of recommendations to ensure that victims of competition law infringements have access to genuinely effective mechanisms for obtaining full compensation for the harm they have suffered.

The White Paper is the latest stage of a policy initiative, the premises of which were already laid down in Regulation 1/2003 that stressed the essential role of national courts in the application of the EC competition rules, for example by awarding damages to the victims of infringements. [4] Given the importance of the right to damages in order to guarantee the effectiveness of the EC competi-

[1] This article has also been published in the EC Competition Policy Newsletter, 2008, number 2, Summer Edition.

[2] Directorate General for Competition, units A1 and B1. The content of this article does not necessarily reflect the official position of the European Commission. Responsibility for the information and views expressed lies entirely with the authors.

[3] White Paper on damages actions for breach of the EC antitrust rules COM(2008) 165, 2.4.2008. The White Paper and the accompanying Staff Working Paper (SWP) are available at http://ec.europa.eu/comm/competition/antitrust/actionsdamages/documents.html.

[4] Council Regulation 1/2003 of 16 December 2002 on the implementation of the rules on competition laid down in Articles 81 and 82 of the EC Treaty, *OJ* L1, 4.1.2003. See in particular recital 7.

tion rules, as acknowledged by the European Court of Justice (ECJ), [5] and in view of the considerable hurdles faced by the victims wishing to exercise their rights in Europe, [6] the Commission adopted in December 2005 a Green Paper [7] that identified potential ways forward.

A. – *From the 2005 Green Paper to the White Paper*

The purpose of the Green Paper was to identify the main obstacles to a more effective system of damages claims, and to set out different options for further reflection to improve both follow-on and stand-alone actions. The Green Paper was met with broad interest in the antitrust community, and achieved its objective of **raising awareness on the right to compensation of victims of competition law infringements, and on the obstacles they face when attempting to enforce their rights**.

Encouraged by the comments on the Green Paper received from stakeholders, from the European Parliament, the European Economic and Social Committee and the Member States, and taking into account the recent case law of the ECJ, the Commission decided to publish a White Paper in order to encourage and further focus the ongoing discussions on actions for damages by setting out concrete measures aimed at creating an effective private enforcement system in Europe.

The Commission also made great efforts to assess the likely benefits and costs of various policy options that could address the current ineffectiveness of antitrust damages actions in the EU. In particular, it commissioned an extensive impact study by independent experts, who used existing scientific knowledge and data to conduct their own economic analysis of the likely effects of various measures to facilitate antitrust damages actions. Building on the findings of the study, the Commission analysed and compared the likely impli-

[5] Case C-453/99, *Courage and Crehan* [2001], ECR I-6297, confirmed in joined Cases C-295/04 to C-298/04, *Manfredi* [2006], ECR I-6619.

[6] See the 2004 Comparative Study commissioned by the European Commission on the conditions of claims for damages in case of infringement of EC antitrust rules, at http://ec.europa.eu/comm/competition/antitrust/others/actions_for_damages/study.html.

[7] Green Paper on damages actions for breach of the EC antitrust rules (the "Green Paper") COM(2005) 672 final. The Green Paper and the accompanying Staff Working Paper are available at: http://ec.europa.eu/comm/competition/antitrust/actionsdamages/documents.html.

cations of the major policy options available.[8] In its White Paper, the Commission further develops the specific policy recommendations which offer a balanced solution to the current, often inefficient and ineffective, compensation systems in place, while avoiding over-incentives that could lead to excessive or abusive litigation of the kind seen in some countries outside Europe.

B. – *The key objectives and underlying principles*

Despite some recent signs of improvement in certain Member States, **the victims of EC antitrust infringements only rarely obtain reparation of the harm suffered**. In that regard, the impact study notes that successful damages actions are still rare, and that the majority of Member States have had no real experience of private antitrust damages actions to date. The ineffectiveness of the right to damages is largely due to various legal and procedural hurdles in the Member States' rules governing actions for damages. Indeed, traditional rules of civil liability and procedure are often inadequate for actions for damages in the field of competition law, due to the specificities of the actions in this field, namely : **complex factual and economic analysis, unavailability of crucial evidence and the often unfavourable risk/reward balance for claimants**.

The general objective of the White Paper is therefore to ensure that all victims of infringements of EC competition law have **access to truly effective mechanisms for obtaining full compensation** for the harm they have suffered. In designing the specific measures aimed at addressing the obstacles identified, the Commission followed three main guiding principles :

- **full compensation** is to be achieved for all victims. This necessarily entails consequences in terms of deterrence of future infringements and greater compliance with EC antitrust rules, particularly when the number of infringements detected increases;
- the legal framework for more effective antitrust damages actions is to be based on a **genuinely European approach**, with balanced measures rooted in European legal culture and traditions;

[8] The external study and the impact assessment report are available at : http://ec.europa.eu/comm/competition/antitrust/actionsdamages/index.html.

– the effective system of **private enforcement** by means of damages actions is meant to **complement, and not to replace** or jeopardise **public enforcement** of Articles 81 and 82 of the EC Treaty by the Commission and the national competition authorities (NCAs) of the Member States.

2. – Compensating the victims of competition law infringements

The focus of the White Paper on compensating victims becomes clearest when considering the scope of the damages and the passing-on of overcharges.

A. – *The scope of the damages*

(i) *Full compensation*

The ECJ confirmed in its *Manfredi* ruling that the principle of effectiveness requires Member States to **ensure that victims of competition law infringements are compensated for the actual loss** (which results from the illegal overcharge) **and the loss of profit** (which results from the reduced sales) caused to them.[9] Moreover, in order to guarantee that this harm is compensated at real (rather than nominal) value, the ECJ requires that **(pre-judgment) interest** shall **also** be paid.

In its White Paper, the Commission fully endorses this broad definition of the harm caused by competition law infringements and the resulting obligation for the Member States (which is addressed both to the national legislator and to the national judge) to enable the victim to receive such full compensation. In its Staff Working Paper, the Commission expresses the hope that this clear instruction from the ECJ will suffice to have all the obstacles to full compensation that still exist in (some of) the Member States removed. However, if it were to appear that such is not the case, the Commission may want to re-examine what further measures are necessary to achieve that objective.

[9] See *Manfredi*, *supra*, n. 4, paragraphs 60 and 95.

(ii) *The calculation of damages*

Even if it is clear under what heads of damage the victim of a competition law infringement may seek damages, the latter may still face difficulties in court because he cannot show (to the required standard) the extent of the harm suffered. For instance, under some circumstances it may be totally impossible for the victim to show the exact amount of the loss. In its White Paper and in the accompanying Staff Working Paper, the Commission formulates two suggestions to overcome these difficulties.

It first recalls that **the principle of effectiveness excludes calculation requirements**, as imposed by law or by the courts, **that make it excessively difficult for victims to obtain the damages to which they are entitled under Community law**. Legislators and, in the absence of their action, judges are thus obliged to mitigate these requirements to a more appropriate level. Naturally, the argument that such mitigation cannot be allowed because it risks deviating from the objective to compensate (the victim may obtain somewhat more, or less, than the actual damage suffered), cannot be accepted. Since compensation remains the objective, judges must do their utmost to ensure that the damages awarded correspond as far as possible to the harm suffered. This approach is clearly reflected more by an approximation of that harm than by a refusal to award damages.

Secondly, the Commission is committed to produce **non-binding guidance on the calculation of damages**, in order to provide judges and parties with pragmatic solutions to these often complicated exercises. The challenge is to produce easily accessible economic calculation models and suitable approximate methods of calculation. In order to assist the Commission in the drafting of the guidance, a study has been tendered, the results of which should be ready in Spring 2009. [10]

B. – *The passing-on of overcharges*

The compensation objective also determined the solution that was put forward in the White Paper for dealing with the passing-

[10] The tender is published under COMP/2008/A5/10, and is available at : http://ec.europa.eu/dgs/competition/proposals2/.

on of overcharges. That thorny issue, on which there is little clarity in the Member States' legislation and case-law, covers both the question (i) whether or not the infringer can invoke the passing-on defence and (ii) whether or not the one to which the overcharge has been passed on can claim damages for the resulting harm.

(i) *The passing-on defence (shield)*

Since the objective of the White Paper is to ensure that victims of competition law infringements receive compensation for the damage they have suffered, it goes without saying that, if ultimately there is no harm suffered, there should also be no compensation.[11] **Purchasers of an overcharged product or service who have been able** (meaning that they have actually done so) **to pass on that overcharge to their own customers should** therefore **not be entitled to compensation** of that overcharge. However, the passing-on of the overcharge may well have led to a reduction in sales. Such loss of profits should obviously be compensated by the one who is responsible for the initial overcharge.

In order to avoid the infringer having to pay damages for an overcharge that has been passed on, the Commission feels that he should be able to invoke the passing-on as a defence. That defence, of course, needs to be proven according to the required standards. In order not to negate the right to compensation, those standards should not be too low. For instance, the fact that a press release states that consumers are harmed by an infringement of competition law cannot constitute sufficient proof of the passing-on of the overcharges to the consumers.

(ii) *The "passing-on" claim (sword)*

The compensation objective implies, as a corollary of the acceptance of the passing-on defence, that the one to whom the overcharge has been passed on, i.e. the ultimate victim, can claim compensation for the resulting harm. However, that ultimate victim, unlike those higher up in the distribution chain, may be less inclined to start an antitrust damages action.

[11] Arguments of enforcement efficiency and deterrence are thus not accepted as autonomous arguments. They can only be accepted as secondary arguments to implement the compensation principle.

The reasons for that reluctance may be manifold, but issues of a low-value claim, an unattractive cost/reward balance, the difficulty of establishing causality with the initial infringement, remoteness, etc. will certainly be among them.

To the extent that those ultimate victims have standing to claim damages,[12] the Commission makes **two types of suggestions** to enable these victims to bring their damages claims. First, it is suggested that they can **aggregate their claims via collective actions**. Secondly, their claim can be facilitated by a **presumption that the overcharge has been passed on in its entirety to their level**. That presumption can be rebutted by the infringer, for instance by referring to the fact that he has already paid compensation for that same overcharge to someone higher up in the distribution chain than the claimant. The latter example is evident when a joint action is brought by claimants from different levels in the distribution chain, but efforts should also be made to have it apply in the case of parallel or consecutive actions. Finally it should be noted that the said rebuttable presumption does not exempt the claimant from its duty to prove the initial infringement and the scope of the damage; the latter aspect is particularly relevant when the overcharge relates to an intermediate product.

3. – Access to justice

A. – *Collective redress mechanisms*

It is clear that victims will rarely, if ever, bring a damages action individually when they have suffered scattered and relatively low-value damage. **In order to avoid these victims remaining uncompensated, it is necessary to provide for some form of collective redress.**

[12] Since the ECJ confirmed that "any individual can claim compensation for the harm suffered *where there is a causal relationship* between that harm and an agreement or practice prohibited under [EC competition law]" (see *Courage and Crehan, supra*, n. 4, paragraph 26, and *Manfredi, supra*, n. 4, paragraph 61), standing could be refused under national law due to the absence of sufficient causality, e.g. in cases of remoteness (see also *Manfredi*, paragraph 64 : "in the absence of Community rules governing the matter, it is for the domestic legal system of each Member State to prescribe the detailed rules governing the exercise of that right, including those on the application of the concept of 'causal relationship', provided that the principles of equivalence and effectiveness are observed").

The issue of collective redress is a sensitive one and has attracted attention in the Member States and at EC level because of its importance for access to justice. This increased attention is also partly due to certain excesses that have been reported from other jurisdictions. This is therefore an area where the Commission has been careful to comply with its second guiding principle of adopting a balanced and genuine European approach, and has designed appropriate safeguards so as to avoid excesses.

The Commission suggests two types of collective redress mechanism. They offer alternative means of court action for the victims, such as final consumers or SMEs, that would otherwise be unable or unwilling to seek compensation given the costs, uncertainties, risks and burdens involved.

(i) *The first mechanism : opt-in collective actions*

An opt-in collective action combines in one single action the claims from those individuals or businesses who have expressed their intention to be included in the action. Such a system improves the situation of the claimants by making the cost/benefit analysis of the litigation more attractive, since it allows them *inter alia* to reduce the costs and share the evidence.

There has been much debate on whether the Commission should suggest an opt-in mechanism, which is closer to the Member States' legal traditions, or rather an opt-out mechanism, whereby the victims represented are all those who do not expressly opt out from the action. Opt-in collective actions are said to make the litigation more complex by requiring the identification of the claimants and the specification of the harm allegedly suffered, whereas an opt-out mechanism allows a wider representation of the victims and can therefore be seen as being more efficient in terms of corrective justice and deterrence. However, combined with other features, opt-out actions in other jurisdictions have been perceived to lead to excesses. On balance, the Commission considered it more appropriate to suggest opt-in collective actions.

(ii) *The second mechanism : representative actions brought by qualified entities*

A representative action for damages is an action brought on behalf of two or more individuals or businesses who are not themselves parties to the action. It is aimed at obtaining damages for the harm caused to the interests of all those represented. **The Commission suggests that a representative action can be brought by two different types of qualified entities**.

The first type of qualified entities covers **entities such as consumer organisations, trade associations or state bodies representing legitimate and defined interests, which are officially designated *in advance* by their Member State to bring representative actions for damages**. In order to be designated, i.e. "endorsed" by their Member State, these qualified entities need to meet specific criteria set in the law. These criteria, together with the risk that the designation is withdrawn in case of excesses, will help prevent abusive litigation.

Given the nature of these qualified entities as well as the designation safeguard, the range of victims they can represent is not defined restrictively. Indeed, they are entitled to represent victims, not necessarily their members, which are identified or, in rather restricted cases, identifiable. While victims shall normally be identified either from the outset or at a later stage, the requirement of strict identification may sometimes be unnecessary, overly costly and burdensome. The possibility to represent "identifiable" victims can be relevant particularly in a case where, in view of the minimal amount of damages to be awarded and the high costs of direct distribution, the court decides that distribution should be indirect, e.g. pursuant to the cy-près doctrine. [13]

The second type of qualified entities covers **entities which are certified on an *ad hoc* basis by a Member State**, as regards a particular antitrust infringement, to bring an action on behalf of (all or some of) their members only. Eligibility is limited to entities whose primary task is to protect the defined interests of their mem-

[13] Cy-près distribution means that the damages awarded are not distributed directly to those injured to compensate for the harm they suffered but are rather used to achieve a result which is as near as may be (e.g. damages attributed to a fund protecting the victems' interests of antitrust infringements in general).

bers other than by pursuing damages claims (e.g. a trade association in a given industry). The various restrictions on standing (i.e. the ability to bring an action) are designed so as to avoid abusive actions, for instance, when led by litigation vehicles specially constituted for the sole purpose of bringing damages actions.

One could assume that opt-in collective actions are likely to be used primarily by businesses or victims having suffered a non-insignificant individual harm, as they require at the outset a positive action from the victims. In contrast, the representative action mechanism is directly targeting the victims' traditional inertia when the harm suffered individually is very low. These two complementary collective redress mechanisms, together with the possibility for the victims to bring individual actions, constitute a set of solutions that will significantly improve the victims' ability to effectively enforce their right to damages.

B. – *Limitation periods*

While acknowledging the importance of limitation periods for establishing "legal peace", the Commission feels that these limitation periods should not be such that they bar claimants from bringing a damages claim when that is still legitimate. To achieve that balance, the White Paper contains suggestions both for stand-alone and for follow-on damages cases.

With regard to stand-alone cases, the main issue relates to the commencement of the limitation period, particularly in the event of a continuous or repeated infringement or when the victim cannot reasonably have been aware of the infringement, for instance because it remained covert for a long period of time. It would clearly be odd if a limitation period were to expire while the infringement is still ongoing or where the victim is simply not aware of the infringement. **The Commission has therefore suggested that the limitation period should not start to run before a continuous or repeated infringement ceases, or before the victim of the infringement can reasonably be expected to have knowledge of the infringement and of the harm it caused him**.

To keep open the possibility of follow-on actions, the Commission considered a number of measures aimed at avoiding the limitation period expiring while public enforcement is still ongoing. One of those options was to suspend the limitation period during the public proceedings. The main drawback of that option, however, is that it may be impossible for parties to calculate the remaining period precisely, given that the opening and closure of proceedings by competition authorities are not always public knowledge. Moreover, if a suspension were to commence at a very late stage of the limitation period, there may not be enough time left to prepare a claim. **The Commission therefore suggests that a new limitation period of at least two years should start once the infringement decision on which a follow-on claimant relies has become final**. The Commission believes that such a rule would not unduly prolong the uncertainty for the infringer, while it would enable the claimant to bring a damages claim once the illegality of the behaviour has been finally established.[14]

C. – *Costs of damages actions*

Taking into account the predominant views expressed during the consultation on the Green Paper, as well as the beneficial effects of the "loser pays" principle as the main costs allocation rule in terms of preventing abusive claims, the Commission decided not to suggest any specific changes to national cost regimes. However, **costs of damages actions represent a major disincentive for victims to exercise their right to damages**, particularly for claimants whose financial situation is significantly weaker than that of the defendant, and/or in situations where cost prevents meritorious claims being brought due to the uncertainty of the outcome. The Commission therefore felt it important to encourage Member States to reflect on their cost regimes, including the level of the court fees, the cost allocation rule and the ways of funding.

In its White Paper the Commission also highlights the **necessity for Member States to give due consideration to mechanisms fostering early resolution of cases**. It notes that the effectiveness of settlement mechanisms is directly related to the effectiveness of the mechanisms for seeking redress through court actions. Indeed, settlement mechanisms alone cannot guarantee the

[14] This suggestion should thus be read in combination with the one on the probative value of NCA decisions (see point 4b below).

exercise of the victims' right to damages without there being an effective and credible judicial alternative. However, where the court alternative becomes credible – and this is the Commission's objective – early settlements are to be encouraged as they can significantly reduce or eliminate litigation costs for the parties and the costs to the judicial system.

4. – Proving the case

Different sections in the White Paper address the specific difficulties that victims of antitrust infringements frequently encounter in proving their case, both in actions following a decision by a competition authority (follow-on actions) and in stand-alone actions.[15] The measures proposed in this context concern, in particular, the disclosure *inter partes*, the effect of decisions of competition authorities and the issue of fault. The sections dealing with the passing-on issue, discussed above, contain a further proposal to facilitate proof for victims.

A. – *Access to evidence : disclosure* inter partes

Victims of antitrust infringements find themselves in a dilemma : antitrust damages cases are very fact-intensive, as the finding of an infringement, the quantum of damage and the relevant causal links all require the often unusually complex assessment of economic interrelations and effects. Much of the corresponding evidence, however, often lies inaccessibly in the hands of the infringers, who sometimes go to considerable lengths to conceal this information. **The current systems of civil procedure in many Member States offer, in practice, no effective means to overcome the information asymmetry that is typical of antitrust cases**. As a result, infringers are able to keep crucial evidence to themselves, which means that victims are discouraged from bringing a claim for compensation and, where they do, judges are not able to decide the case based on a full picture of the facts.

[15] In the White Paper (see section 1.2, *in fine*), the Commission pursues the explicit policy choice to improve the effectiveness of damages actions regardless of whether or not they follow an infringement decision by a competition authority. Even where victims can rely on such an infringement decision, they still face particular difficulties in gathering the evidence required to demonstrate the quantum and the causation of the harm.

In the sections on disclosure of evidence, **the Commission**'s desire to suggest balanced measures becomes particularly apparent. It **proposes a minimum standard** for more effective access to evidence across all EU Member States so as to avoid excesses in both directions. It is committed to avoid, on the one hand, overly wide-ranging, time-consuming and costly disclosure obligations that are prone to abuses (e.g. so-called "discovery blackmail") and, on the other hand, major obstacles to revealing the truth simply because the relevant evidence happens to be under the control of the infringer. Moreover, the White Paper puts forward a solution that is capable of integration even in those systems of civil procedure of the continental legal tradition where obligations to disclose evidence to the court and the other party are less developed.[16] To this end, the White Paper further develops a mechanism that is already part of the Member States' legal orders, namely that underlying the Intellectual Property Directive 2004/48/EC. Under this approach, **obligations to disclose arise only once a court has adopted a disclosure order and they are subject to a strict control by this court**. This central role of the judge corresponds to the systems of civil procedure that applies in the vast majority of Member States. However, for a range of continental European countries, the proposal in the White Paper would mean a significant step forward towards more effective access to evidence.

Judges could order disclosure of information, documents or other means of evidence relevant to the claim once they are satisfied that a range of conditions are met. The first condition is that **the claimant (or the defendant[17]) has asserted all the facts and offered all those means of evidence that are reasonably available to him**, provided that these are sufficient to make his claim a plausible one, i.e. he must show plausible grounds for suspecting that he suffered harm as a result of the antitrust infringement by the defendant. Member States which currently apply very strict requirements in terms of specification of facts and means of evidence would have to allow for an initial alleviation of these strict

[16] The reference to jurisdictions of the continental legal tradition is not meant to suggest homogeneity between these jurisdictions; indeed, particularly in relation to the rules on evidence, significant differences exist on the continent.

[17] For reasons of equality of arms, this disclosure in antitrust damages cases should be available not only to support claims of claimants but also defences by defendants (where in the text above reference is made to "the claimant", the same shall apply *mutatis mutandis* to defendants).

requirements in antitrust damages cases. The general standard of proof for ultimately winning a case would, however, remain unaffected. [18]

The second condition is that **the claimant is unable, applying all reasonable efforts, to produce the means of evidence for which disclosure is envisaged**. The third and fourth conditions require that the claimant has specified sufficiently **precise categories of evidence to be disclosed**, and that the envisaged disclosure measure is **relevant to the case, as well as necessary and proportional in scope**. Specification of circumscribed categories of evidence is needed to allow the court to tailor the disclosure order to what is truly necessary in order to reveal the essential facts and proportionate in view of the nature and value of the claim, the seriousness of the alleged infringement and the addressee of the order. Courts must have some discretion to appreciate the specific circumstances of each individual case, and the Staff Working Paper mentions examples of how categories of evidence can be specified in a sufficiently precise manner while being comprehensive enough not to jeopardise effective access to evidence.

Further important issues addressed include the delicate question of how and to what extent **confidential information**, such as business secrets, can be protected in the proceedings before national courts without *de facto* precluding the exercise of the right to compensation, given the fact that much of the crucial evidence is likely to be commercially sensitive. [19] Another important issue addressed is that **effective sanctions must be available in order to avoid a refusal to hand over evidence and the destruction of evidence**. [20]

Among a number of measures aimed at **preserving the effectiveness of public enforcement** and, in particular, at maintaining the effectiveness of leniency programmes, [21] the White Paper contains an important exception to the disclosure obligations. "Corporate statements", i.e. the voluntary presentations by a company

[18] See SWP, paragraph 91.

[19] See SWP, paragraphs 112 *et seq.* On the need of balancing the right to judicial protection of victims of infringements of EC law and the right to privacy of the infringer see, in a different context, Case C-275/06, *Productores de Música de España (Promusicae) v Telefónica de España SAU* (not yet reported).

[20] See in more detail SWP, paragraphs 128 *et seq.*

[21] See in more detail SWP, chapter 10.

of its knowledge of a cartel and role therein which are drawn up specially for submission under the leniency programme,[22] should be protected against disclosure. This protection applies to all applications (successful or not) submitted under EC and national leniency programmes when the enforcement of Article 81 EC is at issue. A similar form of protection may be appropriate in the context of voluntary presentations as part of settlement submissions.

B. – *Probative value of NCA decisions*

Where a breach of EC antitrust rules has been found in a decision by the European Commission, victims can rely on this decision as binding proof in civil proceedings for damages (see Article 16(1) of Regulation 1/2003). There is a range of compelling reasons for a similar rule in relation to decisions by national competition authorities when they find a breach of Article 81 or 82. At present, such a rule exists in the national law of only some Member States.[23] The Commission suggests that **a final decision by an NCA and a final judgment by a review court upholding the NCA decision or itself finding an infringement should be accepted in every Member State as irrebuttable proof of the infringement in subsequent civil antitrust damages cases**.

Such a rule would not only increase legal certainty,[24] especially for victims of infringements, and enhance the consistency in the application of Articles 81 and 82 by different national bodies. It would also – and this is very important in terms of the effectiveness of antitrust damages actions significantly increase the procedural efficiency of actions for antitrust damages and reduce the difficulties that the victims encounter when they have to prove their case. Without such a rule, infringers would be allowed to call into question their own breach of the law that has already been established in a binding decision by an NCA and, possibly, confirmed by a review court. Victims would have to formally prove, and courts in the civil proceedings would have to re-examine, all the facts and legal issues already investigated and assessed by a specialised public

[22] See points 6 and 31 of the EC Leniency Notice.

[23] See the references in footnote 65 of the SWP to the rules, for instance, in Germany, Hungary and the UK.

[24] See on this aspect in relation to civil proceedings following a Commission decision Case C-234/89, *Stergios Delimitis v Henninger-Bräu AG*, ECR [1991] I-935, paragraph 47.

authority and often by a review court, the latter being the best placed body to ensure the legal and factual accuracy of NCA decisions. Such "re-litigation" would usually entail lengthy disputes between the parties and their legal and economic experts. This would not only add to the already considerable costs and duration of antitrust damages actions, but it would also be a factor which further increases the uncertainty of the victim's action for damages.

The rule suggested in the White Paper is (to some extent) modelled on Article 16(1) of Regulation 1/2003, i.e. based on a legal mechanism that is already part of the Member States' legal order and that is not, as further explained in the Staff Working Paper,[25] at odds with the principles of an independent judiciary and separation of powers.

The Commission does not limit the binding effect of an NCA decision to the domestic courts of the same Member State. This is not surprising given the cooperation and mutual consultation provided for in Regulation 1/2003, and given the objectives of legal certainty, consistency in the application of Articles 81 and 82 and enhancing the effectiveness of antitrust damages claims across the EU. Indeed, limiting the binding effect of NCA decisions to only one Member State would create a serious disincentive for victims of multi-state infringements (found by NCAs of several Member States) to concentrate their claims for compensation in one court. Such concentration of proceedings has obvious advantages in terms of consistency and procedural efficiency for claimants, defendants and the judicial system alike. In the context of multi-jurisdictional cases, Article 6(1) of Regulation 44/2001 explicitly provides for tort victims to be able to cumulate their damages actions against all co-defendants before one court of the country where at least one of them is domiciled.

The Commission sees no need for an exception to the binding effect of NCA decisions from another Member State. All Member States are legally bound to fully respect the rights of defence and fair trial pursuant the European Convention on Human Rights and the EU Charter on Fundamental Rights,[26] and the corresponding possibilities of judicial review exist.[27]

---

[25] See paragraphs 148 *et seq.*, see also footnote 64 of the SWP.
[26] See Article 6 of the Convention and Articles 47(2) and 48 of the Charter.

C. – *The fault requirement*

A final topic that is covered by the White Paper and which is relevant in the context of proving a case relates to the fault requirement. In some Member States it is sufficient to prove the infringement of the EC competition rules (and of course also the damage it has caused) in order to be awarded damages. Other Member States, however, require the claimant also to show that the infringer committed a fault, meaning that he acted intentionally or negligently. The idea behind this additional requirement is that infringers who did not know that they were breaking the law should not be held liable for the negative consequences of their behaviour. The Commission feels that the full application of this requirement to breaches of directly applicable EC public policy rules, such as the EC competition rules, cannot be reconciled with the principle of effectiveness of those rules.[28] That is not only the case because the burden of proving the fault lies with the claimant, who is often unlikely to have information that allows him to show intent or negligence. **The fault requirement in itself also introduces a difficulty to the acquisition of damages which can be disproportionate to the objective it seeks to achieve**.

The Commission understands, however, that **in some exceptional cases, it should be possible for the infringer to escape liability**. Such is the case when the infringer has taken every precaution that can be reasonably expected from him and nevertheless is found to have infringed the competition rules. That kind of **excusable error** on which the infringer can rely by way of defence may occur in novel and complex situations. Mere ignorance of the law, however, clearly cannot render an error excusable; one is bound by the law even if one has no knowledge of it. It will thus normally be irrelevant whether or not the undertaking actually realised that it was infringing Articles 81 or 82. Equally, reliance on wrong legal or other professional advice, as such, cannot exonerate an undertaking. Errors based on incorrect official state-

[27] The Commission, nonetheless, would not object if a Member State were to apply, as a further safeguard, an exception to the binding effect analogous to that contained in Article 34(1) of Regulation 44/2001 with respect to fair legal process; see SWP, paragraph 162.

[28] See, in this context, also the case law of the ECJ which only names the infringement and the damage caused as conditions for a right to damages (cf., the quote of *Manfredi* in footnote 11).

ments by competent public entities, such as competition authorities and courts, should only be excusable where undertakings applying a high standard of care could reasonably rely on such statements.

5. – Outlook

The analysis in the White Paper and its accompanying documents has shown that measures such as those discussed above are indispensable in order to address the obstacles faced by victims and to make the right to damages a realistic possibility for citizens and businesses across the EU. The Staff Working Paper concludes by recalling the Commission's view that some aspects of the issues listed in the White Paper may require EC legislative action to ensure the effectiveness of antitrust damages actions. In addition, it recommends the codification of the key aspects of the *acquis communautaire* and drawing up of non-binding guidance on the calculation of damages.

All of this will, of course, be reflected upon further in the light of the results of the consultation process. The period of public consultation ran until 15 July and more than 170 stakeholders submitted their comments on the White Paper and the accompanying documents, in particular the Staff Working Paper.

THE WHITE PAPER FOR DAMAGES ACTIONS : PUTTING THE COMMUNITY RIGHT TO DAMAGES IN EFFECT

BY

ASSIMAKIS P. KOMNINOS [1]

I. – INTRODUCTION

The publication in April 2008 by the European Commission of the long-awaited White Paper on Damages actions for breach of the EC antitrust rules ("WP") [2] has again brought EC private antitrust enforcement to the forefront. This article attempts to explain how we got to the WP in the first place and how European Community law, in particular the European Court of Justice's rulings, have set the ground for the latest developments. It also proceeds to an appraisal of the WP and of some of its proposals, in light of pre-existing Community law.

[1] Dr Assimakis P. Komninos practices law in Brussels with White & Case LLP and is the author of *EC Private Antitrust Enforcement, Decentralised Application of EC Competition Law by National Courts*, Hart Publishing, Oxford/Portland, 2008. The present views strictly academic and personal.

[2] *Commission White Paper on Damages Actions for Breach of the EC Antitrust Rules*, COM(2008) 165 final. This comes as a follow-up after the publication in December 2005 of a Green Paper but is also a prelude for Community legislation. In the EU jargon, a "White Paper" is a document containing proposals for Community action in a specific area. It sometimes follows a "Green Paper" published to launch a consultation process at European level. While Green Papers set out a range of ideas presented for public discussion and debate, White Papers contain an official set of proposals in specific policy areas and are a prelude to Community legislation. The WP itself is a rather short document that in reality summarises the far more developed Staff Working Paper ("SWP") (*Commission Staff Working Paper Accompanying the White Paper on Damages Actions for Breach of the EC Antitrust Rules*, SEC(2008) 404) and an impressive 600-page long Impact Assessment Study (*Making Antitrust Damages Actions More Effective in the EU : Welfare Impact and Potential Scenarios, Final Report for the European Commission*, 30 March 2008), which is itself usefully summarised in a Commission Impact Assessment Report (*Commission Staff Working Document Accompanying the White Paper on Damages Actions for Breach of the EC Antitrust Rules*, Impact Assessment, SEC(2008) 405). In the present article when reference is made to the "WP", such reference in most cases covers the whole of the recent Commission policy initiative and not just the short document which bears that title.

II. – The road to the White Paper

A. – *The "European" Context of Antitrust Rights and Remedies*

The application of EC competition law by civil courts, though not particularly developed in Europe, has not been a recent phenomenon. Indeed, the very first preliminary reference made by a national court to Luxembourg under the old Article 177 EEC, was a competition case where EC competition law arose in the context of private litigation.[3] Of course, the mere *application* of the competition rules by national courts cannot be said to amount to a system of private antitrust *enforcement*. The term "enforcement" signifies an instrumental role of private actions in the sense of the private litigants not just seeking redress but also in effect becoming themselves actors in enhancing the overall efficiency and effectiveness of the competition enforcement system. It is only very recently that private antitrust enforcement appears for the first time as a meaningful complement – though certainly not an alternative – to public enforcement.

The road was opened by the *modernisation* and *decentralisation* European reforms in the years 1999 to 2004. But it has also come as a consequence of ground-breaking rulings by the European Court of Justice, which has extended the scope of remedies available to individuals by Community law to cover also individual civil liability and has always imposed stringent conditions on national substantive and procedural law, in order to ensure the effectiveness of the EC competition rules. The Court of Justice has indeed been particularly bold in this field due to mainly historical reasons : the Community competition rules have long been recognised as having "horizontal direct effect", i.e. they apply to legal relationships between individuals, and at the same time they have been treated with a high degree of deference as part of the Community's "economic constitution", thus enjoying an increased normative value.

At the heart of private antitrust enforcement in Europe lies the question of the relationship between Community and national laws. At the current stage of European integration, rights and obligations ema-

[3] Case 13/61, *Kledingverkoopbedrijf de Geus en Uitdenbogerd* v. *Robert Bosch GmbH and Maatschappij tot voortzetting van de zaken der Firma Willem van Rijn*, [1962] ECR 45.

nating from Community law are in principle enforced under national law and before national courts. The Community legal order is not a federal one and the Community acts only within the limits of the powers conferred upon it by the EC Treaty. The Community standard is that Community law is enforced primarily by having recourse to national administrative, civil and criminal law before national administrative authorities (*administration communautaire indirecte*)[4] and national courts (*juges communautaires de droit commun*).[5]

Thus, speaking about private law disputes, on the side of *substance*, there is no Community law of contract, tort or unjustified enrichment, or a European Civil Code. Indeed, even if the Community had the power or intention to legislate in such a vast cross-sector area, it would be almost impossible to arrive at a common denominator applicable throughout the EU Member States, taking into account the century-long divisions in the European legal systems and families. Equally, on the side of *procedure*, there are no Community courts of full jurisdiction that could apply Community law and deal with Community law-based claims. Thus national

[4] On this Community transformation of national administrative authorities see in general Dubey, "Administration indirecte et fédéralisme d'exécution en Europe", 39 *CDE* 87 (2003), pp. 87 *et seq.* See also Temple LANG, "The Duties of National Authorities under Community Constitutional Law", 23 *ELRev.* 109 (1998); KAKOURIS, "Special Administrative Courts of the Member States and the Court of the European Communities", in : KAKOURIS (Ed.), *Perspectives, Droit communautaire européen, Théorie générale du droit, Domaine méta-juridique* (Athens/Komotini, 1998), p. 513; SYDOW, "Europäisierte Verwaltungsverfahren", 45 *JuS* 97 (2005), p. 97. See also case C-453/00, *Kühne & Heitz NV* v. *Productschap voor Pluimvee en Eieren*, [2004] ECR I-837, para. 20 : "it is for all the authorities of the Member States to ensure observance of the rules of Community law within the sphere of their competence".

[5] See *inter alia* EHLERMANN, "Ein Plädoyer für die dezentrale Kontrolle der Anwendung des Gemeinschaftsrechts durch die Mitgliedstaaten", in : CAPOTORTI, EHLERMANN *et al.* (Eds.), *Du droit international au droit de l'intégration, Liber Amicorum Pierre Pescatore* (Baden-Baden, 1987), pp. 217 *et seq.*; O. DUBOS, *Les juridictions nationales, juge communautaire, Contribution à l'étude des transformations de la fonction juridictionnelle dans les États-membres de l'Union européenne* (Paris, 2001). On this *dédoublement fonctionnel* as to national authorities and courts see in general R. LECOURT, *L'Europe des juges* (Brussels, 1976), pp. 8-9; D. SIMON, *Le système juridique communautaire* (Paris, 2001), pp. 163-164, 167; RADERMACHER, "Gemeinschaftsrechtliche Staatshaftung für höchstrichterliche Entscheidungen", 23 *NVwZ* 1415 (2004), p. 1416; CANIVET, "Les réseaux de juges au sein del'Union européenne : Raisons, nécessités et réalisations", in : IDOT & POILLOT-PERUZZETTO (Eds.), *Internormativité et réseaux d'autorités, L'ordre communautaire et les nouvelles formes de relations* (Toulouse, 24 Octobre 2003), Petites Affiches, 5-10-2004, No. 199, 45, p. 46. See also case T-51/89, *Tetra Pak Rausing SA* v. *Commission*, [1990] ECR II-309, para. 42 : "when applying Article 86 [now 82]... the national courts are acting as Community courts of general jurisdiction". Compare, however, AG Léger's Opinion in case C-224/01, *Gerhard Köbler* v. *Austria*, [2003] ECR I-10239, para. 66, who sees the *dédoublement fonctionnel* more symbolically than literally : "That expression must not be understood literally, but symbolically : where a national court is called upon to apply Community law, it is in its capacity as an organ of a Member State, and not as a Community organ, as a result of dual functions."

courts act also as "Community courts" of full jurisdiction (*juges communautaires de droit commun*).

It is true that in the last twenty years much has changed, and one can now speak of a *positive integration* drive to unify or harmonise rules on remedies and procedures. However, with very few exceptions, these are sectoral rules applying to very specific areas that are considered important for the attainment of some very specific Community objectives and the reality remains that there are no cross-sector Community rules of administrative or civil law dealing with the enforcement of Community law-based rights. [6]

Consequently, natural and legal persons relying upon Articles 81 and 82 EC would have no other means to pursue their civil claims but through access to national courts and laws. [7] However, the substantive and procedural conditions of civil antitrust enforcement can be quite different in Europe depending on which national law applies and which national court adjudicates. Inconsistencies and inadequacies in national laws on remedies and procedures are certainly a source of serious concern, not just for EC competition law but for Community law in general. In this context, the problem can be identified in three different albeit interconnected levels :

Firstly, there is a problem of *effective or adequate judicial protection*, i.e. the effective protection of Community rights. [8] This is a principle not only of Community law but also of human rights. Indeed, effective judicial protection in the access to the courts configuration derives from Articles 6 and 13 of the European Convention of Human Rights. [9] As far as Community law is concerned, as the Court of Justice has recognised, Articles 81 and 82 EC "tend by their very nature to produce direct effects in relations between indi-

[6] See A.P. KOMNINOS, *EC Private Antitrust Enforcement, Decentralised Application of EC Competition Law by National Courts* (Oxford/Portland, 2008), pp. 142-144.

[7] See, however, below on the new line of case law, in particular the *Courage* and *Manfredi* rulings (cited below).

[8] Among the abundant works on this principle central to Community law, see VAN GERVEN, "Of Rights and Remedies in the Enforcement of European Community Law before National Courts : From the Communitarization of Domestic Law towards the Europeanization of Community Law", VIII(1) *Collected Courses of the Academy of European Law* (1997) 241, pp. 247 *et seq.*; T. TRIDIMAS, *The General Principles of EC Law* (Oxford, 1999), pp. 276 *et seq.*; RODRÌGUEZ IGLESIAS, "Judicial Protection of the Citizen under European Law", in : MARKESINIS (Ed.), *The Clifford Chance Millennium Lectures, The Coming together of the Common Law and the Civil Law* (Oxford/Portland, 2000), pp. 195 *et seq.*

[9] See among others A.D. PLIAKOS, *Le principe général de la protection juridictionnelle efficace en droit communautaire* (Athens/Brussels, 1997), pp. 101 *et seq.*

viduals [and] create direct rights in respect of the individuals concerned which the national courts must safeguard". Failure to afford this safeguard "would mean depriving individuals of rights which they hold under the Treaty itself".[10]

Secondly, there is a problem for the *effectiveness* of the whole system of Community law as such and, more particularly, for the *efficiency* of the Community (competition) rules. There are *two facets* here. One is Community law-specific and the other is competition law-specific. The first facet of the problem is that when citizens pursue their Community rights before the *juges communautaires de droit commun*, in addition to serving their private interests, they are also instrumental for and indirectly act in the Community interest, becoming "the principal 'guardians' of the legal integrity of Community law in Europe".[11] The "direct effect" doctrine was developed partly with this consideration in mind. The second competition law-specific facet refers to the "private attorney-general" role of individuals in antitrust cases. In a mature antitrust system, private enforcement is a necessary complement of public enforcement and by no means inferior or weaker. In such a system, private actions, particularly actions for damages, are crucial for the efficiency of the system as a whole.[12]

Thirdly, the disparities and inadequacies of national legal systems offend against the principle of *consistent and uniform application of Community law*. It has been persuasively argued that the requirement of uniform application or enforcement is not "an all-embracing *principle* which does not allow for national principles".[13] Therefore, national remedial and procedural discrepancies to a certain extent are unavoidable.[14] It is arguable, however, that such

[10] Case 127/73, *Belgische Radio en Televisie and Societé Belge des Auteurs, Compositeurs et Editeurs de Musique* v. *SV SABAM and NV Fonior (I)*, [1974] ECR 51, paras. 16 and 17.

[11] See J.H.H. Weiler, *The Constitution of Europe, 'Do the New Clothes have an Emperor?' and Other Essays on European Integration* (Cambridge, 1999), p. 20.

[12] On this particular point, see below the analysis of the ECJ's *Courage* ruling.

[13] See Van Gerven, "Of Rights, Remedies and Procedures», 37 *CML Rev.* 501 (2000), p. 503 (emphasis in the original text). The author goes on to argue that "although the objective of uniform enforcement of Community law throughout the Community is a fundamental requirement of the Community legal order that must be pursued as much as possible, it is not a Community law principle of the same nature as direct effect, supremacy, or access to a court» (p. 522).

[14] See AG Reischl's Opinion in case 61/79, *Amministrazione delle finanze dello Stato* v. *Denkavit italiana Srl.*, [1980] ECR 1205, at 1233: "That the legal position of the individual may... differ in the various Member States is simply a consequence of the implementation of Community law by the Member States, which is accepted by the Community legal system".

discrepancies are particularly regrettable from an EC *competition* law point of view, because they tend to create variations in the costs of enforcing the EC antitrust rules, and thus lead to unequal conditions of competition among the Member States.

In the decentralised system of EC antitrust enforcement the problem is exacerbated. Competitors and economic actors in general take the likelihood of public or private antitrust action seriously into account in defining their market strategies. In this context, damages have an especially powerful impact on business behaviour. An economic operator's exploitation of its "immunity" from civil actions in damages and failure to compensate victims adequately in one jurisdiction, as opposed to other jurisdictions where companies are constantly successfully or unsuccessfully defending civil antitrust actions and victims can be fully compensated, is hardly compatible with the creation of "a level playing field for agreements, decisions by associations of undertakings and concerted practices within the internal market", as Regulation 1/2003 propagates.[15]

The Court of Justice has consistently recognised the "procedural and institutional autonomy" of the Member States to identify the remedies, courts and procedures that are necessary for the exercise of Community law rights at the national level.[16] The term "proce-

---

[15] *Council Regulation 1/2003 of 16 December 2002 on the Implementation of the Rules on Competition Laid down in Articles 81 and 82 of the Treaty*, *OJ* [2003] L1/1, Recital 8. See also Recital 1, which speaks of the necessity for Arts. 81 and 82 EC to "be applied effectively and *uniformly* in the Community" (emphasis added), and the Impact Assessment Form of the September 2000 Regulation proposal (*Commission Proposal for a Council Regulation on the Implementation of the Rules on Competition Laid Down in Articles 81 and 82 of the Treaty and Amending Regulations (EEC) No 1017/68, (EEC) No 2988/74, (EEC) No 4056/86 and (EEC) No 3975/87 ("Regulation Implementing Articles 81 and 82 of the Treaty")*, COM(2000) 582 final, *OJ* [2000] C 365E/284, p. 56), where reference is made to a "level playing field for companies in the internal market by ensuring more widespread application of the Community competition rules".

[16] The Court of Justice has, until recently, avoided to refer explicitly to the Member States' "procedural autonomy". From 2004 and onwards this is no longer the case. See case C-201/02, *The Queen ex parte Delena Wells* v. *Secretary of State for Transport, Local Government and the Regions*, [2004] ECR I-723, para. 70 : "Under Article 10 EC the competent authorities are obliged to take, within the sphere of their competence, all general or particular measures for remedying the failure to carry out an assessment of the environmental effects of a project as provided for in Article 2(1) of Directive 85/337. The detailed procedural rules applicable in that context are a matter for the domestic legal order of each Member State, *under the principle of procedural autonomy of the Member States*, provided that they are not less favourable than those governing similar domestic situations (principle of equivalence) and that they do not render impossible in practice or excessively difficult the exercise of rights conferred by the Community legal order (principle of effectiveness)" (emphasis added). See also case C-212/04, *Konstantinos Adeneler et al.* v. *Ellinikos Organismos Galaktos (ELOG)*, [2006] ECR I-6057, para. 95; case C-53/04, *Cristiano Marrosu and Gianluca Sardino* v. *Azienda Ospedaliera Ospedale San Martino di Genova e Cliniche Universitarie Convenzionate*, [2006] ECR I-7213, para. 52; case C-180/04, *Andrea Vas-*

dural autonomy" creates the incorrect impression that this principle refers only to national rules of civil, administrative or criminal procedure. In fact its scope is much larger and covers all substantive or procedural mechanisms at national level that can be used for the enforcement of Community law. That is why the term "remedial/procedural autonomy" is preferable. Besides, it is not always clear in the national legal systems where substance stops and procedure begins, or *vice versa*.[17]

More importantly, however, the Court has imposed demanding Community limits and safeguards upon that autonomy. These are the principles of *equality* and *effectiveness*.[18] The first principle means that the enforcement of Community law at the national level should not be subject to more onerous procedures than the enforcement of comparable national law. The second principle is a much more demanding test. It means that although Community-derived rights will have to count on national substantive and procedural remedies for their enforcement, such remedies still have to be *effective* and must not render the exercise and enforcement of those rights impossible or unjustifiably onerous. It reflects a more general guiding principle of Community law, full and useful effectiveness (*effet utile*).

Undoubtedly those two requirements make national divergences less burdensome. The Court of Justice has, nevertheless, proceeded further than that. Starting with such cases as *Francovich*, *Factortame I* and *Zuckerfabrik Süderdithmarschen*,[19] it has also recognised the existence of certain autonomous Community law remedies for

---

sallo v. *Azienda Ospedaliera Ospedale San Martino di Genova e Cliniche Universitarie Convenzionate*, [2006] ECR I-7251, para. 37; case C-1/06, *Bonn Fleisch Ex- und Import GmbH* v. *Hauptzollamt Hamburg-Jonas*, [2007] ECR I-5609, para. 41.

[17] See on this question BERGÉ and SINOPOLI, "Droit des obligations et autonomie procédurale : La distinction fond/procédure sous le double éclairage du droit communautaire et du droit des États membres", *Petites Affiches*, 24-8-2004, No. 169, 7, pp. 8-10.

[18] See e.g. case 33/76, *Rewe-Zentralfinanz eG and Rewe-Zentral AG* v. *Landwirtschaftskammer für das Saarland*, [1976] ECR 1989, para. 5; case 45/76, *Comet BV* v. *Produkschap voor Siergewassen*, [1976] ECR 2043, paras. 12-13; case 130/79, *Express Dairy Foods Ltd.* v. *Intervention Board for Agricultural Produce*, [1980] ECR 1887, para. 12; case 199/82, *Amministrazione delle Finanze dello Stato* v. *San Giorgio*, [1983] ECR 3595, para. 12; case C-261/95, *Rosalba Palmisani* v. *Istituto Nazionale della Previdenza Sociale (INPS)*, [1997] ECR I-4025, para. 27.

[19] Joined cases C-6/90 and C-9/90, *Andrea Francovich et al.* v. *Italy*, [1991] ECR I-5357; case C-213/89, *Regina* v. *Secretary of State for Transport, ex parte Factortame Ltd. et al. (I)*, [1990] ECR I-2433; joined cases 143/88 and C-92/89, *Zuckerfabrik Süderdithmarschen AG* v. *Hauptzollamt Itzehoe* and *Zuckerfabrik Soest GmbH* v. *Hauptzollamt Paderborn*, [1991] ECR I-415, respectively.

Community law-based rights, and has delegated to national law only the very specific conditions for their exercise, as well as the procedural framework rules, always within the limitations of equality and effectiveness. In doing so, it has been guided by the principle *ubi ius, ibi remedium*, under which a Community law right must be protected through an appropriate corresponding remedy, and has relied upon "the full effectiveness of Community rules and the effective protection of the rights which they confer" and upon the duties that Article 10 EC imposes on Member States and their judicial organs.[20]

A former Advocate General of the Court of Justice and eminent scholar of Community law has therefore proposed a more global approach to the issue of remedies in Community law, thus stressing the requirement of effective judicial protection which better describes the Court's case law on remedies. Professor Van Gerven speaks of four already existing Community substantive remedies : a general one, to have national measures that conflict with EC law set aside; and three specific ones, compensation, interim relief and restitution.[21] Individual civil liability is integrated in the first limb of these three specific remedies, beside its admittedly much more developed sibling, state liability. The former Advocate General further makes a distinction between the "constitutive" and "executive" elements of remedies. The first pertain to the principle of the remedy as such; the second to its "content and extent". The first type of elements must be uniform, since they are entirely connected with the Community "right" of which individuals avail themselves. The executive elements, on the other hand, may to a certain extent be governed by national law, but only under more substantial Community requirements. For these elements, Community law should require an "adequacy test", rather than a mere "minimum effectiveness" or "non-impossibility" test which may continue to apply for simple procedural rules.[22]

[20] Joined cases C-46/93 and C-48/93, *Brasserie du Pêcheur SA* v. *Germany* and *Regina* v. *Secretary of State for Transport, ex parte Factortame Ltd. et al. (Factortame III)*, [1996] ECR I-1029, para. 39.

[21] See VAN GERVEN, *supra* note 13, p. 503.

[22] *Idem*, pp. 502-504, 524-526.

B. – *The Court of Justice and Private Remedies in EC Competition Law*

1. *Courage v. Crehan*

Until 2001, the Court of Justice never had the opportunity to rule on the issue of civil liabilities arising from the violation of EC competition rules, although in some instances it referred to possible damages and other civil claims that private parties could pursue before national courts,[23] but without touching upon the question of the Community or national legal basis.

Outside the area of competition law, however, the Court incrementally imposed severe limits on national institutional and remedial/procedural autonomy, first stressing the Community law requirements of non-discrimination/equality and adequacy/effectiveness, and ultimately recognising the existence, as a matter of Community law, of Community remedies available to individuals. Thus there was an impressive development from the early case law, where it was stated that Community law imposed no duties on national laws and courts to introduce new remedies,[24] to a more pro-active approach, notably with rulings dealing with remedies in the fields of social policy and sex discrimination,[25] interim protection[26] and, ultimately, state liability for breaches of EC law.[27] In particular, the Community principle of state liability for breaches of EC law by Member States, established in *Francovich*, increasingly led commentators to argue that a right to damages in cases of EC

---

[23] This was already implicit in *BRT* v. *SABAM I*, *supra* note 10, paras. 16 and 22. Reference should also be made to case C-242/95, *GT-Link A/S* v. *De Danske Statsbaner*, [1997] ECR I-4349, para. 57; case C-282/95 P, *Guérin Automobiles* v. *Commission*, [1996] ECR I-1503, para. 39.

[24] Case 158/80, *Rewe-Handelsgesellschaft Nord mbH and Rewe-Markt Steffen* v. *Hauptzollamt Kiel (Butter-buying Cruises)*, [1981] ECR 1805.

[25] See e.g. case 14/83, *Sabine von Colson and Elisabeth Kamann* v. *Land Nordhein-Westfalen*, [1984] ECR 1891; case C-177/88, *Elisabeth Johanna Pacifica Dekker* v. *Stichting Vormingscentrum voor Jong Volwassenen (VJV-Centrum) Plus*, [1990] ECR I-3941; case C-271/91, *M.H. Marshall v. Southampton and South West Hampshire Area Health Authority (Marshall II)*, [1993] ECR I-4367. All these cases stressed the principle according to which sanctions for enforcement of Community law must be able to guarantee real and effective judicial protection to the discrimination victim, and must have a real deterrent effect on the employer who has breached the pertinent rules.

[26] See in particular *Factortame I*, *supra* note 19.

[27] *Francovich*, *supra* note 18; *Brasserie du Pêcheur/Factortame III*, *supra* note 20. See also, for an analysis of this development of the case law, M. DOUGAN, *National Remedies before the Court of Justice, Issues of Harmonisation and Differentiation* (Oxford/Portland, 2004), pp. 227 et *seq*.

competition law infringements was a matter of EC and not of national law. It was thought that there was no compelling reason to differentiate between state and individual liability for damage caused by infringements of Community law, since the basis for such liability, which is the principle of *effet utile* or effectiveness of Community law, is not affected by the identity of the perpetrator, i.e. whether it is the state or individuals.[28]

Meanwhile, a powerful boost to that line of argument was given in 1993 by Advocate General Van Gerven in his Opinion in *Banks*,[29] in which he argued extensively in favour of recognising a Community right to obtain reparation in respect of loss and damage sustained as a result of an undertaking's infringement of the directly effective Community competition rules.[30] The Advocate General considered in his carefully structured Opinion that the general basis established by the Court in *Francovich* also applied to the case of "breach of a right which an individual derives from an obligation imposed by Community law on another individual" :

> "The full effect of Community law would be impaired if the former individual or undertaking did not have the possibility of obtaining reparation from the party who can be held responsible for the breach of Community law – all the more so, evidently, if a directly effective provision of Community law is infringed."[31]

In competition law, in particular, the Advocate General observed that such a Community right to damages would make the Treaty antitrust rules "more operational", adducing an argument from the US system of antitrust enforcement, where civil suits for damages have played a dominant role.[32] Interestingly enough, he then went on to draw up "detailed rules governing an action for damages in respect of breach of the rules of Community law" and, more specifically, "uniform conditions of liability", relying on the Court's case law on the non-contractual liability of the Community

---

[28] For the first attempts to deduce a Community principle of individual civil liability in EC competition law cases from *Francovich*, see SMITH, "The *Francovich* Case : State Liability and the Individual's Right in damages", 13 *ECLR* 129 (1992), p. 132; HOSKINS, *"Garden Cottage Revisited : The Availability of Damages in the National Courts for Breaches of the EEC Competition Rules"*, 13 *ECLR* 257 (1992), p. 259.

[29] Case C-128/92, *H.J. Banks & Co. Ltd.* v. *British Coal Corporation*, [1994] ECR I-1209.

[30] *Banks*, *supra* note 29, AG's Opinion, paras. 37 *et seq.*

[31] *Op.c it.*, para. 43.

[32] *Op. cit.*, para. 44.

(Article 288(2) EC).[33] In *Banks*, however, the Court declined to address all these fundamental issues, because it reached the conclusion that the only set of rules applicable to the facts, Articles 65 and 66 ECSC, did not have direct effect.

Notwithstanding this missed opportunity, advocates of a Community remedy of damages for antitrust violations drew further support from the progressively more elaborate jurisprudence of the Court of Justice on state liability, notably in *Brasserie du Pêcheur/ Factortame III*, but also from the Court's shift towards a more remedies-oriented case law, where effective judicial protection acquired a central role, as a complement of or corollary to the fundamental principle of direct effect. In 1999, a groundbreaking monograph written by Clifford Jones persuasively argued in favour of a private enforcement system in Europe, after demolishing many of the misconceptions of European scholars as to the exceptionality and non-transposability of the mature US system of private antitrust enforcement.[34] A point central to that study was the view that there was a right under EC law allowing claims for damages from undertakings which had violated Articles 81 and 82 EC, in the line of the *Francovich* and *Brasserie du Pêcheur/Factortame III* judgments.[35] This monograph was to be quite influential with the Court of Justice.

The fundamental issue of the Community or national law basis of the right to damages in EC competition law violations was finally addressed by the Court of Justice in its *Courage* ruling of 20 September 2001.[36] There, the Court recognised a right to damages as a matter of Community rather than national law, and stressed the fundamental character of the EC competition rules in the overall system of the Treaty.

The facts of *Courage* were rather undistinguished. Breweries in Britain usually own pubs which they lease to tenants, while the lat-

---

[33] *Op. cit.*, paras. 46 *et seq.* According to AG Van Gerven, there were three conditions for liability in damages to arise: damage, a causal connection between the breach and the ensuing damage, and the illegality of the alleged conduct. It should be stressed that at that time the Court had not yet accepted the transposability of the then Art. 215(2) EC case law to the liability of Member States, as it did later (*Brasserie du Pêcheur/Factortame III*, *supra* note 20, para. 42), although AG Mischo in *Francovich* had already so suggested (*Francovich*, *supra* note 19, AG's Opinion, para. 71).

[34] C.A. Jones, *Private Enforcement of Antitrust Law in the EU, UK and USA* (Oxford, 1999).

[35] See *idem*, p. 72.

[36] Case C-453/99, *Courage Ltd.* v. *Bernard Crehan*, [2001] ECR I-6297.

ter are under contractual obligations to buy almost all the beer they serve from their landlords. In 1991 Mr. Bernard Crehan signed a 20-year lease with Courage Ltd. whereby he had to buy a fixed minimum quantity of beer exclusively from Courage, while the brewery undertook to supply the specified quantities at prices shown in the tenant's price list. The rent was initially lower than the market rate and it was subject to a regular upward review, but it never rose above the best open market rate. In 1993 Mr. Crehan and other tenants fell into financial arrears, basically blaming this on Courage's supply of beer at lower prices to other non-tied pubs, "free houses". In the same year Courage brought an action for the recovery from Mr. Crehan of sums for unpaid deliveries of beer. Mr. Crehan, alleging the incompatibility with Article 81(1) EC of the clause requiring him to purchase a fixed minimum quantity of beer from Courage, counter-claimed for damages.

There were two specific obstacles to Mr. Crehan's success. The first one was that according to earlier case law, Article 81 EC had been interpreted as protecting only third parties, i.e. competitors or consumers, but not co-contractors, i.e. parties to the illegal and void agreement. The second issue was that under English law a party to an illegal agreement, as this was considered to be by the Court of Appeal, could not claim damages from the other party. This was as a result of the strict construction English courts were giving to the *nemo auditur turpitudinem propriam (suam) allegans* or *in pari delicto potior est conditio defendentis* or *ex dolo malo non oritur causa* rule, which in essence meant that Mr. Crehan's claim in damages would fail, because he was co-contractor in an illegal agreement.

The Court of Justice, following the ruling in *Francovich* which had recognised the principle of state liability as a principle of Community law, and also relying on its *Eco Swiss* ruling,[37] stressed the primacy of Article 81 EC in the system of the Treaty, since it "constitutes a fundamental provision which is essential for the accomplishment of the tasks entrusted to the Community and, in particular, for the functioning of the internal market."[38] It also stressed, with particular reference to "the possibility of seeking compensa-

[37] Case C-126/97, *Eco Swiss China Time Ltd.* v. *Benetton International NV*, [1999] ECR I-3055.

[38] *Courage*, *supra* note 36, para. 20.

tion for loss caused by a contract or by conduct liable to restrict or distort competition", the task of national courts to ensure the full effect (*plein effet*) of Community rules and the protection of individuals' rights conferred by those rules. The full effectiveness (*pleine efficacité*) of the Treaty competition rules and, in particular "the practical effect [*effet utile*] of the prohibition laid down in Article [81(1)]" would be put at risk if individuals could not claim damages for losses caused by the infringement of those rules. The instrumental character of such liability for the effectiveness of the law as such is more than evident in this passage, exactly as was the case with state liability in *Francovich*.[39] And finally, the Court dispelled any doubt as to its pronouncement:

> "Indeed, *the existence* of such a right strengthens the working of the Community competition rules and discourages agreements or practices, which are frequently covert, which are liable to restrict or distort competition. From that point of view, actions for damages before the national courts *can make a significant contribution to the maintenance of effective competition in the Community*".[40]

This last quote makes it clear that the meaning of effectiveness in *Courage* has a double facet. It refers not only to Community law in general, but also to the specific field of antitrust. This is clear from the Court's use of the term "significant contribution" to refer to the role of damages claims for the efficiency of antitrust enforcement in Europe, with a view to maintaining effective competition. More authoritative words in favour of private enforcement and the "private attorney-general" role[41] of the civil litigant could hardly be pronounced.

2. *Manfredi v. Lloyd Adriatico*

More recently, in *Manfredi*,[42] the Court of Justice proceeded to deal further with the "constitutive" and "executive" conditions of

---

[39] *Op. cit.*, para. 26.

[40] *Op. cit.*, para. 27 (emphasis added).

[41] Private antitrust actions, apart from their compensatory function, further the overall deterrent effect of the law. Thus, economic agents themselves become instrumental in implementing the regulatory policy on competition and the general level of compliance with the law is raised. It is for that reason that the private litigant in US antitrust has been called a "private attorney-general" (per J. Jerome Franck, in *Associated Industries of New York State, Inc.* v. *Ickes*, 134 *F.2d* 694, 704 (2d Cir. 1943)).

[42] Joined cases C-295/04 to C-298/04, *Vincenzo Manfredi et al.* v. *Lloyd Adriatico Assicurazioni SpA et al.*, [2006] ECR I-6619.

the Community right to damages. If *Courage* was a *Francovich* type of case, *Manfredi* can be seen as the *Brasserie du Pêcheur/Factortame III* of individual civil liability. This was a preliminary reference case from Italy, where insurance companies had been sued for damages by Italian consumers for prohibited cartel behaviour previously condemned by the Italian competition authority.[43] The ECJ was basically called to decide :

- whether consumers enjoy a right to sue cartel members and claim damages for the harm suffered when there is a causal relationship between the agreement or concerted practice and the harm;
- whether the starting time of the limitation period for bringing an action for damages is the day on which the agreement or concerted practice was put in effect or the day when it came to an end; and
- whether a national court should also of its own motion award punitive damages to the injured third party, in order to make the compensable amount higher than the advantage gained by the infringing party and discourage the adoption of agreements or concerted practices prohibited under Art. 81 EC.[44]

The Court, building on *Courage*, and after making it clear that the basis for individual civil liabilities deriving from a violation of Article 81 EC indeed lies in Community law, seems to have followed former Advocate General Van Gerven's scheme of "constitutive", "executive" and simple "procedural" conditions of the Community right to damages. Thus, the Court makes a fundamental distinction between the "existence" and "exercise" of the right to damages. That the "existence" of the right is a matter of Community law is obvious from the fact that the Court reiterated the most important

[43] Italian courts had earlier sent similar preliminary references to Luxembourg, but the ECJ had held them to be inadmissible because it thought that the referring courts had not included enough information as to the purpose of and necessity for the references : case C-425/03, *Providenza Regio* v. *AXA Assicurazioni SpA*, Order of 19 October 2004, unpublished; joined cases C-438/03, C-439/03, C-509/03 and C-2/04, *Antonio Cannito et al.* v. *Fondiaria Assicurazioni SpA et al.*, Order of 11 February 2004, [2004] ECR I-1605.

[44] The Court was also called to decide whether the nullity of agreements contrary to Art. 81 EC can be relied upon by third parties (its answer was yes), and whether Community law is contrary to a national rule which provides that plaintiffs must bring their actions for damages for infringement of Community and national competition rules before a court other than that which usually has jurisdiction in actions for damages of similar value, thereby involving a considerable increase in costs and time. Another preliminary question sent to Luxembourg in this case related to the applicability of Community law to the anti-competitive conduct.

pronouncements of *Courage*.[45] In this context, it is also clear that the Court proceeded to define, as a matter of Community law, what former Advocate General Van Gerven calls "constitutive" conditions of the right to damages :

> "It follows that any individual can claim compensation for the harm suffered where there is a causal relationship between that harm and an agreement or practice prohibited under Article 81 EC."[46]

In other words, the right to damages is open (a) to "any individual" as long as there is (b) "harm", (c) a competition law violation, and (d) a "causal relationship" between that harm and that violation.[47] In thus defining the Community law constitutive conditions of the right to damages, the Court has produced a broad rule of standing, which includes consumers and indirect purchasers, while at the same time omitting the requirement of fault, which means that national rules following more restrictive rules on standing or requiring intention or negligence for an action for damages to be successful are contrary to the constitutive conditions of the *Courage/Manfredi* right to damages.

To mark the distinction between the existence of the right and its constitutive conditions, governed by Community law, and its exercise and executive conditions, governed by national law, the Court stresses again that "any individual... can claim compensation for [harm causally related with an Article 81 EC violation]", but "in the absence of Community rules governing the matter, it is for the domestic legal system of each Member State to prescribe the detailed rules governing the *exercise* of that right, including those on the application of the concept of 'causal relationship', provided

[45] *Manfredi*, *supra* note 42, paras. 60, 61, 63, 89-91, citing paras. 25-27 of *Courage*. In particular, para. 91 of *Manfredi*, quoting para. 27 of *Courage*, stresses that "the *existence* of such a right strengthens the working of the Community competition rules and discourages agreements or practices, frequently covert, which are liable to restrict or distort competition. From that point of view, actions for damages before the national courts can make a significant contribution to the maintenance of effective competition in the Community" (emphasis added).

[46] *Op. cit.*, para. 61.

[47] Compare also the recent ruling in *City Motors* which again refers to the constitutive conditions of the right to damages in the motor vehicle distribution context : Case C-421/05, *City Motors Groep NV* v. *Citroën Belux NV*, [2007] ECR I-653, para. 33 : "In the event of a breach by a supplier of the condition for application of the block exemption set out in Article 3(4) of Regulation No 1400/2002, the national court must be in a position to draw all the necessary inferences, in accordance with national law, concerning both the validity of the agreement at issue with regard to Article 81 EC and *compensation for any harm suffered by the distributor where there is a causal relationship between that harm and an agreement or practice prohibited under Article 81 EC*" (emphasis added).

that the principles of equivalence and effectiveness are observed." [48] We submit that the Court refers here to the "executive" rules of the Community right to damages. In Van Gerven's scheme these are separate from purely procedural rules, which are again a matter for national law. They are also subject to a higher standard of control under an "adequacy test", rather than a mere "minimum effectiveness" or "non-impossibility" test, which may continue to apply for simple procedural rules.

Indeed, the Court in *Manfredi* makes a clear distinction in its analysis between specific questions pertaining to the causal relationship between harm and antitrust violation and the availability of punitive damages, both seen as "executive" conditions, [49] and questions on limitation of actions and competent national tribunals, both seen as "detailed procedural rules". In addition, the Court seems to share the former Advocate General's conviction that the former affect the very core of the exercise of Community-based rights and should therefore be subject to a more stringent test concerning the Community principle of effectiveness, while the latter can be subject to a more relaxed "non-impossibility" test. It is thus no surprise that in *Manfredi* the Court uses the "non-impossibility" language only in the context of mere procedural rules and not in the context of the "executive" conditions. [50] This means that questions such as causality, nature of harm and damages, and defences, which can be characterised as "executive" conditions, will be subject to a more demanding test of effectiveness/adequacy, while questions such as competence of courts, limitation periods and rules on proof, which are more "procedural" in nature, will be subject to a minimum effectiveness/non-practical impossibility test.

C. – *The Commission's 2005 Green Paper*

The Court of Justice's *Courage* ruling provided the impetus for the Commission to adopt a more pro-active stance on the whole question of private enforcement. Modernisation was now a reality

[48] *Manfredi*, *supra* note 42, paras. 63-64, emphasis added.

[49] *Op. cit.*, paras. 64 and 92 *et seq.*, as to causal relationship and punitive damages, respectively.

[50] Compare paras. 64 and 92, which refer merely to effectiveness, with paras. 71 and 78, which refer to effectiveness seen through the prism of "rendering practically impossible or excessively difficult the exercise of rights conferred by Community law".

and there were, maybe for the first time, serious debates in Europe as to the desirability of introducing measures to enhance private antitrust enforcement. Soon after the Court of Justice delivered its *Courage* ruling, the Commission commissioned a study on the conditions for claims for damages in the Member States in the case of infringement of EC competition rules. Predictably, the study showed an "astonishing diversity and total underdevelopment" of civil antitrust actions in the Member States.[51] Up to mid-2004, there were apparently around 50 judgments as a result of damages actions. Of these judgments, only 28 had resulted in a damages award having been made.[52]

After digesting the results of the Ashurst Study and reflecting further on the appropriate way to move forward, the Commission published on 19 December 2005 for public consultation a Green Paper on damages actions for breach of the EC antitrust rules.[53] The purpose of the Green Paper, which set out a number of possible options to facilitate private damages actions, was to stimulate debate and facilitate feedback from stakeholders.

The Commission was in favour of increased private enforcement, as it believed that this will have a number of advantages for private parties, in particular:

(a) victims of illegal anticompetitive behaviour are compensated for loss suffered;

(b) deterrence of antitrust infringements and compliance with the law are increased;

(c) a competition culture among market participants, including consumers, will develop further, and awareness of the competition rules will be raised;

---

[51] The study is made up of a comparative report (D. WAELBROECK, D. SLATER and G. EVEN-SHOSHAN, "Study on the Conditions of Claims for Damages in Case of Infringement of EC Competition Rules: Comparative Report", 31 August 2004), a report on economic models for the calculation of damages and 25 national reports. See http://ec.europa.eu/comm/competition/antitrust/others/actions_for_damages/study.html.

[52] These statistics are only indicative, since in some Member States not all judgments are published and the comparative report necessarily relies on the national reports, whose quality varies. One must also bear in mind that these statistics do not include cases that were settled with significant damages awarded to the plaintiffs.

[53] *Commission Green Paper on Damages Actions for Breach of the EC Antitrust Rules*, COM(2005) 672 final. The Green Paper was accompanied by a Staff Working Paper which set out the various options more discursively: *Commission Staff Working Paper, Annex to the Green Paper on Damages Actions for Breach of the EC Antitrust Rules*, SEC(2005) 1732.

(d) the Commission and the national competition authorities do not have sufficient resources to deal with all cases of anticompetitive behaviour, and in any event administrative authorities have discretion to pursue other priorities.[54]

We will not enter here into a discussion of the Green Paper, since we are discussing below some of the options that the White Paper espoused.

D. – *National Developments*

It would be inappropriate to end this review of the way to the White Paper without referring to developments in the Member States. Modernisation and decentralisation of Community competition law enforcement and the related European debate on private enforcement, as well as the 2001 *Courage* ruling by the Court of Justice, led to important initiatives at national level. The UK and Germany completely overhauled their legislation and, among other reforms, introduced provisions aimed at enhancing private antitrust enforcement of national and Community competition law. At the same time, there has been a recent surge of damages actions and awards in the national courts, most of them being cases of follow-on claims, i.e. actions relying usually on prior decisions by competition authorities. Whether this last development indicates increased awareness by plaintiffs or changing judicial attitudes is still unclear, but it certainly confirms that the European "wake-up calls" are reaching the Member States.

To start with the UK, the Competition Act 1998 did not contain any direct reference to civil actions or actions for damages, though the availability of such actions was implicit in some other provisions of the Act.[55] The situation was about to change. In 2001 a consultation paper by the Department of Trade and Industry powerfully advocated the desirability of private damages actions; such actions were seen as serving two basic aims: compensation for victims of anticompetitive practices; and drawing private resources into the enforcement process, thus allowing public authorities to pursue the

[54] See Commission MEMO/05/489, *European Commission Green Paper on Damages for Breach of EC Treaty Antitrust Rules – Frequently Asked Questions*, 20 December 2005, accompanying the Green Paper on damages actions, under the title "What in the Commission's view are the advantages of private actions for damages?".

[55] E.g. ss. 55(3)(b) and 58(2) of the Competition Act 1998.

most important cases. These ideas were set in motion with the Enterprise Act 2002. Of particular interest for private enforcement is the conferring on the CAT of jurisdiction to hear claims for damages in competition cases.[56] Damages claims before the CAT presuppose the establishing by either the OFT or the European Commission that an infringement of competition law has occurred. Such a finding of infringement is binding and cannot be re-litigated. These actions must be filed with the CAT within a period of two years, beginning at the time of the public enforcer's final infringement decision or on the date when the cause of action accrued. In addition, UK law provides for the possibility for ordinary civil courts to transfer to the CAT competition issues arising in private civil actions.

Then, section 58A of the UK Competition Act aims at facilitating follow-on civil actions for damages brought before the ordinary civil courts. It provides that findings of infringement of UK or Community competition law by the OFT (or by the CAT on appeal) bind the courts deciding on follow-on civil claims for damages.[57] The UK system provides for another novelty : Section 47B provides for claims for damages brought on behalf of consumers by representative "specified" bodies. These are not meant as US-style class actions, and the claim must specify the consumers on whose behalf the claim is brought.

The recent amendment of the German Competition Act makes another paradigm. German law has long-provided for antitrust damages actions, but the new section 33 GWB marked important progress, in that it provided a legal basis for damages claims for violation not only of German but also of Community competition law. The new provision also abandoned the previous rather restrictive condition for standing, which was conferred only on persons within the "protective scope" of the statute, and stressed that any "person affected", including competitors and "other market participants" can sue for damages. The law also gave standing to associations for the promotion of commercial or independent professional

[56] S. 47A of the Competition Act 1998, as subsequently amended.

[57] It is noteworthy that this provision is different from section 47A of the Act. The former refers only to the UK competition authorities' decisions, while the latter extends the binding effect of infringement findings to decisions of the European Commission. In addition, the provision of section 58A refers to follow-on civil proceedings for damages before the ordinary civil courts (the Chancery Division of the High Court), while section 47A refers to follow-on claims brought before or transferred to the CAT.

interests, including consumer associations. One novel feature was that it is now possible for the courts to calculate the damages taking into account the proportion of the profit which the defendant derived from the infringement. In addition, the passing-on defence is restrained, though not completely banned. Finally, German law goes even further than the UK law by conferring a binding effect not only on European Commission and *Bundeskartellamt*, but also on all other national competition authorities infringement decisions. This binding effect is confined to follow-on civil litigation, basically aiming at offering incentives to claim damages from convicted infringers.

As far as national case law is concerned, in recent years one can speak of a boom in private antitrust enforcement in Europe. It is interesting to note that many of the recent cases, some of which are still pending, are follow-on cases. The *Vitamins* case is the most prominent source of such actions and there are already damages awards and settlements in Germany, England, Sweden and other jurisdictions. A famous example is the *Provimi* judgment decided at the admissibility stage by the English High Court, where as well as English parties, a German party was also claiming antitrust damages.[58] Judgment was given only as to the jurisdictional issues and subsequently the parties settled. There, it was established that where there is an English connecting factor in the private international law sense, i.e. an English element to a cartel, other non-English claimants may also bring claims in London in respect of their non-English based losses, instead of having to pursue separate claims in other jurisdictions.

The *Vitamins* litigation provided also for the first claims that were brought before the CAT as follow-on civil claims for damages under the special procedure of section 47A of the UK Competition Act. These cases, however, did not lead to final judgments, since they were settled, though recently there is a resurgence.[59] Another recent follow-on action brought before the CAT, which was also set-

[58] *Provimi Ltd.* v. *Aventis Animal Nutrition SA et al.* QB (Com.Ct.), [2003] ECC 353.

[59] See *Deans Foods Limited* v. *Roche Products Limited, F. Hoffman-La Roche AG and Aventis SA*, Case No. 1029/5/7/04, settled; *BCL Old Co. Ltd. DFL Old Co. Ltd. and PFF Old Co. Ltd.* v. *Aventis SA, Rhodia Ltd., F. Hoffman-La Roche AG and Roche Products Ltd.*, Case No. 1028/5/7/04, settled. But see also, very recently, *BCL Old Co Ltd. Et al.* v. *BASF AG, BASF plc and Frank Wright Ltd.*, Case No. 1098/5/7/08, currently pending; *Grampian Country Food Group Ltd et al.* v. *Sanofi-Aventis SA et al.*, Case No. 1101/5/7/08, currently pending.

tled, gave rise, however, to an interim award of damages, the first ever award of damages in England for a competition law infringement. This was based on previous infringement decisions by the OFT/CAT in an abuse of dominance case concerning margin squeeze and rebates in the pharmaceutical sector. While the case was still pending, the CAT awarded on 16 November 2006 "interim damages" for an amount of £2 million.[60] That represented, in the court's view, roughly 70 % of the likely final damages award. Meanwhile, more actions for damages have been brought before the CAT, but again for the most part these were settled.[61]

In Germany, the courts' initial rejectionist approach has now changed and the first successful follow-on damages claims in the *Vitamins* litigation are a reality. It is noteworthy that certain German courts adjudicating claims for damages in the post-*Courage* era refused to grant damages to direct purchasers of vitamins on passing-on grounds, and because the cartel was not specifically directed at them but at all market participants.[62] This built on a very restrictive reading of standing under German law that was certainly incompatible with Community law, in particular the *Courage* ruling, which accepted no such limitations but granted a right to damages to all individuals harmed by the anti-competitive conduct. Recent German judgments, however, have reversed this restrictive approach and have rendered the first damages awards.[63]

---

[60] *Healthcare at Home Ltd.* v. *Genzyme Ltd.*, Case No. 1060/5/7/06, [2006] CAT 29. The case was settled. Under English law, interim damages can be an adequate provisional measure, if there is a very good *prima facie* case and if damages appear to be an appropriate final remedy.

[61] See e.g. *The Consumers Association* v. *JJB Sports plc*, Case No. 1078/7/9/07, settled; *ME Burgess et al* v. *W Austin & Sons (Stevenage) Ltd and Harwood Park Crematorium Ltd*, Case No 1088/5/7/07, settled; *Emerson Electric Co et al.* v. *Morgan Crucible Company plc et al.*, Case No 1077/5/7/07. In the latter case, the CAT decided, on a preliminary point, that the time for making a claim for damages pursuant to s 47A of the Competition Act 1998 had not yet begun to run, since appeals were pending before the Community Courts against the Commission's decision which the plaintiffs sought to rely on in their follow-on claims (Judgment of 17 October 2007, [2007] CAT 28). Eventually the CAT granted permission to the plaintiffs to proceed with their damages claims against the immunity recipient, which had naturally not challenged to the CFI the European Commission's – in that case – cartel infringement decision (Judgment of 16 November 2007, [2007] CAT 30) but not against the other addressees of the infringement decisions, whose appeals to the CFI were still pending (Judgment of 28 April 2008, [2008] CAT 8).

[62] LG Mannheim, 11.7.03, 7 *O* 326/02 – *Vitaminkartell*, 106 *GRUR* 182 (2004); LG Mainz, 15.1.04, 12 *HK O* 56/02 (Kart) – *Vitaminpreise* (2004), 54 *WuW* 1179.

[63] LG Dortmund, 01.04.04, 13 *O* 55/02 (Kart) – *Vitaminpreise*, 54 *WuW* 1182 (2004). The damages awarded in this case amounted to the difference between the price paid as a result of the cartel and a hypothetical market price. In addition, the court ruled that the defendant had failed to prove that the plaintiff had passed on his damage to his customers.

Important successful damages claims have also been reported in Austria, France,[64] Denmark,[65] Spain,[66] Sweden,[67] and Italy, where the *Corte di Cassazione* after lengthy tribulations established that consumers could claim damages from a cartel of insurance companies previously convicted by the Italian competition authority.[68]

III. – The White Paper

A. – *Intellectual Debt Acknowledged*

It is only in the aftermath of the Court of Justice's important pronouncements that are described above that the European Commission

---

[64] CA Versailles, 24-6-04, n° 02/07434, *SA Verimedia* v. *SA Mediametrie et al.* The court awarded € 100,000 to the victim of an anti-competitive agreement (on the basis of French competition law). The damages awarded were rather low because *inter alia* of the plaintiff's contributory fault.

[65] Judgment of 20 April 2005, *GT Linien A/S* v. *DSB and Scandlines A/S*, UfR 2005.2171 H. The award of damages amounted to DKK 10 million plus interest and was mostly upheld by the Danish Supreme Court. See also Copenhagen Maritime and Commercial Court, Judgment of 3 October 2002, *EKKO* v. *Brandt Group Norden et al. (EKKO I)*, UfR 2004.2600 S, and Judgment of 15 October 2004, *EKKO* v. *Electrolux Home Products Denmark et al. (EKKO II)*, UfR 2005.388 S.

[66] Juzgado de Primera Instancia, n° 4 de Madrid, 7-6-05, n° 125/2005, *Antena 3 TV* v. *LNFP*. In this case, in a "follow-on" civil action, the court awarded a record € 25 million in damages because LNFP, the Spanish football league, had abused its dominant position by selling broadcasting rights on an exclusive basis to regional public broadcasters, thus foreclosing certain new entrants. The damages claim was based on an earlier national infringement decision, confirmed by the Spanish competent courts. See also Juzgado de lo Mercantil n° 5 de Madrid, 11-11-05, n° 36/2005, *Conduit Europe SA* v. *Telefónica de España SAU*, confirmed in Audiencia Provincial de Madrid (secc. n 28), 25-5-06, n° 73/2006, *Conduit Europe SA* v. *Telefónica de España SAU*. In that case, the court awarded the plaintiff, an Irish communication services provider, € 639,000 for losses incurred as a result of the defendant's abuse of a dominant position, consisting of giving defective and incomplete information in order to block the plaintiff's entry into the market for subscriber directory enquiries.

[67] See Mühlenbock, Salomon and Salwén, "Highlights and Trends in Swedish Competition Law", in : *The European Antitrust Review 2007, Global Competition Review Special Report* (London, 2006), p. 214.

[68] Corte di Cassazione, 4-2-05, n° 2207, *Compagnia Assicuratrice Unipol SpA* v. *Ricciarelli*, 11 *Danno e Responsabilità* 495 (2005). This judgment was decided by the *Sezioni Unite* (a special chamber with an increased number of judges) of the *Corte di Cassazione*. It reversed a previous ruling by the same court that had denied standing to consumers in the same cartel (Corte di Cassazione, 9-12-02, n° 17475, *Soc. Axa Assicurazioni* v. *Isvap and Larato*, 9 *Danno e Responsabilità* 390 (2003)). See Giudici, "Private Antitrust Law Enforcement in Italy", 1(1) *Comp.LRev.* 61 (2004), pp. 73 *et seq.* For other Italian competition law cases where damages have been awarded, see Siragusa, Rizza and D'Ostuni, "Italy", in : *Private Antitrust Litigation 2007, Global Competition Review Special Report* (London, 2006), p. 51. See also indicatively Giudice di Pace di Bitonto, 21-5-07, *Vincenzo Manfredi* v. *Lloyd Adriatico Assicurazioni SpA*, where actually the Italian judge, who was empowered to calculate damages following rules of equity, awarded punitive (double) damages for the specific cartel infringement. Compare the critical comments of Nebbia, "...So What Happened to Mr Manfredi? The Italian Decision Following the Ruling of the European Court of Justice", 28 *ECLR* 591 (2007).

decided to go forward with the publication of its Green and White Papers. In so doing, the Commission availed itself of an increased degree of legitimacy in an area which is always sensitive due to the inevitable intrusion on what is perceived as the Member States' institutional and procedural autonomy. It would have been very difficult for the Commission to go ahead and propose Community legislative action, if it had not been for the Court of Justice's seminal rulings. This intellectual debt is fully acknowledged in the WP, which gives much space to the *acquis communautaire*, as established by the Court.

Indeed, the WP starts from the premises that the right to be compensated for harm caused by an antitrust violation is a right guaranteed by the Treaty itself, as the Court of Justice has stressed in *Courage* and *Manfredi*. This statement itself is an important reminder because the idea that the right to damages finds its basis in Community law is still resisted by some commentators, particularly in the German-speaking theory, who see this purely as a matter of national law, subject only to the Community principles of equality and effectiveness.[69] The Commission is now unequivocal : there are many references to "*the establishment under Community law* of a right to compensation", derived "*directly from Community law*" and to the fact that "this *European law remedy* can as such not be refuted or conditioned by national legislation of any kind".[70] There is also a clear distinction between the *existence* of the right, which is a matter of primary Community law, and its *exercise* which is determined by national legislation but which the White Paper intends harmonising to a certain extent through secondary Community law.[71]

A fundamental quality of the WP is that it codifies and restates the existing *acquis communautaire* involving most aspects of the right to damages for EC competition law violations. The ECJ *Courage* and *Manfredi* rulings are naturally prominent,[72] but there are

[69] See also in favour of the Community law basis of the right to damages, LENAERTS and GUTMAN, "'Federal Common Law' in the European Union : A Comparative Perspective from the United States", 54 *Am.JComp.L* 1 (2006), pp. 91-94, and para. 53 of AG POIARES MADURO's Opinion in Case C-438/05, *The International Transport Workers' Federation and the Finnish Seamen's Union* v. *Viking Line ABP and OU Viking Line Eesti*, [2007] ECR I-10779, which, referring to *Courage*, clearly speaks of a claim "based directly" on Community law.

[70] SWP, *supra* note 2, paras. 308-309, emphasis added. See also section 1.1 of the WP.

[71] SWP, *supra* note 2, para. 309.

[72] For the idea that *Courage* and *Manfredi* already provide at Community level for an exhaustive list of the "constitutive conditions" of the right to damages, see KOMNINOS, *supra*, note 6, pp. 173-176.

also references to other case law that deals with many other questions of remedies and procedures available at national level for the enforcement of Community law. The Commission's choice to dedicate whole sections of the WP to the presentation of the impressive *acquis communautaire* was a wise one. Firstly, because it shows that even if the whole initiative to introduce Community measures for private actions were abandoned, the existing *acquis* itself is a Community minimum from which there can be no departure, and secondly, because it acts as a powerful support and starting point for Community legislation.[73]

Notwithstanding this *acquis communautaire* and the Community law basis of the right to damages, the WP recognises that there are various national legal and procedural hurdles and that therefore there is a need for a strong set of legislative measures to enhance private actions for damages. Community measures, a Regulation and/or a Directive, and most likely a Commission Notice on the quantification of damages, are seen as desirable in order to achieve (i) an effective minimum protection of victims, (ii) a level-playing field and (iii) greater legal certainty.

B. – *The Main Policy Options of the White Paper*

Interestingly, the Commission does not claim a monopoly and speaks of a "combination of measures at Community and national level". It is fair to say that the Commission had never pretended to have an exclusive role in this area but its more deferential attitude to national competencies may be the result of some resistance at national level vis-à-vis Community unification and harmonisation initiatives especially those touching upon matters of national procedural laws. It is indeed the more "procedural" issues that the WP is now proposing to leave to the national level, such as rules on costs, court fees and funding.[74] In addition and to the extent Community legislation is necessary, "procedural" matters such as collective relief and access to evidence, are seen as candidates for harmonisation, through a Directive, rather than for unification, through

[73] Indeed, an argument that is often heard in favour of Community legislation in this area, is that if Community legislation does not step in to deal with the conditions for the exercise of the right to damages (positive integration), the ECJ would have to do this in any way through the preliminary reference procedure (negative integration).

[74] See ch. 9 of the SWP.

a Regulation. Our view is, however, that a Regulation would be more appropriate for core conditions of the exercise of the right to damages, like standing, passing-on and questions pertaining to fault.

The two basic objectives of damages actions, as perceived by the WP, are (a) full compensation for victims, which is presented as "primary objective" and (b) effectiveness of competition enforcement in Europe through increased deterrence, which presumably must be the secondary objective.[75] The Commission also mentions as third objective the development of a competition culture among market participants and the increased awareness of the competition rules.[76]

The WP brushes aside fears expressed in the business world and among practitioners about the import into Europe of a US-style explosive mixture of class actions and adamantly stresses that this is a "genuinely European approach".[77] This is certainly a valid statement, in the sense that there is no proposal about the introduction of punitive damages,[78] opt-out class actions, contingency fees, jury trials, not to mention the "no contribution rule", according to which a defendant who has paid all the damages, as a result of joint and several liability, cannot seek indemnity from other co-defendants.

The main measures and policy choices that the Commission intends to pursue can be summarised as follows:

- standing to sue for damages is recognised for all persons harmed by an EC competition law violation, including competitors, direct and indirect purchasers, and of course consumers;
- direct purchasers in particular should be able to rely on the rebuttable presumption that the illegal overcharge was passed on to them in its entirety ("offensive passing-on");

[75] This hierarchy may also explain the absence of proposals for more "offensive" or "aggressive" mechanisms, such as punitive damages. On the two objectives, see recently NEBBIA, "Damages Actions for the Infringement of EC Competition Law: Compensation or Deterrence?", 33 *ELRev.* 23 (2008).

[76] SWP, *supra,* note 2, paras. 14-15. See also KOMNINOS, *supra,* note 6, pp. 9-11.

[77] WP, *supra,* note 2, section 1.2.

[78] The Commission, however, encourages the award of punitive damages to the extent such damages are available under national law for violations of national competition law (SWP, *supra,* note 2, para. 190) and does not exclude the possibility of introducing punitive damages at Community level in the future, if it were shown that further incentives were necessary for private antitrust enforcement (*op. cit.*, para. 195).

- at the same time, it will be open to defendants to prove that the plaintiff (e.g. a direct purchaser) has passed the illegal overcharge on to his customers; in other words, defensive passing-on should be permitted;
- collective redress should be possible through (i) representative actions by consumer associations, state bodies or trade associations, that are officially certified in the Member States, and (ii) opt-in collective claims for consumers and businesses;
- plaintiffs' access to evidence held by defendants should be made easier; thus the WP proposes in effect a certain relaxation of the "fact-pleading" system and the introduction of some elements of "notice-pleading" under the control of the judge whereby national courts should have the power to order the litigants or third parties to disclose specific categories of relevant evidence;
- final infringement decisions issued by the Commission and by national competition authorities (NCAs) or final judgments on judicial review should be binding on national courts throughout the EU in follow-on civil actions;
- objective (strict) liability should be the rule (no fault requirement) for damages, once the infringement has been established, unless the infringer demonstrates that there is a genuinely excusable error (he bears such burden of proof);
- full compensation should be available, covering not just actual losses, but also lost profits and interest;
- there should be no Community measure on punitive damages;
- the limitation period should not start to run before the day a continuous or repeated infringement ceases, or before the victim can reasonably be expected to have knowledge of the infringement and of the resulting harm;
- for follow-on claims, there should be a new limitation period running for at least two years after an infringement decision has become final;
- corporate statements by leniency applicants (including unsuccessful ones) should not be discoverable, even after the adoption of a final decision;
- the immunity recipient's civil liability should be limited to claims by his direct and indirect contractual partners.

C. – *The Impact of the Pre-existing* acquis communautaire *on the White Paper's Treatment of Certain Questions*

The fact that Community law in the post-*Courage/Manfredi* era itself defines the constitutive conditions of the right to damages, has profound consequences for very important questions such as the rules on standing, in particular for indirect purchasers and consumers, on fault and on the interaction with the leniency programme.

1. *Standing*

Perhaps the most important feature of the WP is the broad rule of standing it advocates, notably for indirect purchasers and of course consumers. At the same time, the WP proposes the retention of the "passing-on defence". The question of the standing of indirect purchasers is closely connected with the prohibition or permission of the passing-on defence. Indeed, standing of indirect purchasers is referred to at times as "offensive passing-on".

Under US antitrust law, indirect purchasers, for example traders that have purchased from retailers rather than from the manufacturer, cannot recover damages, [79] notwithstanding the fact that the harm may have been passed on to them. US law clearly favours compensation only of direct purchasers, and indeed, it disallows the passing-on defence in this case. [80] There is a powerful policy rationale behind this rule, that the direct purchaser is a more "efficient" plaintiff, ultimately preferable to indirect purchasers as a "private attorney-general". In general terms, the US rule seems to take into account certain prudential considerations such as the burden on the judicial system that would result if the private right of action were available in an unlimited way to remotely injured plaintiffs. [81] Denying indirect purchasers standing is also a direct consequence of the exclusion of the passing-on defence, since the defendant and perpetrator of the antitrust violation should not be vulnerable to multiple actions referring to the same acts, while at the same time it is not open to him to rely on the fact that the damage may have

[79] Note, however, that state antitrust laws in the US may allow for indirect purchaser suits.

[80] See the US Supreme Court's judgments in *Hanover Shoe* v. *United Shoe Machines Corp.* (1968), 392 *US* 481 and *Illinois Brick Co.* v. *Illinois*, 431 *US* 720 (1977).

[81] See DAVIS, "Standing on Shaky Ground: The Strangely Elusive Doctrine of Antitrust Injury", 70 *Antitrust LJ* 697 (2003).

been passed-on. In other words, the US system bans the defensive use of the passing-on principle by defendants, while at the same time banning its offensive use by indirect purchasers who base their claims precisely on the fact that the overcharge was passed on to them.[82]

Irrespective of the critique that can be made against this rather inflexible US judge-made rule,[83] in the European context of damages claims, the constitutional status of the Treaty competition provisions and the fact that they form the basis of rights for individuals, mean that the US theories could not have been adopted uncritically. Thus, the *a priori* exclusion of indirect purchasers from the ambit of the persons who can claim damages would therefore not have been compatible with Community law.

In *Courage*, the Court had no difficulty in finding that Article 81 EC not only protected third-party competitors, in that case third-party beer suppliers foreclosed by a specific network of exclusive beer supply agreements, but could also be relied upon by "any individual",[84] including co-contracting parties, in that case tenants.[85] *Manfredi*, as we developed above, built on *Courage* and defined in detail the Community law constitutive condition of standing, explicitly recognising that consumers enjoy standing to sue for harm caused to them by anti-competitive conduct.[86] Such a prin-

[82] See C.A. JONES, *Private Enforcement of Antitrust Law in the EU, UK and USA* (Oxford, 1999), pp. 178-179. It is noteworthy, however, that the bar to the indirect purchaser suits is not applicable to suits for injunctions and is also excluded in the following cases: (a) in cases of pre-existing, cost-plus, fixed quantity contracts, and (b) in cases of vertical resale price maintenance, where the retailer has a claim for lost profits whereas the customer has a claim for the overcharge.

[83] The problem with the total exclusion of indirect purchasers is that there may be times when the direct purchasers benefited from the infringement and are not at all inclined to sue. An upstream cartel may also shield itself from private damages claims by forwarding a share of cartel profits to its direct purchasers. These benefitts dissuade the direct purchasers from exercising their exclusive right to sue for private damages. See further SCHINKEL, TUINSTRA and RÜGGEBERG, "Illinois Walls: How Barring Indirect Purchaser Suits Facilitates Collusion", Amsterdam Center for Law & Economics Working Paper No. 2005-02 (April 2008), also in 39 *RAND Journal of Economics* 683 (2008). It is noteworthy that the recent report of the US Antitrust Modernization Commission proposes overruling *Illinois Brick* and *Hanover Shoe* to the extent necessary to allow both direct and indirect purchasers to sue to recover for actual damages from violations of federal antitrust law (see Antitrust Modernization Commission, *Report and Recommendations*, April 2007).

[84] *Courage*, *supra*, note 36, para. 26.

[85] See BREALEY, "Adopt *Perma Life*, but Follow *Hanover Shoe* to *Illinois*? Who Can Sue for Damages for Breach of EC Competition Law", 1 *Comp.LJ* 127 (2002), p. 128.

[86] *Manfredi*, *supra*, note 42, paras. 60, 61, 63. Compare AG Mischo's Opinion in *Courage*, *supra* note 36, para. 38, stressing that "the individuals who can benefit from such protection are, of course, primarily third parties, that is to say *consumers* and competitors who are adversely affected by a prohibited agreement" (emphasis added).

ciple can also be adduced from the letter of Article 81(3) EC, which speaks of "allowing *consumers* a fair share of the resulting benefit".[87] The WP, indeed, follows that approach and adopts a broad rule of standing, covering also indirect purchasers. It is actually interesting that the White Paper refers to indirect purchasers' standing not as a proposal but rather as part of the already-existing *acquis communautaire*.[88]

Thus, in Europe, the solution will be the opposite from the US : both direct and indirect purchasers will have standing to sue, but at the same time the passing-on defence will be available. Allowing the passing-on defence is a logical consequence of the broad rule of standing, otherwise, as the White Paper accepts, there would be a risk of unjust enrichment of those purchasers that passed on the illegal overcharge to their customers and of multiple compensation of the overcharge.[89]

Finally, since difficulties also arise when the indirect purchaser invokes the passing-on of the illegal overcharge as a basis of his claim ("offensive passing-on"), the WP proposes the introduction of a rebuttable presumption that the overcharge has indeed been fully passed on to the plaintiff – indirect purchaser. This is intended as an alleviation of the victim's burden of proof, without, however, affecting the main conditions of civil liability : in other words, the plaintiff would still have to prove the infringement, the existence of the initial overcharge and the extent the overcharge caused him harm (including causation).[90]

2. *Fault*

Another basic question that was answered in a definitive way by the *Courage/Manfredi* case law and to which the WP gives prominence, is whether liability for damages for breach of Articles 81 and

---

[87] Emphasis added.

[88] SWP, *supra* note 2, paras. 33-37. Of course, the broad rule of standing does not affect the necessity of a causal link between the harm and the infringement of Articles 81 and 82 EC (*op. cit.*, paras. 37 and 205).

[89] SWP, *supra,* note 2, para. 210. At the same time, the WP stresses that the standard of proof for the passing-on defence should not be lower than the claimant's standard to prove the damage. Under this model, the plaintiff must prove that he has suffered loss, but it is open to the defendant to prove that the plaintiff mitigated the loss by passing on the whole or part of the overcharge to downstream purchasers.

[90] SWP, *supra,* note 2, para. 220.

82 EC presupposes fault or whether it is strict. The answer to this question is that in principle it is only strict liability that renders the prohibitions of those Articles meaningful.[91] The Treaty rules on competition do not generally require subjective intent to contravene the relevant prohibitions,[92] so civil liability for EC competition law breaches should not be based upon such a condition.

Of course, we must distinguish conceptually between fault in the context of the *anti-competitive conduct* and fault in the context of *civil liability* and *civil damages*. Although interconnected, the two questions are different. The Court of Justice in *Courage* stressed this conceptual difference in the following terms :

> "Contrary to the submission of Courage, making a distinction as to the extent of the parties' liability does not conflict with the case-law of the Court to the effect that it does not matter, for the purposes of the application of Article [81] of the Treaty, whether the parties to an agreement are on an equal footing as regards their economic position and function. That case-law concerns the conditions for application of Article [81] of the Treaty while the questions put before the Court in the present case concern certain consequences in civil law of a breach of that provision."[93]

It is the second context that we deal with here, i.e. whether culpability should play a role for the establishment of civil liability flowing from a proven antitrust violation, and the answer is that it should not. In all such cases, liability for EC competition law violations is strict. Indeed, the requirement of intention or negligence for the imposition of fines and periodic penalty payments by the Commission or national competition authorities in the context of administrative public enforcement[94] should be distinguished, because such penalties do not aim at compensating the victims of

---

[91] See in this sense A. Jones and B. Sufrin, *EC Competition Law, Text, Cases, and Materials* (Oxford, 2004), p. 1219.

[92] With regard to Art. 81 EC, the critical factor is the *objective* meaning and purpose of the agreement in its economic context, while the *subjective* intention of the parties is immaterial. Vice versa, an agreement might not have as its object the restriction of competition merely because the parties subjectively aimed at this. In Art. 82 EC, again, abuse is an objective concept and the intention of the dominant undertaking is irrelevant. However, exceptionally, intention may play a role in establishing an abuse of dominant position in predatory pricing cases, and in cases where the abuse takes the form of vexatious litigation which is part of a systematic campaign or strategy of the dominant undertaking to intimidate, harass, and exhaust competitors by raising their costs unreasonably.

[93] *Courage*, *supra*, note 36, para. 35. The Court was of course dealing in that specific case with the issue of the plaintiff's contributory fault, but its clear distinction between fault for the establishment of the antitrust violation and fault for the civil liability is of general importance.

[94] See Art. 23 Reg. 1/2003, *supra*, note 15, with regard to fines. The same is also accepted for periodic penalty payments.

the anti-competitive practices, but rather at punishing and deterring their perpetrators.[95] Civil liability, on the other hand, while also containing deterrence elements, predominantly compensates the harm caused by anti-competitive conduct, and this harm should not be compensated only in cases of the perpetrator's fault.

Strict liability, therefore, differentiates individual civil liability for violation of Community competition law from its older sibling, state liability, which arises only where the Member State has committed a "sufficiently serious breach" of Community law.[96] There is, however, no compelling reason for accepting such a requirement in individual liability cases. Indeed, as some authors argue, there are inherent features in state liability which justify and necessitate the "sufficiently serious breach" condition, but that cannot be transposed to individual liability for Community law violations.[97] Such a limitation has been imposed on public policy grounds in order to limit the liability of Member States when acting in their sphere of legislative discretion. On the other hand, when Member States do not enjoy legislative discretion, liability according to the Court of Justice is strict.[98] Therefore, strict liability is more appropriate for breaches of the Treaty competition rules.[99]

The strict liability principle was indeed recognised by the Court of Justice in *Manfredi*, which enumerated the constitutive conditions of individual civil liability but left the requirement of fault out.[100] This

[95] Compare Case T-59/02, *Archer Daniels Midland Co.* v. *Commission*, [2006] ECR II-3627, para. 351 : "In so far as the damages at issue amount to compensation for European Union purchasers, the Court considers that the proceedings at issue and the payments demanded by the Commission, on the one hand, and by the United States authorities on the other clearly do not pursue the same objectives. *Whilst in the first case the Commission seeks to sanction an infringement of competition law* in the Community or the EEA *by means of a fine, in the second case the United States authorities seek to compensate victims of ADM's dealings*" (emphasis added).

[96] *Brasserie du Pêcheur/Factortame III*, *supra*, note 20, paras. 51, 55 *et seq.*

[97] See M. Brealey and M. Hoskins, *Remedies in EC Law, Law and Practice in the English and EC Courts* (London, 1998), p. 124; Saggio, "La responsabilità dello stato per violazione del diritto comunitario", 6 *Danno e Responsabilità* 223 (2001), p. 242; P.P. Craig and G. De Búrca, *EU Law : Text, Cases and Materials* (Oxford, 2008), p. 1084.

[98] Case C-5/94, *Regina* v. *Ministry of Agriculture, Fisheries and Food ex parte Hedley Lomas (Ireland) Ltd.*, [1996] ECR I-2553, para. 28.

[99] See, in this sense, Winckler, "Remedies Available under French Law in the Application of EC Competition Rules", in : Ehlermann & Atanasiu (Eds.), *European Competition Law Annual 2001 : Effective Private Enforcement of EC Antitrust Law* (Oxford/Portland, 2003), p. 128; Van Gerven, "Harmonization of Private Law : Do we Need it?", 41 *CMLRev.* 505 (2004), p. 522.

[100] *Manfredi*, *supra*, note 42, para. 61. See, however, *contra* Eilmansberger, "The Green Paper on Damages Actions for Breach of the EC Antitrust Rules and Beyond : Reflections on the Utility and Feasibility of Stimulating Private Enforcement through Legislative Action", 44 *CMLRev.* 431 (2007), p. 458, who thinks that *Manfredi* did not touch upon the question of fault.

sits in stark contrast to some national laws, such as the Swedish Competition Act, which require intention or negligence for a right to damages to arise.[101] Some form of fault is also required in Finnish,[102] Austrian,[103] Danish, and Greek law.[104] While national law can provide for detailed "executive" rules on the right to damages, these rules cannot go as far as to affect the constitutive conditions of individual civil liability, as set out in *Courage* and *Manfredi*, by adding stricter ctriteria based on the nature or degree of the infringement or fault. Such restrictive conditions are plainly incompatible with the specific constitutive conditions of the Community right to damages. This is not really a question of national remedial/procedural autonomy, to be dealt with under the Community principle of effectiveness, but rather a question of supremacy of Community over national law.[105]

The White Paper seems to accept the above[106] and, indeed, notes that the rule should be that of strict or objective liability for damages once an infringement of EC antitrust rules has been proven.[107] The Commission also proposes to qualify the strict liability rule by allowing the defendants to exculpate themselves if their breach of the antitrust rules was due to an "excusable error".[108]

---

[101] Art. 33(1) of the Swedish Competition Act.

[102] Art. 18a(1) of the Act on Competition Restrictions of 1992, as amended in 2004.

[103] See EILMANSBERGER and THYRI, "Austria", in: CAHILL (Ed.), *The Modernisation of EU Competition Law Enforcement in the European Union, FIDE 2004 National Reports* (Cambridge, 2004), p. 54.

[104] In English law, however, liability for breach of statutory duty is usually strict and absolute.

[105] Compare JACOBS and DEISENHOFER, "Procedural Aspects of the Effective Private Enforcement of EC Competition Rules: A Community Perspective", in: EHLERMANN & ATANASIU (Eds.), *European Competition Law Annual 2001: Effective Private Enforcement of EC Antitrust Law* (Oxford/Portland, 2003), p. 216, who make a distinction between substance and procedure. While, according to the authors, national substantive rules are vis-à-vis Community law subject to the principle of supremacy, procedural rules must only comply with the principles of equivalence and effectiveness. In our view, the constitutive conditions of individual civil liability, as defined by Community law itself, would fall under those authors' "substance" definition, and should thus supersede any contrary national rule, pursuant to the principle of supremacy, rather than the principle of effectiveness.

[106] See, in particular, SWP, *supra*, note 2, paras. 170-171.

[107] This, of course, does not affect or eliminate the requirement of causation. The causal link between the antitrust infringement and the damage itself must still be proven.

[108] The Commission views "excusable error" rather restrictively and it will remain to be seen how this whole rule will be applied by the courts. Particularly problematic may be liability in cases of unclear or novel abuses of dominant positions (monopolisation cases) or non-hardcore agreements which may have certain pro-competitive benefits but are considered on balance to be unlawful. In such cases, a strict liability rule with a very restrictive "excusable error" defence will give rise to serious concerns. Therefore, it is advisable that this defence be available to cover conduct which is not clear to be *a priori* anti-competitive. A horizontal co-operation agreement whereby the parties genuinely believed that they were acting lawfully or the conduct of a dominant company that is considered to be abusive for the first time should be such cases.

Of course, the "excusable error" qualification by no means affects the strict liability rule, which remains a matter of primary Community law, since it is only exceptionally that some form of fault must be required for civil liability to arise, in order to avoid excesses. A useful example is offered by the defective products liability Directive,[109] which introduces the principle of strict liability, but also includes in Article 7 exceptions to the rule under which the producer has the burden to prove certain exonerating facts.[110] This shows that a rule of strict liability can accommodate a relaxation in order to comply with basic notions of fairness or some specified public policy.[111]

3. *Interaction with the Leniency Programme*

Where the WP may give rise to a discussion as to its compatibility with the *Courage/Manfredi* case law is its proposal to limit the civil liability of successful immunity recipients to claims by their "direct and indirect contractual partners". The aim is basically to safeguard the effectiveness of the Leniency Programme, which might have been put at risk as a result of the Commission's drive for an enhanced system of private actions in Europe.

The particular question of reducing the civil liability of successful leniency or total immunity applicants is quite complex and goes to the core of the relationship of public with private enforcement. It also touches upon the fundamental issue of the objective of private

---

[109] *Council Directive 85/374/EEC of 25 July 1985 on the Approximation of the Laws, Regulations and Administrative Provisions of the Member States Concerning Liability for Defective Products*, [1985] *OJ* L210/29, as amended by European Parliament and Council Directive 1999/34/EC of 10 May 1999, [1999] *OJ* L141/20.

[110] Art. 7 : "The producer shall not be liable as a result of this Directive if he proves : (a) that he did not put the product into circulation; or (b) that, having regard to the circumstances, it is probable that the defect which caused the damage did not exist at the time when the product was put into circulation by him or that this defect came into being afterwards; or (c) that the product was neither manufactured by him for sale or any form of distribution for economic purpose nor manufactured or distributed by him in the course of his business; or (d) that the defect is due to compliance of the product with mandatory regulations issued by the public authorities; or (e) that the state of scientific and technical knowledge at the time when he put the product into circulation was not such as to enable the existence of the defect to be discovered; or (f) in the case of a manufacturer of a component, that the defect is attributable to the design of the product in which the component has been fitted or to the instructions given by the manufacturer of the product".

[111] The public policy concerned here is that to apply an unqualified strict liability rule to a horizontal co-operation agreement whereby the parties genuinely believed that they were acting lawfully or to the conduct of a dominant company that is considered to be abusive for the first time, would risk stifling healthy competition and innovation.

antitrust damages actions: if the paramount objective is compensation, then limitations of a successful immunity beneficiary's liability will be difficult; if, on the other hand, the main objective is deterrence and effectiveness of enforcement as such, then it will be easier to protect the integrity and attractiveness of the leniency programme by limiting civil liability.

The 2005 Green Paper on damages had examined two options. One was to grant a successful immunity applicant the option to claim a rebate on any damages claim facing him, in return for helping claimants bring damages claims against all cartel members.[112] The claims against the other infringers, jointly and severally liable for the entire harm, would have remained unchanged.[113] The other option was to remove joint and several liability for the successful immunity applicant and limit his liability to the share of the harm corresponding to his share in the cartelised market.[114]

The WP, however, no longer pursues any of these options and makes instead a proposal to limit the civil liability of successful immunity recipients[115] to claims by their "direct and indirect contractual partners". In other words, the immunity recipient would be liable only to persons that bought directly from him the products or services in question (direct contractual partners) or those down the supply chain who bought these products or services from the direct contractual partners themselves.[116] Thus, a victim that did not buy cartelised products or services[117] directly or indirectly from him and, more interestingly, a harmed competitor, a shareholder[118] or the victim of so-called "umbrella pricing"[119] will not be

---

[112] Option 29 of the Green Paper.

[113] If there had been a system of double damages for horizontal cartels, this rebate would have de-doubled the award for the immunity recipient, thus restoring single damages as the content of the claim which he faces.

[114] Option 30 of the Green Paper.

[115] This proposal does not cover the other leniency applicants that did not receive full immunity.

[116] SWP, *supra*, note 2, para. 305.

[117] An issue is what happens with cartels that do not involve sale of goods or services to contractual partners (e.g. a cartel not to sell in a particular market or to a particular client).

[118] Whether shareholders or other persons related to a company that has breached the antitrust rules, such as employees, can sue for damages, is debated. See BREALEY, *supra*, note 85, p. 134; MILUTINOVIÇ, "Private Enforcement: Upcoming Issues", in: AMATO & EHLERMANN (Eds.), *EC Competition Law: A Critical Assessment* (Oxford/Portland, 2007), pp. 734-735. In our view, the broad language in *Courage* should cover these persons too, assuming they can identify and prove harm and, more importantly, causation.

[119] These are customers who did not purchase from cartel members but from fringe firms outside the cartel, but within the same relevant market, that charge a higher price as a non-cooperative response to the cartel price. See further Impact Assessment Study, *supra*, note 2, p. 413.

able to claim damages. At the same time, this rule would in effect remove the immunity recipient's joint liability,[120] since, as the Commission, explains in an example, "where 30 % of a victim's total purchases of cartelised products originate from the immunity recipient, the latter would only be liable for 30 % of the total harm suffered by this victim due to the overcharge of the cartelised products".[121]

The question is whether the limitation of the right of competitors and others not falling under the Commission's definition of "direct and indirect contractual partners" is at odds with primary Community law, i.e. with the Treaty itself and the ECJ rulings in *Courage* and *Manfredi*, which stress that the right to damages should be open to "any individual".

In principle, while some compromise between the principle of effective judicial protection (compensation of all harmed individuals) and effectiveness of competition law enforcement (safeguarding of the effectiveness and attractiveness of the leniency programme) is desirable and Community law can accommodate this, a secondary Community legislative measure (a Regulation or a Directive) cannot result in the total exclusion of the right to damages for certain categories of persons, as guaranteed by primary Community law. For example, protecting the successful immunity recipient from potential punitive damages at national level, or at Community level, should the Community proceed to the introduction of such a system in the long term, would not raise concerns, because the Community right to damages could still be exercised by all harmed individuals with regard to the immunity recipient's liability to pay single damages for the part of the damage that is attributable to him.

The problem here is that the WP proposes to totally bar certain classes of individuals from claiming damages against an undertaking that has infringed Article 81 EC. In particular, it proposes that

[120] The WP considers that removal of joint liability by itself is not sufficient to effectively limit the immunity recipient's liability (SWP, *supra*, note 2, para. 304). Compare, however, para. 322 of the SWP, where removal of joint liability is surprisingly mentioned as a separate proposed measure. Perhaps the reference in paragraph 322 was left in from a previous draft by mistake.

[121] *Op. cit.*, fn. 160.

competitors and other potential plaintiffs should not be able to claim damages from that undertaking.

If we look closer, however, at the proposed solution, we see that in reality the WP does not propose to affect the exercise of those persons' right to damages against the other cartel members that did not receive full immunity from fines. Indeed, joint and several liability of these cartel members continues to be the rule, so they would still be jointly and severally liable to pay damages to a potential harmed competitor for the whole of his harm. Thus, in reality what the WP proposes is not to totally bar some persons from suing for damages but rather it would make those persons only slightly worse off by slightly increasing their risk in case of the insolvency of all or some of the other cartel members with the exception of the immunity recipient. This is a rather low risk.[122] In fact, irrespective of this WP proposal and of what primary Community law dictates, all plaintiffs always bear the risk of all the cartel members' insolvency. So, it seems to us that the proposed solution would most likely not seriously affect the existence of the Community right to damages, while at the same time it would undoubtedly strengthen the effectiveness of one aspect of the leniency programme, the race to the authority to be the first undertaking that self-reports, thus ensuring full immunity status.[123] Being second or third would not only mean the loss of full immunity but also exposure to damages liability for the whole of the harm.[124]

In fact, an even better solution would be to completely exclude the immunity recipient's liability also for claims by his direct and indirect contractual partners. Again, as above, this would not dramatically affect the exercise of the right to damages by these persons, since they could still claim compensation for the whole of their damage against the other cartel members, who would remain jointly and severally liable. As a safety valve, the law could provide that this total exclusion of liability would not apply to the exceptional case of insolvency by one or more of the jointly and severally

[122] The cartels that are prosecuted by the Commission under Article 81 EC are likely to concern activity and companies of a certain size and therefore the risk of insolvency of any of these companies is extremely low.

[123] See also Impact Assessment Study, *supra*, note 2, p. 521.

[124] Note, however, that the Commission does not propose to disallow contribution among the (non-immunity recipient) cartel members.

liable (other) cartel members.[125] While not affecting the right of compensation, such a solution would even more enhance the effectiveness of the leniency programme.[126] Indeed, this has now been adopted in the amended text of the Hungarian Competition Act, which, with the intention to increase the attractiveness of the leniency policy, provides that a leniency applicant receiving full immunity from fines will not be liable to pay damages to third parties, until and if such damages can be collected from other cartel members (i.e., from those which did not receive full immunity under the leniency policy).[127]

Besides, ensuring that the leniency programme remains attractive and thus effective is quite beneficial for private enforcement and potential plaintiffs. First, the plaintiffs become aware of the cartel infringement, which is more effectively exposed to the public authority by the leniency applicants, second, the facts are established during the administrative proceedings, third, courts or plaintiffs could under certain circumstances ask for documentary evidence in the hands of the public enforcer, in order to establish the liability and/or the damage, and fourth, a final public decision, depending on the applicable rules, may have a binding effect on the follow-on civil proceeding or may constitute *prima facie* evidence of the cartel violation.

[125] In such a case, the plaintiffs would have to sue first the other cartel members and, in case of insolvency of the latter, they could then bring a new action against the immunity recipient for the part of harm that is attributable to him (in other words, removal of joint liability for him should here be the rule).

[126] Of course, a debate is still possible, if one views *Courage* and *Manfredi* not only as authority for a Community *right* to damages available to victims but also as authority for a Community law *obligation* imposed on infringers (to compensate the victims). In that case, indeed, any exclusion of an infringer's liability to certain classes of victims would be contrary to primary Community law. In our view, however, the language in *Courage* and *Manfredi* (*supra*, notes 36 and 42, paras. 26-27 and paras. 89-91, respectively), which is rights- and not obligations-centred, and the underlined powerful rationale of effectiveness would allow for a compromise in order to safeguard the effectiveness of public enforcement and thus by implication the *effet utile* of Article 81 EC.

[127] The amended text has not yet come into force due to a pending review by the Constitutional Court, because of certain concern on new rules imposing liability on management. Although the amendments were due to take effect in September, the entire amending act is now suspended until the Constitutional Court concludes its review. In any case, the new provisions on damages actions are not subject to the ongoing constitutional review, so they are likely to enter into force as they stand now.

COMPETITION LAW AS A STRATEGIC ISSUE FOR COMPANIES: DOES PRIVATE ENFORCEMENT CONSTITUTE A GREATER THREAT?

BY

Christophe ROQUILLY

Professor of Business Law
Director of LegalEdhec Research Centre
EDHEC Business School

This superb conference, jointly organised by the Federation of Enterprises in Belgium and the Institute for European Legal Studies at the University of Liège, deliberately asks a sophisticated question: Do alternative enforcement techniques constitute a new paradigm of EC Competition Law? This welcome line of questioning is an opportunistic follow-up on the White Paper on Damages Actions for Breach of the EC Antitrust Rules[1], which in turn followed the Green Paper of 2005.[2] During this conference, brilliant specialists of competition law from diverse backgrounds (academics, practitioners, members of regulatory bodies) endeavoured to dissect the White Paper, identifying its satisfactory or problematic elements, as well as those points that either confirmed or left open to debate our current understanding of this area. My modest contribution will be to place this question of private enforcement in the more general context of the relationship between competition law and companies, with a particular focus on the strategic (or otherwise) nature of this relationship from a corporate point of view. In a perfect and positivist – and perfectly positivist – world, companies would seek total compliance with competition law. In a world where companies are above all guided by a certain economic ration-

[1] Commission White Paper on Damages Actions for Breach of the EC Antitrust Rules, COM(2008) 165 final.

[2] Commission Green Paper on Damages Actions for Breach of the EC Antitrust Rules, COM(2005) 672 final.

ale, this is not necessarily the case : they reason in terms of cost/advantage or threat/opportunity. It is undeniable that competition law poses a legal risk for companies that form part of certain cartels or abuse their dominant position on the market. That this risk can be considered a threat in the strategic sense of the term is less clear, however.

The first part of this paper serves as a reminder of some basic considerations regarding corporate objectives and strategy development, before going on to make it clear how the strategic nature of competition law can be formulated. The second section considers what influence the development of private enforcement has had on this strategic element, particularly in France.

I. – Competition law as a threat to companies

First of all it is important to explain the title of this section. My intention is not to suggest that competition law *per se* is a threat to companies, as to do so would suggest a serious paradox, given that one of the main objectives of this branch of law is to encourage the development of free competition. In principle, freedom is after all primarily a source of opportunity and not threat. Rather my aim is to ask whether competition law can represent a threat for certain companies according to their strategy, the way in which they deploy and use their resources, and the intentions of regulatory authorities and judges. We must first ask why a company's search for performance might be at odds with the rules of competition law, and then consider to what extent this conflict is strategic in nature.

A. – *Performance, competitive advantage and potential conflict with competition law*

Whatever strategy they may adopt, companies seek to develop their performance and generate sustainable competitive advantages. Most scholars in the fields of management and strategy consider that a superior and sustainable performance comes from a sustainable competitive advantage.[3] However, definitions of a sustainable

[3] See T. Powell, "Competitive Advantage : Logical and Philosophical Considerations", *Strategic Management Journal*, 2001, 22(9), 875-888.

competitive advantage vary. For some, it requires the securement of above average profit by the company owners. For others, an economic rent must be generated, or a company must have a superior ability to attract clients.[4] Such an ability implies that the company creates and captures more value than its competitors, as explained by Pisano and Teece.[5] To do this, the most appropriate strategy must be developed. The notion of strategy is multidimensional, as Hax and Majluf have shown.[6] It can be defined at once as a means by which to set long-term objectives and one's priorities in relation to the allocation of resources, as the definition of a company's competitive domain, as a coherent amalgam of decisions, as a response to external threats and opportunities and internal strengths and weaknesses, or as a means by which to invest in tangible and intangible resources with a view to developing capabilities that will secure a sustainable competitive advantage.

In the historic model – that of industrial organisation – external variables constitute the determining elements of corporate strategy.[7] It shows the external environment as being divided into three segments : general (demographical, economic, socio-cultural and technological data, etc.), industrial (threat of new entrants, client power, supplier power, threat of substitute products, etc.) and competitive (determining the intentions, actions and responses of competitors). The legal dimension of this external environment is of course widely recognised. The (external) legal sphere comprises of elements from the three segments just mentioned : legislative and regulatory texts, and court decisions; professional standards and codes of good practice; rights owned or controlled by competitors such as intellectual property rights or legal structures, etc. Some scholars even recognise that elements of the legal sphere can contribute to the development of strategic industry factors.[8] However

[4] On the absence of a uniform definition, see R. Lal, M. Sarvary and R.W. Coff, "When competitive advantage doesn't lead to performance : The resource-based view and stakeholder bargaining power", *Organization Science*, 1999, 10(2) : 119-133.

[5] G.P. Pisano and D.J. Teece, "How to Capture Value from Innovation : Shaping Intellectual Property and Industry Architecture", *California Management Review*, 2007, 50(1) : 278-296.

[6] A.C. Hax and N.S. Majluf, *The Strategy Concept and Process*, 2nd ed., NJ : Prentice Hall.

[7] M.E. Porter, *Competitive strategy : Techniques for analyzing industries and Competition*, 1980, Free Press : New York.

[8] See G.S. Hansen and B. Wernerfelt, "Determinants of firm performance : the relative importance of economic and organizational factors", *Strategic Management Journal*, 1989, 10(5) : 399-411; R. Amit and P.J.H. Shoemaker, "Strategic assets and organizational rent", *Strategic Management Journal*, 1993, 14(1) : 33-46.

this dominant theory has come up against some criticism, which has questioned whether a company's performance can be explained by external elements. An approach referred to as "resource-based" has now developed, emphasising that it is the possession of certain resources, capabilities and core competencies that provides a company with a sustainable competitive advantage, and not the key factors behind an industry's success. [9] So as not to exceed the scope of my contribution, I will simply point out that the legal dimension is also present in the resource-based approach. Resources can be legal (contracts, intellectual property rights, corporate legal structures, etc.), and their role is to protect, develop and capture the value of other resources. [10] They are the result of a company's capacity to build legal solutions using elements from the legal sphere, but can also carry legal risks (they can come into conflict with regulatory provisions or with the legal resources of other companies).

Competition law is of course a component of the legal sphere, and can constitute a legal risk for companies. According to Verdun, legal risk is the result of an encounter (or confrontation) between a legal norm and a particular event that has considerable consequences. [11] Collard defines it as the same encounter, but with consequences that may affect the value of the firm and/or threaten its objectives. [12] The legal norm in question, to use the expression of Collard and Roquilly, reflects the desire of the State (or States) to structure the relationships of rivalry and cooperation between companies within the framework of their efforts to acquire or preserve a clientele. [13] Rivalry and cooperation are clearly essential for a vibrant economic market. To seek to dominate the market is not in itself a reproachable objective, as long as companies develop their own efficiency without endangering that of others. [14] The secure-

---

[9] For an overview of the resource-based approach, see E. MÉTAIS, *Stratégie et Ressources de l'Entreprise*, 2004, Paris : Economica.

[10] For an illustration of the use of legal resources, see C. ROQUILLY, "Les Ressources Juridiques au Service de la Stratégie d'Entreprise : Le Cas de l'iPhone", *Petites Affiches – La Loi*, 2008, March : 7-18.

[11] F. VERDUN, *La Gestion des Risques Juridiques*, 2006, Paris : Editions d'organisation.

[12] C. COLLARD, "Le risque juridique existe-t-il? Contribution à la définition du risque juridique", *JCP-Cah. dr. Ent*, 2008, 1 : 8-13.

[13] C. COLLARD and C. ROQUILLY, "Droit de la concurrence et droit de la consommation", in *Droit de l'entreprise*, 2008, Paris :Lamy, p. 659.

[14] E. ELHAUGE, "Defining better monopolization standards", *Stanford Law Review*, 2003, 56(2) : 253-344.

ment of a competitive advantage must come from a company's superior use of its resources and capacities, and not from unfair domination or manipulation of the market,[15] regardless of whether this is the result of individual or concerted action. It is therefore important for a company to anticipate the risk of competition law being applied, as shown by Fried and Oviatt.[16] The management of legal risk – that is, the risk of an encounter between a rule of competition law and an action by a company, with possible negative effects for the latter – is only possible if the company is in a position to identify, evaluate and make a decision in relation to this risk. The worst scenario is that in which the company (or more precisely some of its representatives) is unaware of the existing risk. Such unawareness can lead to non-compliance, the ramifications of which for the company have not been analysed. The implementation of competition law compliance programmes within a company can prove extremely useful as a means of training all relevant staff members to recognise those actions that might save or ruin the company.[17] It is only by respecting this organisational condition that companies can adopt their own rationale with regard to the risks of confrontation between their actions and competition law. One might counter that these programmes are costly and perhaps place SMEs at a disadvantage, but the risk of conflict with competition law – at least its provisions on anticompetitive practices – is probably less significant for SMEs than for larger corporations, except perhaps in the case of cartels. A compliance programme in this domain should not be costly given that the number of internal parties concerned would be low.

Companies have several options as to what decision to take in regard to risk. They can avoid the risk completely by deciding against any action that would infringe the rules of competition law. Or they can circumvent the rule of law; this implies finding another way to complete a given project without abandoning it. A third

[15] See R. Boscheck, "Competitive advantage: Superior offer or unfair dominance?", *California Management Review*, 1994, 37(1): 132-151.

[16] V.H. Fried and B.M. Oviatt, "Michael Porter's missing chapter: The risk of antitrust violations", *Academy of Management Executive*, 1989, 3(1): 49-55.

[17] On compliance programmes, see L. Ancrum, "Are EC Competition law compliance programmes compulsory?", *Accountancy*, 1992, 109(1183): 59-62; B. Mounier-Khun and E. Dieny, "Responsabilité des dirigeants et collaborateurs de l'entreprise dans le cadre des pratiques anticoncurrentielles: Perspectives", *JCP* éd. E, 2008, n°s 7-8, 1232, p. 20 onwards.

option is to confront the rule of law: a company thereby takes a deliberate decision to enter into conflict with the provisions of competition law. Finally, companies can seek to transform the relevant provisions by using various forms of lobbying to bring about a change in the law, thereby neutralising the risk or even transforming it into an opportunity.[18] Let us simplify the problem in the following terms: what analysis must a company undertake in order to choose between rejection and confrontation of the risk? This may appear provocative as it suggests that a company might benefit from non-compliance with competition law. In an approach based on a strict economic rationale, the question can be raised in these terms, and the cost/advantage analysis is familiar to many companies. It therefore remains to determine the criteria according to which such an analysis can be developed, and whether risk can, in certain cases, be seen as a strategic threat.

B. – *The reality of strategic threat*

A company driven by rational behaviour must ask the following question: given the risk of confrontation with the provisions of competition law, does a particular planned action create or destroy more value for the company? In other words, is the value created by this action greater than the value it destroys? I wish to isolate the two extreme hypotheses in which top managers would have a particularly strong or particularly weak aversion to risk.[19] The question of measuring the creation or destruction of value is an especially delicate one, as it is multi-faceted. Financial value is not

---

[18] Lobbying is considered to be closely linked to strategy. See in particular D.B. Yoffie and S. Bergenstein, "Creating Political Advantage: The Rise of the Corporate Political Entrepreneur", *California Management Review*, 1985, 28 (1): 124-139; B. Shaffer, "Firm-level Responses to Government Regulation: Theoretical and Research Approaches", *Journal of Management*, 1995, 21(3): 495-514. This lobbying does not only target the legislature; it can also target the various regulatory agencies and authorities; see E. Tiller and J. De Figueiredo, "The structure and conduct of corporate lobbying: How firms lobby the Federal Communications Commission", *Journal of Economics and Management Strategy*, 2001, 10(1): 91-122; G.L.F. Holburn and R. Vanden Bergh, "Influencing agencies through pivotal political institutions", *Journal of Law, Economics and Organization*, 2004, 20(2): 458-483.

[19] Several theses have been put forward in this area: for that of expected utility, see P.J.H. Shoemaker, "The Expected Utility Model: Its Variants, Purposes, Evidence and Limitations", *Journal of Economic Literature*, 1982, 20(2): 529-563; for that of prospect theory, see D. Kahneman and A. Tversky, "Prospect theory: An analysis of decisions under risk", *Econometrica*, 1979, 47(2): 263-291; for that of rigidity, see B.M. Staw, L.E. Sandelands and J.E. Dutton, "Threat-rigidity effects in organizational behavior: A multilevel analysis", *Administrative Science Quarterly*, 1981, 26: 501-524.

the only type to be taken into consideration, and it is not always possible to transform other types of value into financial value. Some scholars have even begun to study value management in its diverse forms.[20]

Companies compare two options : is the value created greater than the value destroyed in accordance with the decision to comply or not to comply with the provisions of competition law? This question, which is considerably more complex than it may appear, implies another : does competition law create a framework that prompts companies to be compliant? Companies can use economic analytical tools to help them rationalise their choice, such as the formula for probable litigation cost (CJP – Coût Judiciaire Probable) devised by Collard on the basis of studies by Cailloux and *alii*,[21] where CJP = ά x CJM, with ά = (CG x CRJ)/PT. CJM represents the average litigation cost (Coût Judiciaire Moyen), taking into account the sanctions imposed in the type of case being heard. ά is the weighting factor, while CG (Coefficient de Gravité) is the severity factor that takes into account the particular nature of the facts under consideration and the fact that judges can impose varying sanctions in accordance with the severity of these facts. CRJ represents the trial success factor (Coefficient de Réussite Juridictionnelle) and is based on the analysis of relevant decisions, with the aim of determining the chances of success in an action related to facts of this nature. PT, finally, is the potential for settlement (Potentiel de Transaction) and measures the capacity to reach a compromise with the other party.[22] The PT element of this formula must be neutralised if one adapts it to the specific evaluation of the risk of pecuniary sanctions being imposed by a competition authority. At a European level, companies can look to the European Commission Guidelines to refine their application of this formula.[23] The competition authorities can only create an incentive for compliance

[20] O. Jokung-Nguéna, J-L. Arrègle, Y. De Rongé and W. Ulaga, *Introduction au Management de la Valeur*, 2001, Paris : Dunod.

[21] J.P. Cailloux, H. Bidaud and P. Bignon, *La fonction juridique et l'entreprise*, 1995, Paris : Eska.

[22] See C. Collard, "Le management juridique – une nouvelle pratique au sein de l'entreprise", *Entreprise Ethique*, 2005, 22, 34-40.

[23] Guidelines on the method of setting fines imposed pursuant to Article 23(2)(a) of Regulation No 1/2003, *Official Journal*, C 210, 1.09.2006, pp. 2-5. For an analysis of these guidelines, see W.P.J. Wils, "The European Commission's 2006 Guidelines on Antitrust Fines : A Legal and Economic Analysis", *World Competition : Law and Economics Review*, Vol. 30, No. 2, June 2007.

if they are in a position to determine effectively the profits generated by the company whose behaviour is at issue, and consequently set the amount of penalties to be imposed. However, the immediate profits generated by a company (for example an increase in sales) does not necessarily cover its overall strategic gains, which might explain why companies can in some cases run the risk of financial sanctions that are greater than their immediate profits, but where a strategic advantage can be gained. Competition law can only constitute a threat in the strategic sense of the term if it can damage the actions a firm takes in order to acquire a strategic advantage. In other words, it is necessary to reflect on the possibility of any detriment to one of a company's strategic assets. The amount of a financial sanction is far from being the only element a company must take into consideration. Beyond such sanctions, companies may be ordered to modify or even abstain from particular behaviour. The prohibition of a certain type of distribution contract, which might undermine a company's marketing strategy, or an order to disclose certain technological information, and therefore risk the loss of a competitive advantage over time, are examples of the kind of sanctions that might be seen as a strategic threat. However, the time frames involved in such procedures allow companies to anticipate and perhaps even reconfigure their strategy. Another element not to be neglected when determining the possibility of a strategic threat is the potential damage to a company's corporate image, which can mean significant destruction of value that is difficult to measure. Finally, the destruction of value brought about by sanctions can cause the financial markets to react negatively. Certain studies, however, show that this creates no significant effect, although they contain some bias that should be eliminated.[24]

In light of all these elements, it can be suggested that the risk of sanctions under competition law is only strategic in nature in the most restricted of cases, and the incentives to comply are often insufficient in terms of a company's anticipated profits or its strategic objectives. One might nonetheless ask whether, when added to these elements, the risk of private enforcement would not increase the risk of a strategic threat. The objective of those victims of anticompeti-

[24] See A. Jerson, F. Le Roy and P. Sentis, *L'impact boursier des annonces des pratiques anticoncurrentielles*, XVIIIème Conférence Internationale de Management Stratégique, AIMS, 28-31 May 2008, Sophia Antipolis.

tive practices who take civil liability actions against the parties responsible for such practices is not to increase the risk taken by these parties, but rather to encourage legitimate compensation for the victims in such cases. However, from a company's point of view, the purely mechanical effect of the development of various types of sanctions is necessarily an increase in the level of risk taken. The risk of civil liability being invoked is nothing new,[25] and the evaluation of such liability can be done using the formula outlined above. It is also possible to use more sophisticated formulae, such as that developed by Hylton.[26] He argues that a company will have to be compliant – and therefore abandon any action that might infringe competition law – as soon as $x < [v1p(1 - h1) - v2qh2]L + (v1p - v2q)Cd$, where x is the cost of compliance, given that :

- v1 is the probability of injury, where the firm violates the law;
- v2 is the probability of injury, where the firm complies with the law;
- *p* is the probability of a lawsuit, where the firm violates the law;
- q is the probability of a lawsuit, where the firm complies with the law;
- cd is the defendant's litigation cost;
- h1 is the probability of the plaintiff losing, where the defendant violates the law;
- h2 is the probability of the plaintiff winning, where the defendant complies with the law;
- L is the liability (damages).

The question of what is covered by the "cost of compliance" remains. At the very least, one would have to include unrealised profits (i.e., which would have been realised if the company had gone ahead with an action that was in breach of competition law). Several other points need to be clarified, however : does the company have sufficient information to make an adequate calculation of the diverse probabilities ? What is the margin of error between a forecast of compliance and one of non-compliance (absence or pres-

[25] An article had already been devoted to this in the 1960s : R. Houin, "Les conséquences civiles d'une infraction aux règles de concurrence", *Annales de la faculté de droit de Liège*, 1963, p. 27 onwards.

[26] K.N. Hylton, *Antitrust Law – Economic Theory & Common Law Evolution*, 2003, Cambridge : Cambridge University Press.

ence of evidence of anticompetitive behaviour; ambiguity as to the relevant market – made all the greater in a highly dynamic environment)? Inversely, does the relevant competition authority and/or judge have access to serviceable information in order to determine the profits realised by a company that has decided not to comply, especially where these profits are partly indirect?

I now propose a study of the specific risk related to private enforcement in an effort to determine whether its development can really increase the potential of a strategic threat to companies. Any response to this question will depend on the difficulties inherent in civil liability actions, particularly in terms of the burden of proof and litigation costs.

II. – Private enforcement and increased threat

A certain number of elements currently limit the potential impact of private enforcement on the compliance of companies with regard to competition law. The White Paper on Damages Actions for Breach of the Antitrust Rules attempts to provide some answers. One succinct example can be taken from the case of French law.

A. – *Limits on the risk of implementing private actions*

First and foremost, it is important to stress that not all victims of anticompetitive practices have the same profile. There is a gulf between the two extremes of the spectrum – major corporations at one end and consumers at the other – in terms of access to information and expertise, as well as the financial means available to enter into litigation. One might counter that the potential level of injury sustained is also radically different. However, a more objective approach requires a comparison of the damages caused to a major company and the sum of those suffered by individual consumers (rather than one individual consumer). Companies concerned by the risk of civil liability actions based on anticompetitive practices can in some cases benefit from the presence of significant obstacles to the effectiveness of such actions. In other words, certain factors constitute an impediment on recourse to private action and actually prevent the potential development of a strategic threat that might force companies to comply with the provisions of the law. The first such impediment can lie in a victim's isolation; this is where an individual suffers minor damage, perhaps without even realising it, especially where the damage is caused indirectly. The second impediment is related to the legal factors that must be proved by the victim : fault committed, damage, chain of causality. There exists, as the European Commission highlights in its White Paper, a "*structural information asymmetry*", which it says "*it is essential to overcome*",[27] and it can prove extremely delicate for the victim to identify the key evidence. As for damage, the victim may come up against the difficulty of a judge invoking not only *damnum emergens*, but also *lucrum cessans*, not to mention the fact that the chain of causality will not necessarily be established automatically.[28] The third impediment is of course related to the cost of litigation, particularly in a domain where the search for proof and the demonstration of damage sustained can lead to significant costs for the plaintiff.

In its White Paper, the European Commission attempted to provide a certain number of clarifications in order to eliminate these impediments, or at least reduce them, so as to encourage Member States to facilitate the effectiveness of private actions. It was in the interest of companies – especially those with the greatest concerns about their strategy and in particular the way in which they deploy their resources – to anticipate what are for the moment the recommendations of the Commission, and to try to influence the future implementation of new regulatory measures within Member States in an effort to prevent private actions from posing a real strategic threat. The European Commission has proposed certain solutions to facilitate the damages actions taken by victims of anticompetitive practices. To enable victims of all categories – including indirect purchasers – to exercise their rights effectively, and to ensure they are not impeded by their isolation (or feeling of isolation), the development of two complementary actions has been suggested : representative actions and opt-in collective actions.[29] Given that

[27] See 2.2 Access to evidence (*inter partes* disclosure).

[28] In relation to these elements, see D. FASQUELLE, *Les dommages et intérêts en matière concurrentielle*, DGCCRF web site : http://www.finances.gouv.fr/fonds_documentaire/dgccrf/02_actualite/ateliers_concu/civilcomm3a.htm.

[29] Jenny explains, however, that the judicial systems in which indirect victims may take civil liability actions are much more costly than those in which only direct victims may do so; see F. JENNY, *L'action au civil et le droit de la concurrence : les expériences étrangères*, Colloque sur

the costs of antitrust damages actions can also impede such actions, the Commission encourages Member States to favour settlements, to set court fees in a pertinent manner, and to give national courts the possibility of issuing cost orders derogating from the normal cost rules. On the question of key evidence and the fault committed, the Commission suggests that a minimum level of *inter partes* disclosure be guaranteed under the control of the courts, and that proof of a breach of Articles 81 or 82 should be sufficient to show that a fault has been committed. With regard to evaluating damages, it intends to create a framework to develop methods by which to calculate compensation for any damage – but for damage alone.

It may seem that the impediments outlined here are in fact nothing out of the ordinary in terms of civil liability, but they are made all the more significant by the specific characteristics of anticompetitive behaviour, in particular the possible complexity of the facts and the difficulty of access to information. Two other difficulties must be mentioned in relation to the fact that civil action against anticompetitive practices is not an isolated mechanism; it must coexist with other mechanisms, and this risks tensions that would be unfavourable to the effectiveness of the civil action itself. So how then will civil liability actions relate to the leniency programmes? Using the prisoner dilemma, Lévèque compellingly shows the complexity of the effect the leniency programmes have on the detection and formation of cartels.[30] Their effectiveness in the long term, both from the point of view of the identification and disappearance of existing cartels, and that of the emergence of new cartels, has yet to be demonstrated. If a company, by denouncing the existence of a cartel in which it participates, then finds itself more at risk of a civil liability action, the mechanism can be said to be a disincentive, and the result will then be contrary to that sought by the regulator, except where the amount of damages to be paid is less than the financial sanction which the company will escape. The Commission White Paper suggests that "*adequate protection against disclo-*

la réparation du préjudice causé par une pratique anti-concurrentielle en France et à l'étranger : bilan et perspectives, 17 October 2005, Cour de Cassation, Paris. Komninos stresses that such a system is in contrast to that of the US, and explains that the solution proposed by the European Commission places the damages awarded above any objective of efficiency; see A.P. Komninos, "The EU White Paper for damages actions : A first appraisal", *Concurrences*, 2008, 2, 84-92.

[30] F. Lévêque, "L'efficacité multiforme des programmes de clémence", *Concurrences*, 2006, 4, 31-36.

sure in private actions for damages must be ensured for corporate statements submitted by a leniency applicant".[31] It also indicates that the possibility of limiting the civil liability of the immunity recipient in relation to its direct and indirect contractual partners must be studied carefully. The second difficulty lies in the relationship between civil action and public action. Civil action cannot, in principle, be substituted for public action, as their objectives are not identical. Three possibilities can be envisaged : civil action as a complement to public action ("follow on"); civil action as parallel to public action; and civil action as autonomous from public action ("stand alone"). The victim's choice of one option over another will have different consequences in terms of recourse to proof, the duration of the dispute, compatibility between the different judgements, etc. The strategic management of legal risk (*sensu lato*) that a company implements must take into account these different scenarios. In its opinion dated 21 September 2006, the French *Conseil de la concurrence* analysed three options, highlighting the various advantages and disadvantages, as outlined very briefly in the table below.[32] This analysis might be seen to prefer "follow on enforcement" if seen in terms of efficiency for the victim.

Stand alone private enforcement		*Parallel private enforcement*		*Follow on private enforcement*	
+	-	+	-	+	-
No dependence on public enforcement	No specific competencies held by the court to judge questions relating to anticompetitive practices		Potential conflict between the decision delivered by the competition authority and that of the Court	Possibility of referring to the decision delivered by the competition authority	Longer duration of dispute
Possibility of assistance from public authority	Potential difficulty in establishing proof of facts		Potential conflict between procedures		

[31] See 2.9.

[32] Avis du Conseil de la concurrence dated 21 September 2006 relating to the introduction of group actions in the domain of anticompetitive practices : http://www.conseil-concurrence.fr/doc/classactions.pdf.

The risk for a company of seeing a rise in the level of strategic threat represented by a position of non-compliance with competition law will only increase as a result of civil action where the victim has the means by which to take such an action successfully. As emphasised above, this question is more sensitive for some victims than for others. One of the most controversial points (controversial because of its determining role in the level of risk facing companies) is that of group, or collective, actions. I will now focus on the particular case of France in order to illustrate this.

B. – *Implementing group action : a source of increased risk for companies*

The isolation and lack of means facing certain victims – mainly consumers – eliminates at the outset whatever little strength a civil action might have. In cases of quite significantly anticompetitive behaviour, companies are therefore protected from a potentially high economic risk. Under French law, Article L.422-1 of the consumer code (*Code de la consommation*) already provides for actions to be taken by joint representation. Its use has remained highly confidential up to now and has never presented a major risk for companies. Each consumer must expressly mandate the recognised body, and it is forbidden to solicit other consumers that might be concerned by advertising or via a call for witnesses. The introduction into French law of collective action could make it possible to overcome the ineffectiveness of the current provision and make the legal risk more credible for companies willing to transgress the rules of competition law. The French employers' organisation, MEDEF, has spoken out against this mechanism.[33] It raises fears – some legitimate – of perverse effects, which might be eliminated if the provisions were made sufficiently secure. Other arguments seem less convincing, in particular that based on the efficiency of consumer law. It is however no surprise that the Union Fédérale des Consommateurs (federal union of consumers) and the CLVC (national association for consumers and service users) both came out strongly in favour of collective action, or, more accurately, group action, to employ the preferred terminology. They seek an opt-out collective action, and cleverly show that they feel more closely aligned with

[33] See position adopted in July 2006 : http://www.medef.fr/main/core.php?pag_id=55014.

the model developed in Quebec than that in the US.[34] For its part, the *Conseil de la concurrence* clearly stated its preference[35] (as did the First President of the *Cour de cassation* in May 2006[36]), but did not however specify which system should be chosen between the opt-in and opt-out. In its report on group action, submitted to the Minister for the Economy and the Minister for Justice on 16 december 2005, the task force chaired by Messrs Cerutti and Guillaume suggested two options, outlining the advantages and disadvantages of both but without really adopting a position. It did however indicate that the opt-out would be less advisable if it were to be reserved for recognised consumer associations alone.[37] It is clear that various influential powers have voiced their concerns to the legislature. On 17 June 2008, a bill to modernise the economy was adopted by the deputies of the French National Assembly. The text was later examined by the Senate, on the 30 June 2008. Despite the intervention of certain deputies – in particular Mr Charié, who presented an amendment to insert a Chapter III after Article L.422-3 of the *Code de la consommation* with specific reference to group action[38] – the bill contains no provisions whatsoever relating to collective action. Communicating with the legislature – whether directly or indirectly – in an effort to prevent the emergence of a possible strategic threat, or at least of additional legal risk, is an integral part of strategic management. Even if group action were to be introduced into French law in the near future, its potential efficiency would not necessarily be realised; two instruments that would contribute to its success would still be missing. First, the discovery procedure. This might initially seem very useful for the establishment of proof; however, as correctly pointed out by the task force on group action, it would appear that this procedure would not transfer easily to the French judicial system.[39] Indeed, it is highly criticised in the US, where even large numbers of law-

[34] See : http://www.ensemblenjustice.org/actionGroupe.php.

[35] Judgement dated 21 September 2006 relating to the introduction of group action to the domain of anticompetitive practices : http://www.conseil-concurrence.fr/doc/classactions.pdf.

[36] According to him, the introduction of collective action into French law is "unavoidable"; see interview in *La Tribune*, 16 May 2006.

[37] Report published by Documentation Française in 2005, Paris (Ministère de la Justice). Available at : http://www.ladocumentationfrancaise.fr/rapports-publics/054004458/index.shtml.

[38] Amendment n° 351 : http://www.assemblee-nationale.fr/13/amendements/0842/084200351.asp.

[39] See footnote n° 36.

yers are challenging the exorbitant costs it generates for companies, especially since the development of e-discovery. Secondly, the French legal system prohibits contingency fees; in principle this would disallow a law firm from assuming responsibility for the costs of a group action on the basis of subsequent remuneration from a percentage of the monies awarded by the civil courts. Once again, however, there is the risk of perverse effects, as revealed by a scandal involving the lawyers of an American firm, who were accused of having manipulated the mechanisms of class action.[40] Punitive damages are another issue that might be raised – a concept that is totally alien to French law. Civil action would provide for compensation for injury sustained by the economy; as highlighted by Vogel, this would strengthen the role of private action and weaken that of public action.[41] If group action were to be introduced into French law, the probable litigation cost (*Coût Judiciaire Probable* – see above) to be incurred by companies responsible for the behaviour in question would be radically modified. The potential for settlement would be affected and the *Coût Judiciaire Moyen* could most likely no longer be calculated on the same basis. The tools by which legal risks are measured would therefore have to be refined.

To employ a notion that is dear to Ost and van de Kerchove, the law is a game,[42] and the players involved all have different strategies. The State and its institutions strive for a competitive market that conforms to a chosen model and just compensation for damage caused to private parties. As for companies, their attitude towards the risk of non-compliance with competition law can vary in accordance with various considerations. Their capacity to anticipate and manage this risk can manifest itself prior to legislative changes via lobbying and communication, and, following such changes, via effective management of legal disputes. The development of private enforcement, if this does indeed go ahead, will result in greater complexity in the strategic management of potential conflict with the provisions of competition law. One important factor will be the aptitude of victims – be they professionals or con-

---

[40] See : http://www.law.com/jsp/llf/PubArticleLLF.jsp?id=1190883782451.

[41] L. Vogel, *L'articulation entre le droit civil, le droit commercial et le droit de la concurrence*, Colloque sur la réparation du préjudice causé par une pratique anti-concurrentielle en France et à l'étranger : bilan et perspectives, 17 October 2005, Cour de Cassation, Paris.

[42] F. Ost and M. van de Kerchove, *Le droit ou les paradoxes du jeu*, 1992, Paris : PUF.

sumers – to make use of the means placed at their disposal. It is my contention that in a liberal economy, information asymmetry must be reduced as much as possible, which implies that perpetrators of anticompetitive behaviour must be in a position to identify the risks they are taking, and in particular the methods applied by the regulatory authorities and relevant judges in determining the fault committed and the damage sustained, and also that the victims of such practices must be able to access the information required for them to exercise their rights effectively. That notwithstanding, we must endeavour to avoid a shift towards a system that could generate unjustified costs, both for companies and for society as a whole, and also favour the kind of opportunistic behaviour so well highlighted by Jenny : impeding the threat of a hostile takeover bid; deliberately and illegitimately damaging a company's reputation; harming strategies of innovation; enticing a competitor or partner into an unwanted transaction, etc.[43] Regardless of the authority that applies it or the economic entity that invokes it, competition law must above all avoid becoming a threat to economic progress, innovation and the acquisition of clientele. Lawmakers must therefore find the right balance between a competition law that poses almost no threat to companies willing to flout its provisions, and one which is a source of unjustified costs, or, if one takes this reasoning to its extreme, a source of strategic threat even for those companies that choose the path of compliance.

[43] F. Jenny, *op. cit.*, n° 29.

PRIVATE ENFORCEMENT – THE BUSINESS COMMUNITY'S VIEWPOINT

BY

Philippe LAMBRECHT

Secretary General, Federation of Enterprises in Belgium

AND

Charles GHEUR

Advisor, Federation of Enterprises in Belgium

I. – Introduction

Competition law is a key issue for a federation like ours. FEB's mission is to defend the interests of all Belgian companies, whatever their size, market share or sector. That just shows how much importance FEB attaches to the proper application of competition law, protecting all companies and all consumers. We firmly believe in the need for vigorous competition, which contributes to the growth of the economy, in line for instance with the Lisbon Strategy. However, the European Commission's latest initiatives in this area are causing concern in the business world.

On 2 April 2008, Competition Commissioner Neelie Kroes published a White Paper on damages actions for breach of the EC antitrust rules. [1] The Commission's objective was to enable the victims of breaches of competition law to efficiently exercise their right to reparation for damage they had suffered.

We should first point out that FEB is a strong supporter of developing and maintaining a competitive commercial environment in the EU. We are convinced that competition provides the best incentive for businesses to be efficient, encourages innovation and

[1] White Paper on damages actions for breach of the EC antitrust rules, COM(2008) 165 final, http://ec.europa.eu/comm/competition/antitrust/actionsdamages/documents.html.

guarantees consumers the best possible choice. Antitrust law is crucial and its public and private enforcement is fundamental to creating and maintaining a competitive economy, in the same way as the public and private enforcement of other Community rules, such as those related to the free movement of goods, is fundamental to the efficient operation of the internal market.

Nevertheless, one thing will surely have escaped no one's attention : with the laudable aim of supporting compensation for damage caused by anti-competitive practices, the Commission has proposed solutions that could seriously clash with the principles firmly anchored in Member States' civil liability law or procedural law.

II. – The *Belgian* business community's viewpoint

The title of this article is "Private enforcement – the business community's viewpoint". But perhaps it would be more appropriate to talk about "the *Belgian* business community's viewpoint", as how FEB's sister federations – the other national employers' organisations – view the White Paper may vary depending on the legal situation in the different EU countries. Their level of concern will reflect the legal traditions and culture of individual Member States.

For example, the Commission's proposal for the fault requirement[2] will not be a matter for concern in Belgium because in the eyes of Belgian law a breach of a legal requirement (and thus a provision of the EC Treaty) is a fault for which the infringer is liable under Article 1382 and the following articles of the Civil Code. Therefore proof of a breach of the EC Treaty must be considered sufficient reason to bring a damages action – not because of the existence of a presumption of blame, but because of the equivalent nature of competitive and civil faults, given that undermining the market is in itself an element that incurs liability.

[2] For Member States that require fault to be proven, the Commission proposes a measure to make it clear that : (i) once the victim has demonstrated a breach of Article 81 or 82, the infringer should be liable for damage caused unless he demonstrates that the infringement was the result of a genuinely excusable error; (ii) an error would be excusable if a reasonable person applying a high standard of care could not have been aware that the conduct restricted competition.

However, the example just given doesn't mean that we approve of the European Commission's approach. A remark that needs to be made before discussing the different issues relevant for damages actions is that FEB regards as inappropriate the use of EU competition law to harmonise important aspects of Member States' law of tort and procedural law. National rules relating to issues such as fact-finding, unlawfulness, burden of proof, causation and defences have evolved gradually in the different Member States' legal systems and perform their role within the context of those systems. Such traditional concepts of national law should not be harmonised on the basis of the Commission's legislative competence in the field of competition.[3]

Many people before us have found themselves asking a question about the legal basis : "Which provision(s) of the EC Treaty is the Commission using as its basis to make the proposals in the White Paper?" Indeed, we might raise legitimate questions about the legal grounds of any action taken by the European Union in these areas, as its competition law mandate does not entitle it to fundamentally change the general rules of civil procedure of the Member States – not to mention the question of establishing whether the Commission's initiatives actually conform to the subsidiarity principle, which is a moot point.

III. – Causes for relief *vis-à-vis* the Green Paper

The White Paper conjures up a number of reservations in the business world, as we shall see below. But let us start by expressing an initial sense of relief. Certain options in the Green Paper published in late 2005 had made us fear the worst,[4] but the most "extreme" seem to have been abandoned by the Commission in its White Paper.

(a) For example, we are delighted that the idea of introducing a discovery process in Europe has not been retained. Discovery (as seen in the United States) means that a company has to divulge

[3] This is also BusinessEurope's position – cf. its responses to the White Paper on the Commission's website : http://ec.europa.eu/comm/competition/antitrust/actionsdamages/white_paper_comments.html.

[4] Green Paper on damages actions for breach of the EC antitrust rules, COM(2005) 672 final.

all its commercial documents during a hearing. The system is extremely dangerous because it entails an obvious risk of being abused by a competitor so as to gain access to confidential information or business secrets.

(b) The White Paper doesn't retain the possibility of an opt-out in collective actions, which would have allowed all the victims to take part in these actions without even having to officially register. Redress actions of this type, launched on behalf of an indefinite group of people, without any official legal mandate, goes against many principles of Belgian law, and in particular the principle of the authority of *res judicata*.

(c) In the White Paper the Commission no longer proposes a system of multiple damages, but rather a system of single compensation, in alignment with the case law of the European Court of Justice. The aim of paying out damages is solely to provide reparation, rather than to encourage victims to demand reparation. The Commission will probably have taken note of the risks of unjust gain for victims and consequently market imbalance as well as the risk of legal actions being abused by parties stubbornly insisting on competition law so that they can receive higher compensation.

(d) The Commission doesn't appear to want contingency fees either. In this system, the plaintiffs' lawyer is paid a set percentage of the sum awarded to the group. This means of paying lawyers must be avoided at all costs, otherwise lawyers, as seen in the United States, will do all they can to precipitate and bring to a successful conclusion court actions, since their fees are based on success in such actions. Moreover, the system of contingency fees goes against the prohibition, in force in Belgium, on lawyers being paid based on a *de quota litis* clause.

(e) Happily, another characteristic of the US system, punitive damages, seems to have been spurned by the Commission. In the US this possibility means that the prospects of significant damages over and above what would be needed to compensate the plaintiffs is an added incentive for lawyers to bring class actions. But this system would be completely out of place in Belgian law : Belgium's law on civil liability – like that of many other Member States – is based on the principle that damages must compensate the victim for all the losses suffered but are not punitive in any way.

We were relieved, then, to note that the Commission had rejected these options, many of which are specific to the US system of class actions. However, the fact that the Commission White Paper doesn't recommend opt-out, contingency fees, punitive damages and so on in its White Paper doesn't mean that these aspects of the American system won't resurface. The White Paper doesn't offer any guarantee that they won't be retained – maybe in national legislation. We shall come back to this.

IV. – Main causes for concern

A. – *Collective redress*

Despite the series of improvements with respect to the Green Paper of 2005 we have just listed, the recent White Paper is continuing to cause companies a great deal of consternation. Our main concern about the White Paper is the Commission's proposal to introduce collective redress mechanisms.

Our first comment is on a methodological issue. We are dismayed that Commissioner Kroes has produced her White Paper before her colleague, Commissioner for Consumer Affairs Meglena Kuneva, has finished her work, as we know that Commissioner Kuneva has launched a range of studies and surveys on the issue of collective redress mechanisms.[5] The results of her consultations are expected by the end of 2008.[6] However, following agreement with the other members of the Commission, Commissioner Kroes has pre-empted her colleague with her White Paper. However, we think an issue as delicate and important as this one deserved more reflection. FEB only wants to see moves being made towards a reform if very detailed impact assessments are taken as the basis. In our opinion, the principles of better regulation demand the utmost prudence to ensure that an ill-thought-out reform doesn't lead to collective

[5] (1) K.U.Leuven's study on alternative means of consumer redress other than redress through ordinary judicial proceedings, http://ec.europa.eu/consumers/redress_cons/collective_redress_en.htm; (2) evaluation of the effectiveness and efficiency of existing collective redress mechanisms; (3) analysis of problems faced by consumers in obtaining redress for mass claims, and the consequences of such problems for consumers, competitors and the relevant market (results to be published autumn 2008).

[6] Communication on consumer collective redress (to be published in December 2008) will involve consultation on the options relating to consumer collective redress (cf. E-2020/08EN Answer given by Commissioner Kuneva on behalf of the Commission).

actions being abused, as has been seen for example in the United States.

Indeed, knowing the effects of class actions on the other side of the Atlantic, we can only shudder at the idea of a more or less identical system being introduced here. The annual cost of damages actions in the US is put at some 240 billion dollars a year – a figure larger than the Belgian budget. Class actions have thus become a real "business" in the United States, with benefits primarily for a few specialist lawyers. The perverse consequences of class actions led the US Congress to adopt the Class Action Fairness Act in 2005. This legislation aims to cut down on the abuses involved in class actions. It would be paradoxical if we were to embark on a path of introducing class actions in Europe while the US has been trying for a number of years to remedy the adverse effects of this type of action.

Admittedly, the Commission isn't proposing to introduce class actions, but more balanced collective redress actions, which don't involve the failings of the North American procedure.

The White Paper proposes two additional collective redress mechanisms for competition law : (1) representative actions brought by consumer associations or trade associations on behalf of their members – whether they are identified or identifiable victims; and (2) opt-in collective actions (in which victims expressly decide to combine their individual claims into a single action).

We already mentioned that the Commission has retained the opt-in, which is the only system to respect the rights of the defendant and the principle of the authority of *res judicata*. This rule protects the litigant by preventing him from being bound by a ruling from actions in which he wasn't involved.

Referring to the representative action, we think that qualified entities shouldn't be able to be certified on an *ad hoc* basis by a Member State for a particular infringement. It is preferable for these entities to be officially designated in advance, based on clearly defined conditions, so as to avoid associations being set up for the needs of a particular case. To avoid "windfall" effects, damages must be awarded to only the victims. At any rate, damages must not be awarded to the consumer associations themselves for their collective loss. Otherwise this type of action could be a means of the associations gathering funds.

In addition to these technical observations, FEB maintains an objection in principle to collective redress mechanisms. We firmly believe that collective actions are not an appropriate solution for the reasons, both legal and socioeconomic, summarised below.

(a) Collective actions go against basic principles of Belgian law. The first principle is that there must be a personal interest for bringing an action : *"Nul ne plaide par procureur"*. The case law of the Court of Cassation is strict in its defence of collective interests.[7] An association cannot in principle go to court to defend its statutory purpose or the collective interest of its members. An association can only start legal proceedings connected with its own interest.[8] Legal derogations exist but they have a strict interpretation (for example, legal action by human rights organisations regarding racism, injunctions proceedings brought by recognised consumer associations).

(b) Moreover, collective actions conjure up the false impression that concentrating on a single litigation case would reduce costs and increase efficiency in identical or similar disputes having the same cause and involving many individuals. That isn't the case. Collective actions will continue to contribute to log-jams in courts which will be incapable of handling these cases, in terms of expertise, management of evidence, procedural incidents, and so on. Since the 1980s, there have been alarming warnings about the overload of our legal system. Do we really want to make the court backlog even worse?

(c) In our current legal system, plaintiffs can always join together, in a spirit of pragmatism, to share the costs and available resources. Nor does anything prevent a party, such as Deminor, from asking the general public for mandates to launch a "collective" action.

(d) Collective redress actions are a huge risk for companies because of such factors as the impossibility of determining and assessing the consequences of such an action, an increase in the number of actions not meeting actual requirements, individuals being encouraged to bring a case and the establishment of associations that aim to obtain landmark rulings.

---

[7] See the landmark judgements of 9 December 1957, 25 October 1985 and 19 September 1996.

[8] Article 17 of the Judicial Code.

(e) A large number of actions are pooled, which exposes companies to exorbitant claims for damages, which inevitably leads in turn to an increase in insurance premiums and even to certain risks becoming uninsurable.

(f) The publicity surrounding such cases has the potential to harm the image of a company, and so have a negative impact on, for example, its stock market value. Companies are forced to compromise under the pressure of a media spotlight, without their liability necessarily being proven or established in the final ruling.

(g) We also note that victims are sometimes conspicuously absent from these procedures, which are often "hijacked" by law firms or various interest groups, as proved by experience with the US system of class actions. This means that the cost of these procedures, which is borne by society as a whole, are generally not paid out to victims, but line the pockets of intermediaries instead.

(h) Legal precedent in the US shows that the main objective of this type of action is no longer to obtain damages for allegedly injured parties, but to put pressure on companies. Private action is now taking the place of the public action. Sometimes such actions are even destabilising manœuvres by unscrupulous competitors. It is very clear that there are significant risks of abuses and destabilisation of companies and of the market if it becomes too easy to bring collective actions.

(i) Adopting a harmonised litigation system similar to the one in the US, even if adapted to the situation in the EU, has the potential to lead – as seen in the US – to a culture of excessive litigation with a resulting increase in costs for the EU economy.

For these reasons, FEB opposes any reinforcement of collective redress mechanisms. Of course, the Commission is not proposing class action, but rather a watered down version that strips class action of its most worrying aspects. However, although the Commission is refraining from introducing the American system, the risk remains nonetheless that Europe could be soon confronted with class action derivatives.

In fact, the introduction of new collective redress mechanisms in Europe is likely to lead to other aspects of the US litigation system being adopted in Europe, including the "no costs" rule and liberal discovery procedures. In addition, contingency fees or other funding incentives which are already being introduced in European countries such as Italy, risk being adopted by other European countries and even by the EU, thus increasing the financial incentives for plaintiff attorneys to litigate. The US class action procedures require these other features if they are to deliver the perceived benefits to plaintiffs that they do in the US. The experience in Australia and Canada has shown that once class actions are introduced, these other features are likely to follow in one form or another. This would result in some of the worst features of US litigation making their way into Europe, with considerable adverse effects on the EU economy.

A balance needs to be found between offering easy access to the courts and the economic cost of this easy access. This is why we believe that, whenever possible, disputes should be settled via out-of-court procedures. Therefore, we think that greater emphasis should be placed on promotion and reinforcement of alternative dispute resolution mechanisms (ADRs). Member States have implemented various forms of ADRs which are fine-tuned to their specific situation. Non-judicial means of redress make it possible to reach a solution acceptable to both parties more rapidly, at a lesser cost and helping to maintain a less confrontational atmosphere between parties. Therefore, these should also be taken into consideration before further action is taken on collective means of redress.

B. – *Access to evidence : disclosure* inter partes

We have already welcomed the fact that the Commission has rejected the discovery system in the strict sense that exists in the United States. We are aware of the drastic consequences discovery can have for a company faced with the procedure.

The Commission suggests that national courts should, under specific conditions, have the power to order parties to proceedings or third parties to disclose precise categories of relevant evidence. Whilst the Commission's proposal is perhaps not unreasonable, it does not settle all of our concerns. Are the Commission's planned safeguards sufficient? Our main concern is about the Commission's proposals on access to evidence : what is meant by "categories of evidence"? Doesn't this hide the discovery system that we thought we had escaped?

Under Belgian law, Articles 870 et seq. of the Judicial Code govern evidence and presentation of documents. The principle is that each of the parties is responsible for proving the facts it puts forward as allegations.[9] The judge may, however, order each litigating party to produce the evidence in their possession.[10] When there are presumptions that are serious, precise and consistent that one of the parties or a third party holds *a document* containing relevant evidence, the judge may order the party concerned to present this document, or a certified copy, so that it may be included in the case file.[11]

We feel that it is excessive that the Commission suggests that a claimant can demand the disclosure of "precise categories of relevant evidence". In fact, the claimant's power to bring nuisance suits would, in this case, be disproportionate to the defence of his/her legitimate interests. We believe that the preferable option is, as is the case under Belgian law, the disclosure of individual relevant documents that are adequately identified and that this should all be done under the supervision of the judge.

Finally, if access to evidence is facilitated in the way the Commission proposes, we think that, as a counterbalance, the rights of defence and protection of trade secrecy must be guaranteed. The Commission's proposal regarding access to evidence makes the need to recognise once and for all the benefit of professional secrecy for in-house lawyers in preparing their opinions even more pressing. It is essential therefore to urge the Commission and the Member States to grant qualified in-house counsel legal privilege. When in-house counsel is properly qualified and complies with adequate rules for professional ethics and discipline, their valuable legal advice should be privileged. When consulting their own in-house lawyers, executives must be able to rely on their counsel's professional secrecy and should not be discouraged from consulting them because there is a risk that confidential deliberations could be disclosed.

[9] Article 870 of the Judicial Code.
[10] Article 871 of the Judicial Code.
[11] Article 877 of the Judicial Code.

We are referring here to the Akzo ruling handed down by the Court of First Instance of the European Communities in 2007.[12] In this case, the Court of First Instance ruled that in order to take advantage of legal privilege, i.e. confidentiality of counsel in a European context, the party providing this counsel must be independent. To define this notion, reference is made to the sense specified in social legislation : an independent worker is a person not bound by a contract of employment. This ruling, therefore, deprives in-house lawyers of legal privilege. FEB, along with the Belgian Institute of Corporate Lawyers and the European Company Lawyers Association (ECLA), does not support the court's argument. We believe that if the determining criterion for identifying lawyers who are entitled to legal privilege is independence, greater account should be taken of intellectual independence and the issue should not be limited to the strict interpretation under social legislation.[13]

C. – *Damages*

The Green Paper that preceded the White Paper raised the following question : should the purpose of awarding damages simply be to provide compensation or should it also help to deter the infringers and encourage victims to claim compensation ?

In principle, FEB believes that damages should be awarded with reference to the loss suffered by the claimant as a result of the infringement by the defendant. Definitions of damages which go beyond compensation would unjustly enrich plaintiffs and could reduce incentives to apply for leniency. It would also introduce punitive elements into a system that should be about compensation. Unlike the US, where public enforcement is less developed than in the EU, punishing breaches of Community law in the EU should be a matter for the public authorities.

The definition provided by the Commission in the White Paper no longer includes punitive aspects and no longer mentions the gain made or doubling the amount of compensation. This is good, but FEB would also like the Commission to explicitly exclude punitive

[12] Court of First Instance of the European Communities, 17 September 2007, *Akzo Nobel Chemicals Ltd v. Commission*, joined cases T-125/03 and T-253/03.

[13] *"If a lawyer is subject to a set of rules that guarantee his intellectual integrity and independence, he should be treated in the same way as external advisers."* J. Cattaruzza, President of the Institute of Company Lawyers (IBJ/IJE) in IBJ/IJE's *2007 annual report*, p. 9.

damages : we should be fully aware of the risks of unjust gain for victims and therefore the market imbalance that punitive damages could entail.

The Belgian system is based on the principle of full compensation of damage whereby the infringer is only required to provide compensation for the loss suffered by the victim. FEB supports this principle and believes that a clear distinction must be maintained between the regulatory role granted to competition authorities whereby these authorities have the powers to issue sanctions, and the role granted to courts to redress the loss incurred.

As we have just mentioned, Belgium's law on civil liability – like that of many other Member States – is based on the principle that damages must compensate the victim for all the losses suffered but are not punitive in any way. Given the substantial increase in the size of the fines issued by the European Commission and the national competition authorities, we can safely say that this objective is being achieved without the need for the additional application of punitive damages.

D. – *Costs of damages actions*

Starting legal proceedings is by no means a trivial matter. As a result, all measures that could remove responsibility from litigants must be avoided.

FEB does not support the proposal to give courts discretionary powers to order, at the start of the case, that the claimant will not be required to pay costs even if the case is rejected.

The development of whimsical or improper actions should not be encouraged by excessively reducing the financial risk to claimants represented by the cost of proceedings. Moreover, such a proposal conflicts with our procedural law and, in particular, with new rules on the recoverability of lawyers' fees. [14]

[14] Law of 21 April 2007 regarding recoverability of lawyers' fees and expenses (*"Loi relative à la répétibilité des honoraires et des frais d'avocats"* published in the *Belgian Official Gazette* of 31 May 2007). Under this law, the party that loses the case is ordered to pay an *indemnité de procédure* (procedural indemnity) consisting of a fixed-sum contribution towards the lawyers' fees and expenses that have been incurred by the winning party.

If a claimant did not have to cover court costs, there is no doubt that many questionable claims would flood the courts and reduce the efficiency of competition law.

V. – Conclusion

Those were our main comments and concerns regarding the White Paper on damages actions for breach of the EC antitrust rules. For the rest, we refer to the responses that FEB submitted to the Commission (specifically with regard to the binding effect of national competition authorities' decisions, passing on overcharges and limitation periods). [15]

In general, we feel that the White Paper lacks precision and that its proposals are inadequately explained. Greater clarity is needed on many of the issues the Commission presents, for example with regard to access to and disclosure of evidence.

By way of conclusion, FEB reiterates its desire that damage caused by cartels and abuses of dominant positions should be better compensated. However, the European model should not be distorted. The Community model has a certain sense of originality : it combines, on the one hand, market protection guaranteed by the competition authorities and, on the other, protection of private interests guaranteed by the judge responsible for drawing conclusions, at civil level, on the existence of anti-competitive practices. The combination of these two aspects should deter companies from undermining competition law.

We think that the right balance needs to be found : if the fate of victims needs to be improved as the Commission suggests, care also needs to be taken not to weaken certain fundamental rights, such as the rights of defence and protection of business secrets.

Is Commissioner Kroes aware that she is preparing to open a Pandora's box? She has of course removed the most harmful options from the Green Paper, and we welcome this move. But having said that, the concerns of the business world have not been set-

[15] See FEB's responses to the White Paper on damages actions for breach of the EC antitrust rules, http://www.vbo-feb.be/index.html?page=58&lang=fr. The stakeholders' comments on the White Paper received by DG Competition are available at : http://ec.europa.eu/comm/competition/antitrust/actionsdamages/white_paper_comments.html.

tled. The proposal aims to provide minimum guarantees for redress at EU level but does not take into consideration the risk that – once the existing balance in national system is broken – Member States might end up going too far and adopting more far-reaching rules. These rules, on the one hand, might not provide effective results for the consumers and, on the other hand, imply excessive burdens for companies (e.g. more far-reaching collective action mechanisms, contingency fees, etc.) This would result in an even more fragmented playing field in Europe. The Commission should at least set the red lines that must not be crossed more explicitly.

The paper affects 27 different legal systems and different approaches to litigation and tort law. These are delicate features of national legal systems and – as we said – competition law is not the most appropriate instrument for pushing for harmonisation. National rules related to issues such as fact-finding, unlawfulness, burden of proof, causation and defences have evolved gradually in the different Member States' legal systems and perform their function within the context of these systems. External intervention in such delicate aspects of national legal systems risks upsetting these systems with unforeseeable effects on their inner balance.[16]

FEB warns against the risks of creating a "litigation industry". By making access to the courts too easy, the measures proposed by the Commission if not accompanied by robust safeguards will gradually plunge Europe into a litigation society paralysed by disputes.

To sum up, we are in favour of a competition culture, but against a litigation culture that has a devastating impact on growth and employment and paralyses the spirit of entrepreneurship.

[16] This is also BusinessEurope's position: http://ec.europa.eu/comm/competition/antitrust/actionsdamages/white_paper_comments.html.

A FEW THOUGHTS ABOUT REPRESENTATIVE ACTIONS

BY

ANNE-LISE SIBONY

LECTURER (*CHARGÉE DE COURS*) IN EUROPEAN LAW
CO-DIRECTOR OF IEJE
UNIVERSITY OF LIÈGE

In this session, we have so far heard the respective points of view of the Commission, of the Belgian national competition authority, of the representatives of the business community, but not that of consumers. I have no particular authority to voice the point of view of consumers and it is not my intention to try to do so. After all, not taking sides is a rare privilege of academics. Rather, I would like to share a few thoughts relating to a topic addressed in the *White paper*, which is of particular interest to consumers, plaintiff lawyers, as well as companies who could be either plaintiffs or defendants in such actions.

Collective action mechanisms have called a lot of individual and collective attention from scholars,[1] national legislators[2] as well as

[1] Among many references see POLVERINO, F., "A class action model for antitrust damages litigation in the European Union", *World competition*, 2007, vol. 30, n° 3, pp. 479-499. In France, there has been an ongoing discussion about the adoption of a class action mechanism for years. See *inter alia* CABALLERO, F., "Plaidons par procureur! De l'archaïsme procédural à l'action de groupe", *RTD civ.*, 1985; GUINCHARD, S., "L'action de groupe à la Française", *RIDC*, 1990 n° 2, p. 599; BORÉ, L., "Pour mieux réparer les préjudices collectifs : une 'class action' à la française ?", *Gaz. Pal.*, September 29th 2001, p. 5; GOLDNADEL, J.-M., "L'introduction des *class actions* en France", *Gaz. Pal.*, September 25-27th 2005, pp. 3-6; CANIVET, G., "Des obstacles juridiques à l'action de groupe, Conference UFC – Que choisir November 10th 2005", *Pour de véritables actions de groupe : un accès efficace et démocratique à la justice*, http://www.courdecassation.fr/; GUINCHARD, S., "Une class action à la française", *D.*, 2005, p. 2180; Conference *Les* "class actions" *devant le juge français : rêve ou cauchemar*, University of Evry, Novembre 18th 2004, *Les Petites Affiches*, Special Issue, June 10th 2005, n° 115. For an economic approach, see DEFFAINS, B., DORIAT-DUBAN, M. and LANGLAIS, E., *Economie des actions collectives*, PUF, 2008.

[2] About the new Italian law, see FIORELLI, G.I., "Collective actions and EU strategy for consumer protection : the draft bills introducing the class action in Italy", *The European legal forum : Forum iuris communis Europae*, 2007, vol. 7, n° 3, pp. I-120-I-122. In France the long-discussed legislation has not been adopted yet. See CERUTTI, G., and GUILLAUME, M., *Rapport sur l'action de groupe remis au ministre de l'économie et au ministre de la justice le 16 décembre*

from the business communities and consumer movements. Among different types of group actions, "representative actions", which are presented in the *White paper* as a mechanism complementary to that of "collective actions"[3] have been somewhat less discussed than class actions. Yet, they too raise a number of questions. The first questions which come to mind are of course "who will represent victims of antitrust violations?" and "who will be able to be represented?". As the *White paper* is rather elusive on both questions, it is perhaps useful to look for analogies in other areas of EC law. In this respect, the area of access to justice in environmental matters may offer some insights. While it is not possible here to draw an exhaustive comparison, I will first indicate a few points which may deserve further consideration. I would then like to briefly touch upon the type of procedure in which representation occurs. Surely, representative actions are envisaged in relation to formal judicial proceedings. But we heard that companies voice a strong preference for alternative dispute resolution techniques, which are perceived as less harmful for the reputation of the defendant firm than formal judicial procedures because of their confidential character. The question here is whether both kind of procedure meet to the same extent consumers' aspirations.

Who will represent whom?
Insights from environmental law

In relation to this elementary question, the *White Paper* is rather vague. It merely states that representative actions will have to be brought "by qualified entities, such as consumer associations, state bodies or trade associations, on behalf of identified or, in rather restricted cases, identifiable victims".[4] As regards the question of how an entity may become qualified to bring a representative action, the *White paper* states that there should be two mechanisms. Entities could be "either (i) officially designated in advance

2005, http://www.justice.gouv.fr/publicat/rapport/rappactiondegroupe.pdf; following up on this report, several legislative proposals have been submitted, including, to quote only the more recent ones, proposal n° 424 of November 21st 2007, http://www.assemblee-nationale.fr/13/pdf/propositions/pion0424.pdf and proposal n° 324 of November 24th 2007, http://www.assemblee-nationale.fr/13/pdf/propositions/pion0324.pdf.

[3] *White paper*, at 2.2.

[4] *White paper*, p. 4.

or (ii) certified on an *ad hoc* basis by a Member State for a particular antitrust infringement to bring an action on behalf of some or all of their members".[5]

First of all, one may first wonder why the European legislator should attempt to define qualified entities and why some administration of a Member State should be empowered to decide what entities are allowed to represent consumers. After all, it is in principle a matter for the court seized to assess standing. But the rules on standing usually refer to impairment of a subjective right, a condition which may not be met by a consumer association who is not itself a victim of the antitrust infringement. One reason to legislate on qualified entities is therefore to give associations a broader standing than they would otherwise have under current national laws. Another likely reason for defining qualified entities is that civil procedure laws differ to a large extent across the Member States. Therefore there may be a need to harmonise the rules on standing at the European level in order to avoid forum shopping. But if these are the rationales, it is clear that precise rules will have to be designed. It will *inter alia* be necessary to define who will be in charge of "officially" recognising that an entity is qualified, what the criteria for recognition will be and whether refusal to recognise an entity as qualified will be subject to appeal.

Similar questions have arisen in the field of environmental law. This came about in the wake of the Århus convention, signed by the European Community and its Member States on 25 June 1998. This international treaty consists of three pillars. The first pillar grants the public the right of access to environmental information. The second grants the right to take part in decision-making processes. The third pillar, which is of particular interest for present purposes, provides for a right of access to justice. The analogy with competition law is not only formal, as the Århus convention is premised on the idea that environmental laws will be better enforced if citizens are empowered to trigger their judicial application. Just like in competition law, there is an element of private enforcement besides the purely private dimension of litigation. In both fields, private actions are not only encouraged for the redress

[5] *Ibid.*

they provide for the successful claimant, but also for their deterrent effect on infringers.

Interestingly, the proposed directive on access to justice in environmental law matters[6] provides for criteria which could apply by analogy in the field of competition law. Article 8 of the proposed directive relates to criteria for recognition of qualified entities. It provides as follows :

> In order to be recognised as a qualified entity, an international, national, regional or local association, organisation or group shall comply with the following criteria :
>
> (a) it must be an independent and non-profit-making legal person, which has the objective to protect the environment;
>
> (b) it must have an organisational structure which enables it to ensure the adequate pursuit of its statutory objectives;
>
> (c) it must have been legally constituted and worked actively for environmental protection, in conformity with its statutes, for a period to be fixed by the Member State in which is constituted, but not exceeding three years;
>
> (d) it must have its annual statement of accounts certified by a registered auditor for a period to be fixed by each Member State, in accordance with provisions set out by virtue of paragraph 1 (c).

Each of these conditions could be discussed in detail, but one perhaps deserves special attention, namely the condition relating to the purpose of the qualified entity. In the field of environmental law, it has been debated whether an association ought to have the protection of environment as its sole purpose or whether, for example, a consumer association could also qualify if it had the protection of environment as one of its objectives.[7] In the field of competition law, one question that would arise in relation to the stated goals of qualified entities is whether the notions of a consumer association and of a trade association are mutually exclusive. While this question may seem somewhat surprising if taken out of context, in relation to competition law litigation it may have an actual bearing. Indeed, there are a number of goods that are bought both by natural and legal persons (*e.g.*, IT equipment, airplane tickets or banking services). Assuming that an antitrust violation occurred in relation to such a product and assuming further that the relevant market was not defined along the lines of different categories of customers, consumer associations and trade associations could be inter-

[6] COM(2003) 624 final.

[7] In this respect, art. 8(a) above is somewhat ambiguous.

ested in bringing a private suit. Because a trade association may face an internal conflict – if some of its members are suspected of having committed a violation while others claim to be victims of the same – they may be less likely to take action. In such a situation, representative actions would be more effective if aggrieved firms could take side with consumers and be represented by the same entities.

While firms and consumers may have similar procedural interests when they are both victims of an antitrust infringement, the same cannot be said when considering defendant companies and consumers. Defendant companies have a clear preference for confidential procedures while private persons may be wary of such proceedings. This brings me to the second set of remarks I would like to make.

Formal judicial proceedings v. alternative dispute resolution mechanisms

Defendant companies have an interest in avoiding public proceedings, because of their high cost, but also because of the bad publicity they bring. Plaintiffs in principle also have an interest in reducing the cost of proceedings (although this may be lessened if they are confident that the defendant will have to pay for these costs at the end of the proceedings). However, bad publicity may be a point on which plaintiffs and defendants have divergent views in the sense that consumers precisely desire the publicity that companies seek to avoid. In saying this, I am only offering a hypothesis which would need to be tested empirically. The reason why this point may deserve consideration has to do with the very rationale for collective actions : each victim of an antitrust violation has a small financial stake. This not only deters individual action, it also raises a question of what a satisfactory compensation is. What matters more for a consumer of, say, football shirts[8] or mobile telephone services :[9] is it getting her money back – presumably some 30 € – or having a court of law let it be known that the firm from which she purchased this good or service has misbehaved ? In other

[8] *Allsports Limited v. Office of Fair Trading*, Case 1021/1/1/03.

[9] French Competition Council, Case 05-D-65, November 30th 2005 relating to practices in the mobile communication sector.

words, the principle according to which justice must not only be done but also be seen to be done may reflect a preference of consumers.

Such a preference might by be called by economists a preference for moral satisfaction. If this is taken into account, cost and speed are not the only relevant variables when reflecting on the best procedural mix. The outcome of the proceedings in terms not only of money but also of publicity may be essential in order to secure active engagement of victims in private enforcement. In legal theory terms, it may be said that bad publicity earned by violators of competition law must be viewed as an element of restorative justice. Whatever the terms, it would make sense for the European legislator to allow for the possibility that consumers – and consumer associations – prefer formal proceedings because they are public. This is why, in the case of private actions in the field of competition law, formal representative actions are surely at least as important as mediation[10] if not more.

[10] Directive 2008/52/EC of the European Parliament and of the Council on certain aspects of mediation in civil and commercial matters, *OJ* 2008 L136/3.

PART II.

Settlements and Commitments

THE EUROPEAN COMMISSION'S NEW SETTLEMENT PROCEDURE FOR CARTEL CASES : A DEFENSE COUNSEL'S PERSPECTIVE

BY

David W. HULL

Partner, Covington & Burling, Brussels

AND

Michael J. CLANCY

Associate, Covington & Burling, Brussels

On 30 June 2008, the European Commission introduced a new procedure designed to facilitate the early settlement of cartel cases.[1] Under this procedure, if a defendant voluntarily acknowledges its involvement in the cartel as well as its liability, the Commission can reduce the fine. The system is designed to alleviate some of the procedural burdens arising in a full administrative procedure, which include granting full access to the file, conducting an oral hearing, and drafting and defending a full statement of objections and final decision. In addition, the system will likely reduce the significant number of appeals to the Community Courts in cartel cases. The Commission hopes that the new system will allow it reduce its backlog of cartel cases and free up resources to investigate new cases.

[1] The Commission's settlement package consists of the implementing regulation, Commission Regulation (EC) No 622/2008 of 30 June 2008 amending Regulation (EC) No 773/2004, as regards the conduct of settlement procedures in cartel cases ("Implementing Regulation"), the Commission Notice on the conduct of settlement procedures in view of the adoption of Decisions pursuant to Article 7 and Article 23 of Council Regulation (EC) No 1/2003 in cartel cases ("Settlement Notice"), the FAQ document, Antitrust : Commission introduces settlement procedure for cartels – frequently asked questions ("Settlement FAQs"), and a press release, Antitrust : Commission introduces settlement procedure for cartels ("Settlement Press Release"), all available at http://ec.europa.eu/comm/competition/cartels/legislation/settlements.html.

This paper analyses the new settlement procedure from the standpoint of defense counsel. First, we provide an overview of the settlement procedure and discuss certain limitations inherent in the procedure that may limit its overall effectiveness, particularly in more complex cases. We then discuss the main factors that a defendant should take into account in deciding whether to settle a case.

I. – Overview of the Settlement System

A. – *Which Cases Are Suitable for Settlement?*

The Commission is under no obligation to enter into settlement discussions and has emphasized that it retains a broad margin of discretion in deciding which cases may be suitable for settlement. [2] In deciding whether to open settlement discussions in a given case, the Commission will consider "the probability of reaching a common understanding regarding the scope of potential objections with the parties involved within a reasonable time frame, in view of factors such as the number of parties involved, foreseeable conflicting positions on the attribution of liability, extent of contestation of the facts." [3] It will also consider "the prospect of achieving procedural efficiencies... including the scale of burden involved in providing access to non-confidential versions of documents from the file." [4]

It will be interesting to see whether the Commission only uses the settlement procedure in straightforward cases or whether it also will offer to open settlement discussions in more complex cases. While it may be easier to reach the requisite "common understanding" with the parties in straightforward cases, the greatest procedural efficiencies will be in complex cases, particularly if this allows the Commission to avoid having to defend its decision in the lengthy appeals process. Even where the Commission manages to overcome the hurdle of reaching a common understanding in factually complex cases with multiple parties, the settlement procedure may not offer the parties sufficient incentives to settle. In a complex case, a

[2] Settlement Notice, p. 5.
[3] Settlement Notice, p. 5.
[4] Settlement Notice, p. 5.

defendant may have more options available to it in terms of arguments and defense strategies and may be unwilling to surrender these options in return for only a 10 % reduction in its fine. As discussed below in Section II, there are a number of disadvantages to choosing to settle a case, and, the more complex the case, the greater these disadvantages would seem to be.

B. – *Settlement Discussions*

Where the Commission believes that a case is suitable for settlement, it will invite all of the defendants to submit a written request within two weeks if they are interested in entering into settlement discussions.[5] Thereafter, the Commission will control the timing and order of settlement discussions and will provide each defendant with the envisaged objections, range of likely fines and the relevant supporting evidence, upon which each defendant will be given an opportunity to state its views.[6] Any reduction in fine received in connection with a settlement would be in addition to any reduction received under the Leniency Notice.[7]

The settlement procedure is not intended to be the kind of plea-bargaining system used in the United States. The Commission has emphasized that it will not negotiate the use of evidence or the level of fine imposed.[8] Despite the one-sided nature of the settlement discussions, defendants may have some ability to influence the contours of the case and the level of fines as the Commission will give defendants an "opportunity to assert their views on the potential objections against them."[9] Thus, there may be some room for the Commission to make the settlement option more attractive to a defendant during the course of discussions by changing its views on various aspects of the case that enter into the calculation of the fine in response to the arguments put forward by the defendant. However, the Commission will be constrained in its ability to do so by its need to avoid discrimination among the defendants during the settlement process as well as by the terms of its own Fining Guidelines, which are aimed at making the Commission's fining policy

[5] Settlement Notice, p. 9.
[6] Settlement Notice, p. 15.
[7] Settlement Notice, p. 33.
[8] Settlement Press Release.
[9] Settlement Notice, p. 16.

more predictable and consistent and, thus, necessarily limit the Commission's discretion in setting fines. As a result, once certain facts are established, the Commission's ability to offer individual defendants extra incentives to settle may be limited.

The absence of any meaningful room to negotiate on the part of the Commission could undermine the overall effectiveness of the settlement procedure. In light of the various disadvantages to settlement that are discussed below in Section II, it is questionable whether the settlement procedure as currently envisaged would offer many defendants adequate incentives to settle, particularly in complex cases. Unless the Commission is able to find ways of improving its offer by having some flexibility in how it arrives at a fine, settlements may only be reached in the simplest, most straightforward cases.

While the incentives offered to defendants to settle under the new procedure seem generally weak, there could be one notable exception : where the defendant is a large company, the limitation placed on the increase for deterrence (it may not exceed a multiple of two for settling defendants) could represent a significant incentive to settle. Taking the extreme example of a party facing a deterrence multiple of five,[10] the advantage of settling would be a 64 % reduction of its fine.[11] It is not yet clear how the Commission will apply the deterrence multiplier under the 2006 Fining Guidelines, but the cap on this multiple could be a compelling incentive for large companies. In these cases, the concern may not be the lack of incentives, but rather the possibility of coercion as a defendant may prefer to settle a weak case than see its liability potentially increase several fold.[12]

---

[10] See Commission Decision, Case IV/37.614/F3 *PO/Interbrew and Alken-Maes*, p. 344.

[11] Assuming a base amount of 100, the fine after a 5X deterrence multiple would be 500, while the fine after a 2X deterrence multiple and the additional 10 % settlement reduction would be 180, a 64 % net reduction.

[12] See Wouter P.J. WILS, *The Use of Settlements in Public Antitrust Enforcement : Objectives and Principles*, pages 20-21, available at http://papers.ssrn.com/sol3/cf_dev/AbsByAuth.cfm?per_id=456087 ("large settlement rewards may allow competition authorities to obtain settlements in weak cases (or including weak parts of cases), which, in the absence of the settlement option, would never have been opened, or would have been discontinued by the competition authority. In such cases the voluntary nature of settlements could be contested on the ground that the competition authority has placed the defendant into an unfavorable choice situation, compared to the situation in which the defendant would have been if no possibility of settlement had existed").

C. – *Settlement Submission*

Where the Commission and a defendant reach a common understanding regarding the scope of the objections and the range of likely fines, the defendant will be given at least 15 working days in which to put forward a final settlement submission.[13] The specific language of the settlement submission will reflect the settlement discussions with the Commission, and must contain an acknowledgement of liability and an indication of the maximum fine accepted by the parties.[14] The defendant must also waive its right of access to the file and to an oral hearing. Once submitted, the defendant is not allowed to revoke or withdraw the settlement submission unless the Commission does not meet the settlement request.[15] In contrast, the Commission may withdraw from the settlement procedure at any time. For instance, if one defendant decides not to submit a settlement submission, the Commission may decide to withdraw from the procedure. As discussed below, the possibility of such a withdrawal is one of the disadvantages of the procedure that will need to be taken into account by defendants in deciding whether to settle.

D. – *Statement of Objections and Decision*

After the settlement submission has been finalized, the Commission will issue a short-form statement of objections, to which the defendant will have the chance to respond. If the defendant confirms that the statement of objections reflects the content of the settlement submission, the Commission will proceed to the adoption of a final decision. However, the Commission retains the discretion at any point prior to the final decision to depart from the settlement procedure, in which case it will revert to the standard administrative procedure and issue a full statement of objections.

A settlement decision will include the Commission's conclusions that the settling parties have infringed EC competition law, and conclude the proceedings against each settling defendant for the scope and duration of the cartel infringement covered by the settlement submission. Private plaintiffs can thereafter rely on such

[13] Settlement Notice, p. 17.
[14] Settlement Notice, p. 20.
[15] Settlement Notice, p. 22.

decisions in actions for damages before national courts as proof that the addressee of the decision infringed Article 81 or 82 EC. Further, pursuant to Article 16(1) of Regulation 1/2003, national courts have an obligation not to take decisions counter to a Commission decision. Settlement decisions may be appealed before the Community Courts.

II. – To Settle or to Litigate?

A. – *Advantages of Settlement*

In the Settlement Notice, the Commission offers two incentives to defendants agreeing to settle.[16] First, it offers a 10 % reduction of the fine imposed. Second, it agrees that any specific increase in the amount of the fine for deterrence will not exceed a multiple of two. While often overlooked, this second benefit is potentially of much greater significance for large companies for the reasons discussed above.

In addition to the specific incentives set out in the Settlement Notice, settlement may offer a defendant an opportunity to convince the Commission to lower the fine through arguments put forward during the settlement discussions. As discussed above, while the Commission has stated that it will not negotiate settlements and its discretion is limited under the current system in any event, it still may be possible to obtain some additional reductions during the settlement process.

Finally, settlement offers a means of achieving prompt resolution of the matter and certainty regarding the level of fine imposed, thus allowing companies to move on with their business and avoid the additional cost and distraction of extended administrative proceedings and possible appeals.

---

[16] Settlement Notice, p. 32.

B. – *Disadvantages of Settlement*

1. *Forgoing the Opportunity to Appeal*

From the defendant's perspective, perhaps the most significant downside of settling a case is that it effectively gives up its right to appeal. While the Commission has emphasized that a settlement does not prevent a defendant from appealing to the Community Courts,[17] the practical effect of admitting liability, waiving access to the case file, and accepting a maximum level of the fine is that the scope for appeal will be drastically reduced. If a defendant has good arguments, giving up the ability to appeal a case is a step that should not be taken lightly.

A statistical study of cases between 1998 and 2007 determined that fines were appealed to the Community Courts in 45 out of 50 cartel cases (90 %) by one or more defendants. Further, 16 of the 27 decided appeals resulted in a fine reduction, with these reductions averaging 19.3 %.[18] While there are signs that the Community Courts may be less likely to grant reductions going forward, at the very least, these results suggest that a defendant with good grounds for challenging the Commission's position will need to consider carefully whether it would be better off litigating rather than settling.

In addition to giving up its ability to challenge aspects of the Commission's decision dealing with its involvement in the cartel, a defendant who enters into a settlement may be effectively giving up its ability to challenge certain features of the Commission's fining policy that are questionable. For example, a settling defendant would be giving up its ability to challenge the legality of holding a parent liable for its subsidiary's conduct, an issue that is the subject of numerous appeals before the European Court of First Instance as well as the European Court of Justice.[19] If the Commu-

[17] Settlement FAQs, page 6.

[18] Case Associates, C. VELJANOVSKI, *European Commission Cartel Prosecutions and Fines, 1998-2007 – A Statistical Analysis* (2007).

[19] See e.g., Case 509/06, *Akzo Nobel v Commission* ("The CFI appears to have erred in law in finding that liability for an infringement committed by a Community undertaking can be attributed not only to its parent companies but also – and primarily – to the head holding company which indirectly holds the shares in one of the two parent companies.") and Case C-97/08, *Akzo Nobel and Others v Commission* ("The applicants consider that the Court of First Instance has misapplied the concept of 'undertaking' within the meaning of Article 81 EC and Article 23 (2) of Regulation 1/2003[1], as interpreted by the Court in its case-law on the imputation of the unlawful conduct of a subsidiary to its parent company.").

nity Courts disagree with the aggressive stance taken by the Commission on the attribution of liability from a subsidiary to its parent, this ruling will result in significant limits on the fine that the Commission may impose because the cap on the total fine (10 % of an undertaking's total turnover in the previous fiscal year) would apply to the subsidiary's turnover rather than the parent's. Settlement would prevent the defendant from challenging the legality of the 2006 Fining Guidelines, which have yet to be tested in court, but which would seem susceptible of challenge if they are used to impose fines completely out of proportion to those imposed in the past.[20]

2. *Limited Access to File May Lead to Disadvantageous Settlement*

In considering whether to settle, a defendant will need to consider whether the limitation on its rights of access to the file could result in its agreeing to pay a fine that is much higher than it would have had to pay in the event it had decided to litigate the case through the normal procedure. In connection with settlement discussions, the Commission will inform the defendant of "the essential elements taken into consideration... such as the facts alleged, the classification of those facts, the gravity and duration of the alleged cartel, the attribution of liability, an estimation of the range of likely fines, as well as the evidence used to establish the potential objections."[21] Upon request, the Commission will also provide the defendant with a list of all accessible documents in the case file, and the defendant may obtain access to the non-confidential version of any of these documents to the extent such access is justified for the purpose of enabling the defendant "to ascertain its position regarding a time period or any other aspect of the cartel."[22]

Thus, the defendant's right of access to the file will be limited in that it will have to justify why it should have access to a given document, which may be hard to do if the defendant is not sure what is in a given document. Moreover, the Commission places an addi-

[20] Guidelines on the method of setting fines imposed pursuant to Article 23(2)(a) of Regulation No 1/2003, *Official Journal* C 210, 01/09/2006, P. 0002-0005. Judge Vesterdorf, the former President of the Court of First Instance, has expressed doubts regarding the purpose and effect of the Commission's 2006 Fining Guidelines, see *Handelsblatt*, 20 June 2007, *Berlin lehnt Haftstrafen für Kartellsünder ab Vorstoß eines hohen EU-Richters stößt auf Vorbehalte*.

[21] Settlement Notice, pp. 15-16.

[22] Settlement Notice, p. 16.

tional caveat on access to the file in the context of settlement discussions: it will only provide access where the "disclosure does not jeopardize the overall efficiency sought with the settlement procedure."[23] This caveat is reasonable in light of the purpose of achieving procedural efficiencies through the settlement system. Nevertheless, it provides the Commission with a significant degree of discretion in granting access to the file.

As a result of these limitations on access to the file, the settlement procedure is one where the Commission sees all the cards, but the defendant only sees some of them. The danger for the defendant is that it may agree to settle where the Commission has a weak case because it is not able to obtain a complete picture of the Commission's case. In straightforward cases where the facts are clear and the defendant was fully aware of the violation, the lack of access to the file may be less of an issue. However, in complex cases where the facts are not clear or in cases where the defendant does not know the extent of its involvement in the cartel (perhaps because the participants in the cartel were sales managers who are not able or willing to provide a complete picture of the cartel), the lack of access to the file may put the defendant at a greater disadvantage in deciding whether to settle because it will not be in a good position to judge whether the allegations made by the Commission are accurate or to determine whether exculpatory evidence is available.

If the settling defendant is also a leniency applicant, the limitations on access to the file may also affect the defendant's ability to verify that the Commission has provided the appropriate leniency reward. Pursuant to the Leniency Notice, the value of a defendant's leniency application is measured in comparison to the information in the Commission's file at the time of the application. It is therefore necessary to see the Commission's file in order to make this comparison. As a settling defendant will not receive full access to the file, it may not be able to verify whether the value ascribed by the Commission to its leniency application is appropriate. While it would seem to be the rare case where the benefit of challenging the level of leniency granted by the Commission would outweigh the reward for settlement, where the leniency reduction is potentially significant, it is a factor to be taken into account.

---

[23] Settlement FAQs, page 3. See also Regulation 773/2004 (as amended), Article 10a(4).

3. *Risk that Defendant's Position Will Be Prejudiced If Settlement Is Rejected at a Later Stage*

A defendant contemplating settlement must take into account the possibility that the Commission may later decide to abandon the settlement and revert to the normal procedure. The Settlement Notice makes it clear that the Commission may withdraw from settlement discussions or reject the settlement at any time up to the adoption of the final decision.[24] As a practical matter, the situation in which the Commission would seem most likely to break off settlement discussions is when it is unable to convince all parties to settle as it would not be able to realize the procedural efficiencies that it wants to achieve in the settlement process. Otherwise, it is likely that the Commission will be loathe to depart from a settlement save in exceptional cases because such a departure could undermine the Commission's credibility, thus making it harder for the Commission to bring defendants to the settlement table in the future.[25] Nevertheless, a defendant entering into settlement discussions and making a settlement submission will have no guarantee that the submission will be accepted and must take this possibility into account.

If the Commission were to break off settlement discussions or reject a settlement at a later stage in the procedure, there is a danger that the settlement discussions and submission will taint the impartiality of the Commission's case team going forward. The Commission addressed this issue in part by making it clear in the Settlement Notice that any settlement submissions may not be used as proof against the party should the Commission depart from the settlement.[26] However, the Commission did not take the additional step of putting into place measures designed to insulate the officials conducting the settlement negotiations from those prosecuting and ultimately deciding the case. As the CFI emphasized in the recent *Akzo* judgment, once the Commission official sees the evidence, the damage is done: "The mere fact that the Commission cannot use privileged documents as evidence in a decision imposing a penalty

[24] Settlement Notice, pp. 27 and 29.

[25] Even the Commission acknowledges that departure from settlements "should occur only exceptionally if the usefulness of the settlement instrument is to be preserved." Settlement FAQs, p. 6.

[26] Settlement Notice, p. 29.

is thus not sufficient to make good or eliminate the harm which resulted from the Commission's reading the content of the documents."[27] The same concern would seem to apply in the context of settlement discussions – once a defendant has admitted certain facts, it will be difficult to convince the case team otherwise in the event that settlement discussions are terminated and the case proceeds on the normal track. Likewise, if the defendant puts forward its best arguments in the context of settlement discussions, it would be unrealistic to expect the case team not to take these arguments into account when planning its prosecution strategy.

4. *Admission of Liability Could Lead to Higher Fines in Future Cases*

A defendant considering settlement will have to take into account the fact that it could face higher fines in any future cartel cases in which it is involved because it will be considered a recidivist as a result of its admission of liability in the settlement. Under the Fining Guidelines, the basic amount of the fine may be increased by up to 100 % for each infringement established.[28]

5. *Additional Exposure to Damage Claims in Private Litigation*

Finally, a defendant considering settlement will need to take into account the potential effect on its exposure in private litigation involving claims for damages. One of the primary topics of comments in the consultation process preceding the adoption of the settlement procedure concerned the protection of a company's settlement submission from discovery in such private litigation. The genesis of this concern was primarily the requirement in the draft Settlement Notice that the settlement submission had to be "written."[29] As such a written statement could have potentially been discoverable in litigation, in particular in the United States, companies making such a submission could have faced additional financial exposure.

The Commission acknowledged these concerns – the final text of the Settlement Notice provides that a settlement submission may

[27] Joined Cases T-125/03 and T-253/03, p. 87.
[28] Fining Guidelines, p. 28.
[29] Proposed Settlement Notice, p. 20.

be submitted orally, with the only recording of the statement maintained by the Commission itself.[30] In this respect, the Commission's procedure for settlement submissions now mirrors that allowed for leniency applications. However, the Commission did not extend this protection to the written declaration that parties must submit declaring that they envisage engaging in settlement discussions in view of possibly introducing settlement submissions at a later stage.[31] While it is currently unclear whether private litigants would see this as a useful document, it is unclear why the European Commission does not allow companies to also make such declarations orally.

Finally, while the Settlement Notice protects the confidentiality of the settlement submission during the course of the proceedings, third parties will nevertheless be able to obtain the same information from the public version of the resulting Commission decision. Further, as discussed above, entry into a settlement will mean that this decision will be released earlier into the public domain. For parties admitting participation in a global cartel, the release of this information will significantly impact their positions in litigation abroad.

The natural result of the streamlined settlement proceedings is that the Commission will quickly issue decisions in settlement cases. As a result, third parties seeking private damages will be able to bring follow-on litigation against a party sooner. While some companies may see this as an advantage, as it allows them to resolve their liability and put the entire matter behind them more quickly, other companies may wish to delay such private actions for as long as possible.

III. – Conclusion

The new settlement procedure lends itself to relatively straightforward cases where the Commission has strong evidence establishing the main features of the case. In these cases, the scope for defendants to contest liability is limited, so that the advantages of settlement may well outweigh the disadvantages. In addition, these

[30] Settlement Notice, p. 38.
[31] Settlement Notice, p. 11.

are the cases where all defendants are more likely to be willing to settle, which generates the kind of procedural economies that the Commission is seeking before choosing to go down the settlement route.

In more complex cases where the Commission's case is less compelling and there is more room to argue about the facts, the settlement procedure may be less attractive, both for defendants as well as the Commission. If the defendant believes it has strong arguments to contest its liability or is unsure of the degree of its participation in a cartel, it may prefer to litigate rather than settle for a modest decrease in its fine. As noted, the calculus may be slightly different for large companies that are subject to a deterrence multiplier because the benefit of the cap on this multiplier resulting from settlement could be significant. From the Commission's perspective, complex cases may not lend themselves to settlement because it may have difficulty in bringing all of the defendants to the table. If there are holdouts, the settlement process may not generate sufficient procedural economies to warrant settlement.

Going forward, there are several factors that could affect the overall attractiveness of the settlement procedure. First, rulings by the Community Courts in pending cases could affect the willingness of defendants to settle. For example, if the Community Courts show that they are less inclined to reduce fines than in the past, defendants may find the settlement option more attractive. Likewise, if the Community Courts eliminate uncertainty regarding issues such as the attribution of liability from a subsidiary to a parent or certain aspects of the Commission's fining policy, defendants will have fewer arguments on appeal and may be more inclined to settle. Second, if the Commission shows a willingness to engage in a dialogue with defendants during the settlement process and gives serious consideration to their arguments regarding various features of the case, it may be able to make the settlement option more attractive for defendants. Finally, the greater the transparency that the Commission is able to introduce in the process in terms of access to the file and the greater the certainty in terms of potential fines, the more likely defendants will be to settle as they will view settlement as less of a gamble.

The new settlement procedure is clearly a positive step in the direction of offering all parties an option to protracted litigation.

However, it remains to be seen to what extent the new procedure offers sufficient incentives to bring a meaningful number of cases to settlement. As it has done with its leniency procedure, it is to be hoped that the Commission will not hesitate to revise its settlement procedure to take into account its early experience or lack thereof should few cases proceed to settlement.

COMMITMENT DECISIONS UNDER REGULATION 1/2003

BY

JOHN TEMPLE LANG[1]

CLEARY GOTTLIEB STEEN AND HAMILTON LLP, BRUSSELS AND LONDON
PROFESSOR, TRINITY COLLEGE, DUBLIN
VISITING SENIOR RESEARCH FELLOW, OXFORD

REGULATION 1/2003 ON COMMITMENT DECISIONS

Regulation 1/2003 introduced a new kind of decision, called here a "commitment decision", into Community competition law.

Recital 13 of Regulation 1/2003 reads:

> *"Where, in the course of proceedings which might lead to an agreement or practice being prohibited, undertakings offer the Commission commitments such as to meet its concerns, the Commission should be able to adopt decisions which make those commitments binding on the undertakings concerned. Commitment decisions should find that there are no longer grounds for action by the Commission without concluding whether there has been or still is an infringement. Commitment decisions are without prejudice to the powers of competition authorities and courts of the Member States to make such a finding and decide upon the case. Commitment decisions are not appropriate where the Commission intends to impose a fine."*[2]

Article 9 of Regulation 1/2003 reads:

> *"Where the Commission intends to adopt a decision requiring that an infringement be brought to an end and the undertakings concerned offer commitments to meet the concerns expressed to them by the Commission in its preliminary assessment, the Commission may by decision make those commitments binding on the undertakings. Such a decision may be adopted for a specified period and shall conclude that there are no longer grounds for action by the Commission."*

The last sentence of Recital 13 means that commitments are not cases for plea-bargaining. Imposing a fine necessarily involves a finding that there has been an infringement, and in commitment

[1] Cleary Gottlieb is involved in several of the cases discussed in this paper.

[2] See generally TEMPLE LANG, *Commitment Decisions and Settlements with Antitrust Authorities and Private Parties under European Antitrust Law*, in HAWK (ed.), 2005 Fordham Corporate Law Institute (2006) 265-324.

decisions the Commission does not make any finding whether there was an infringement.

The Commission has accepted commitments in only a limited number of cases, although commitments are being considered in others. The Commission has not yet developed a policy on commitments under Article 9. The Commission initially believed that commitment decisions would be unusual and rare, and has been rather surprised that, for various reasons, there have been so many cases in which commitments have already been suggested either by companies or by Commission officials.

The Commission's Commitment Cases so far

Bundesliga

The *Bundesliga* case[3] concerned joint selling of television and radio broadcasting rights for football matches in Germany. According to the Commission's preliminary assessment, the clubs were prevented from dealing independently with television and radio companies, and competition in the sale of the rights was excluded. The Commission ultimately allowed joint selling by the clubs, on the basis that the football interests committed themselves to offer rights for live broadcasts in several packages, by an open non-discriminatory procedure, for a maximum of three seasons at a time. Each club would be free to sell rights to deferred broadcasts to free television and radio, and on mobile phone networks and the internet, but these should not interfere with the various packages.

Such complicated and detailed provisions could only have been arrived at by negotiations.

Coca-Cola

The *Coca-Cola* case[4] involved commitments throughout the EU. The company agreed to make no exclusive supply arrangements and to offer no growth or target rebates. Customers which want to

[3] *OJ* No. C-229/13, 2004; *OJ* No. L-134/46, May 27, 2005; *OJ* No. C-130/2 and C-130/4, decision dated June 22, 2005; Wilbert, *Joint selling of Bundesliga media rights, Commission, Competition Policy Newsletter 2005,* No. 2, pp. 44-46. The text of the Decision and the Bundesliga commitment is available online from the Commission.

[4] *OJ* No. C-289/10, Nov. 26, 2004.

buy the best-selling brands will not be obliged to buy others as well. Rebates will not be made conditional on buying the other brands as well as the best-selling ones, or on reserving shelf space for the entire range. Where Coca-Cola provides a free cooler, and there is no other chilled drinks capacity in the outlet to which consumers have access, the operator may use 20 % of the cooler for other companies' products.

Again, such detailed obligations could never have resulted without negotiations.

Repsol

In the *Repsol* case,[5] the Commission's concerns related to non-compete clauses in distribution agreements for motor fuel with service stations. Repsol gave commitments allowing cancellation of agreements, imposing a maximum duration of five years for new agreements, and agreed not to buy any service stations not supplied exclusively by it. Repsol will advertise in advance the expiry of agreements. An independent auditor will verify compliance and report annually to the Commission.

This commitment decision is now being challenged in the Court of First Instance[6] by a service station that had a supply contract with Repsol, arguing that the decision is not effective to deal with its competition concerns. The challenge is based on a change in the status of the service station under an act in 2007 of the monitoring trustee.

Alrosa

In *De Beers-Alrosa*,[7] the companies first offered to reduce progressively De Beers' purchases of rough diamonds from Alrosa, the second largest diamond producer in the world, over the five year period to which their initial agreement related, and to limit the purchases after that, "in 2011 and thereafter". Later in the Commission's procedure De Beers committed itself to buy <u>no</u> diamonds from Alrosa, after a transitional period. Two independent trustees

[5] *OJ* No. C-258/7, Oct. 20, 2004.
[6] Case T-45/08, *Transportes Evaristo Molina*, *OJ* No. C-92/36, April 12, 2008.
[7] Commission Press Release IP/04/1513; *OJ* No. C-136/32, June 3, 2005.

were to monitor the companies' commitments. (This case is discussed below).

Santiago Agreement

In a case involving the "Santiago Agreement" between European performing rights Societies, the Commission sent a statement of objections arguing that two clauses in the agreement were contrary to Article 81. The clauses limited the territorial scope of multi-repertoire licences for online performance to licencee users in the same Member State as the licensor Society, and required each Society to give equally favourable licensing terms to all other Societies which are parties to the agreement. Several of the Societies gave commitments not to enter into any agreements including similar clauses.[8]

Cannes Extension Agreement[9]

The Cannes Extension Agreement was a reciprocal agreement between collecting Societies concerning mechanical reproduction rights. The Commission criticised a clause providing that, before granting a rebate to a record company in the context of a Central Licensing Agreement, the Society needed the consent of the "relevant member". A second clause prohibited the Societies from ever entering the music publishing or the record production markets. The Societies offered commitments to delete the second clause, and to revise the first to allow rebates to be given, without prior consent, out of the administrative expenses of the Society in question.

Joint selling of media rights to the FA Premier League[10]

This case raised the same kinds of concerns as the *Bundesliga* case. The football clubs in the UK Premier League collectively sold the media rights to the matches involving clubs that play in the League, whether or not the matches are part of the League competition, through a company with exclusive rights to sell them. The

---

[8] *BUMA* and *SABAM* – Santiago agreement, *OJ* No. C-200/11, August 17, 2005; cp. Commission decision *IFPI Simulcasting*, *OJ* No. L-107/58, April 30, 2003; TEMPLE LANG, *Media, Multimedia and European Community Antitrust Law*, in HAWK (ed.), 1997 Fordham Corporate Law Institute (1998) 377-448, 416-429.

[9] Commission decision, *OJ* No. L-296/27, November 15, 2007.

[10] Case Comp/C-2/38.173, March 22, 2006.

Commission was concerned that selling the rights in large packages, or selling all the "live" TV rights to a single buyer, would foreclose competition in television markets, and would restrict output.

The Commission accepted commitments under which the number of matches available for live TV transmission would be increased. TV rights would be sold in a number of packages. No one buyer would be allowed to buy all the rights. Mobile and internet rights would be given more quickly after matches. The duration of the agreements would not exceed three years. The rights would be sold in a transparent and non-discriminatory procedure, to facilitate *ex ante* competition for the rights. Unused rights would go back to the clubs.

Draft commitments were made more precise, after consultation, to limit the discretion of the League. It was agreed that there would be six evenly balanced packages of rights. An increased number of radio rights would be made available, and if one buyer bought them all and there was still unmet demand, extra packages would be offered. Clubs could exploit certain rights on a deferred basis. Bids linked to other packages would be disregarded. A Trustee would oversee the selling process.

Distrigaz[11] *– The Commission explained why its decision was proportional*

The Commission adopted a preliminary assessment concerning Distrigaz's gas supply contracts with a variety of customers including industrial users, electricity producers, and resellers. Long term contracts would prevent customers switching supplier, and so would limit the scope for other gas suppliers, and foreclose their access to the market. This would hinder the development of competition following liberalisation of the market. The Commission was concerned by both the duration of the contracts and the volumes of gas tied to Distrigaz. Only very large buyers could in practice have more than one supplier.

Commitments were accepted under which in each year at least 65 % of the gas supplied to industrial users and electricity producers would be available for competing suppliers to bid for. No new

[11] Case Comp/B-1/37.966, October 11, 2007.

contract with industrial users or electricity producers would be for longer than five years. Existing contracts for more than five years can be terminated. Contracts with resellers must not exceed two years. There will be no clauses for tacit renewal. The commitments are to apply for four years, (regarded as the period of liberalisation of the Belgian gas market) but only as long as Distrigaz has a market share of more than 40 %, and at least 20 % more than its nearest competitor. No contracts are to include restrictions on resale or use.

The Commission was clearly anxious to show that the *Alrosa* judgment (discussed below) had been taken seriously. So the Commission included in the decision a long discussion explaining that the commitments were proportional. Distrigaz can still bid for the business of customers whose contracts are ending, and can still use both long term and short term contracts at the same time, provided that it complies with its overall obligations. When the preliminary assessment was made, Distrigaz had only one contract lasting more than five years, so the main effect of the commitments was to ensure that Distrigaz did not make its contracts longer-lasting than previously. There are specific exceptions that lessen the effect of the commitments. The ban on contracts with gas resellers for more than two years is to prevent Distrigaz from making long term contracts with the largest resellers.

Less convincingly, the Commission said that it would reconsider the terms of the commitment if for example a buyer wanted a contract for more than five years. The Commission should not approve commitments that would involve it in detailed supervision and reconsideration. It would be inefficient to have a new Commission decision each time a commitment needed to be altered, and it would be wrong to delegate important decisions to officials.

Austrian Airlines and Skyteam[12]

In two airline cases, draft commitments have been published for comments, but not yet approved or made binding. In each case, airlines had made arrangements that caused the Commission to raise "competition concerns" (not fully explained, but presumably due to

[12] *OJ* No. C-233/18, Sept. 22, 2005 and *OJ* No. C-76/12, March 27, 2002.

closer cooperation on certain city-pair routes on which those airlines were the principal operators flying).

In the *Austrian/SAS* case, the routes were within Europe. The parties committed themselves to make slots available for two frequencies per day on each route, if a new entrant could not get slots otherwise, but if the number of flights provided by independent competitors fell, the parties would make more slots available. However, they would not have to reduce their frequencies or capacity below 60 % on the route in question. Slots not used by the new entrant would have to be returned to the parties. Slots provided under the commitments would not be paid for. Preference would be given to the new entrant planning the highest number of frequencies. The Commission must approve the parties' choice of new entrants. The parties also committed themselves to make interlining, prorate, and frequent flyer agreements with the new entrants. The parties also agreed to limit their frequencies for four IATA seasons on routes on which a new entrant begins to operate. However, if a new entrant operated 50 % or more of the frequencies, the parties would be able to match any frequency increase.

In addition, the parties also agreed to make intermodal agreements with companies providing surface transport as part of a journey including the city pair routes in question.

In the *Skyteam* case, there were both long haul and European routes in question. Skyteam includes Air France, Alitalia, Delta, KLM and Northwest. A Monitoring Trustee is to supervise implementation of the commitments. Although more detailed than the suggested commitments in the *Austrian/SAS* case, and more complex because of the greater number and variety of routes, the substantive obligations are similar.

In general, it is undesirable for the Commission to seek or accept commitments, the effect of which is to restrict the freedom of the companies in question to compete legitimately (in the airline cases, to increase the frequency of their flights). Any such restriction is in essence regulatory, and not based on competition law. Such a commitment is also likely to be disproportionate, since it can rarely if ever be appropriate to restrict legitimate competition to deal with a competition concern. This is now clear, if it was not clear before, after the *Alrosa* judgment.

Performing Rights Societies – CISAC

This is the third commitment case involving collecting and performing rights Societies. The Commission sent a Statement of Objections to the European performing rights Societies saying that two kinds of clauses in the CISAC model agreement and in a number of reciprocal agreements were contrary to Article 81. The clauses had the effect of preventing owners of performance rights from joining or granting their rights to any Society outside their own State, and granted exclusive rights for each State to the Society in that State. Some of the Societies offered commitments[13] under which they would remove clauses of these two kinds from their reciprocal agreements. In addition, the Societies in question undertook to licence their own performing rights repertoires to internet services, satellite services and cable services directly across the EEA, or to mandate each signatory Society to grant multi-repertoire multi-territorial licences for these kinds of services, with various limitations. However, the Societies could exclude services from the network of reciprocal agreements.

It is curious that the Commission thought it worthwhile to publish for comments commitments that the Societies had explicitly reserved the right to withdraw. Presumably the Commission did not consider that publication for comments necessarily implied that the Commission believed that the commitments were sufficient.

A complete solution to all of the issues raised for European Societies as a result of internet, satellite and cable technology would involve changes going further than those necessary to deal with the Commission's concerns as set out in the Statement of Objections. So, on the basis of the *Alrosa* judgment discussed below, the Commission would presumably have to write its commitment decision in such a way that it made binding only those commitments that were related to its concerns as they had been stated. The European Societies and big music publishers are now discussing several scenarios for new arrangements for distribution of music online. Two of them would be likely to give rise to new competition concerns, but all of them, if they were revised if necessary so as to make them lawful, could be made the subject of commitments. However those aspects

[13] Notice pursuant to Article 27(4) of Reg. 1/2003, Case COMP/38 698 – *CISAC*, *OJ* No. C-128/2, June 9, 2007; *OJ* No. C-200/11, August 17, 2005.

of a comprehensive overall solution that were not necessary to deal with competition concerns expressed by the Commission could be the subject of contractual arrangements between the Societies themselves, and made binding in that way. In multi-enterprise cases, results involving commitment decisions need not be incomplete[14].

Liechtensteinische Kraftwerke and Telecom Liechtenstein

The EFTA Surveillance Authority has published a Notice[15] inviting comments on an agreement to discuss infrastructure development, under which LKW agreed to achieve the infrastructure requirements of Telecom Liechtenstein, and the parties agreed not to compete with one another. The Authority was concerned that the agreement would obstruct or foreclose existing competitors and new entrants. The parties agreed to remove the non-competition clause and the provision for strategic alignment. LKW agreed to find out, at least once a year, the infrastructure requirements of all service providers, and to consolidate their requirements into a non-discriminatory network plan.

The judgment in Alrosa v. Commission[16]

Alrosa challenged the Commission's decision accepting the commitments made by De Beers, on two grounds. Alrosa argued that the commitment that the Commission had ultimately obtained from De Beers was disproportionate, and that the Commission had not given Alrosa an opportunity to comment on the terms that were finally accepted. Three-quarters of the judgment of the Court of First Instance deals with the question of proportionality, which is obviously important in cases under Article 9, and which is the reason why the Commission has appealed to the Court of Justice.

[14] Since this was written the Commission adopted a prohibition decision under Article 7 of Regulation 1/2003, and refused to accept the commitments offered: Commission decision 38.698 CISAC, dated July 16th 2008. A number of the Societies have brought proceedings in the Court of First Instance for the annulment of this decision: see e.g. Cases T-398/08, 401/08, and 422/08. The President of the Court of First Instance refused to suspend the Commission's decision.

[15] *OJ* No. C-118/31, May 15, 2008.

[16] Case T-170/06, July 11, 2007. Compare the Commission decision *IFTRA-Aluminium*, *OJ* No. L-228/3, 1975.

The Court of First Instance stressed that a decision making a commitment binding is not a mere acceptance of a proposal, but a decision that puts an end to an infringement or a possible infringement. A decision may have effects *erga omnes*, by making a particular type of conduct binding in relation to third parties. The Commission argued that the principle of proportionality should apply in a different way to commitment decisions. The Court said (para. 99) that the judicial review of proportionality is an objective review, since the appropriateness of and the need for the decision must be assessed in relation to the aim pursued by the Commission in the specific case. Under Article 9, the aim is to address the concerns expressed in the Commission's preliminary assessment. The Commission must establish the reality of the competition concerns that justified it in envisaging a decision under Articles 81-82, and which allow it to require the company to comply with certain commitments. This necessitates an analysis of the market and an identification of the infringement envisaged which, although not definitive, must be sufficient to allow judicial review of the appropriateness of the commitment. It follows that the Commission cannot adopt a commitment decision prohibiting absolutely all future trading relations between two enterprises unless such a decision is necessary to re-establish the situation which existed before the infringement. The fact that a company has offered commitments does not necessarily mean that they are necessary, and does not limit the review which the Court conducts of the justification for making them binding (para. 107). Unlike Merger Regulation cases, in which the Commission is obliged to carry out an analysis of the future, commitment cases concern existing practices, and therefore the review by the Court is <u>not</u> limited to manifest errors of assessment.

Under the principle of proportionality, where there is a choice between several appropriate measures, the least onerous must be chosen, and the disadvantages created must not be disproportionate to the aims pursued. In this case, since the presumed infringement resulted from the agreement between Alrosa and De Beers, it might have been enough simply not to allow the parties to implement that agreement. But the Commission's concerns also related to long-standing relations which were strengthened and perpetuated by the agreement, which the Commission said prevented Alrosa from establishing itself as an effective competitor and an alternative source of supply. The question therefore was whether De Beers' commitments were necessary (para. 121). The Commission had said that it had not carried out a complex economic assessment, which would have justified limiting the scope of judicial review. But it should have provided an analytical framework sufficient to allow effective judicial review of proportionality. The Court concluded that there was a manifest error of assessment. Solutions less onerous than the complete prohibition of all transactions between Alrosa and De Beers were possible to pursue the aims of the decision, their determination presented no particular technical difficulties, and the Commission should have considered them. *Prima facie*, the most appropriate way to end the supposed abuse would be to prohibit any agreement reserving to De Beers the whole, or even a material part, of Alrosa's exports.

The Commission is not required to give reasons when it concludes that commitments are not suitable or are insufficient. But proportionality requires that, when less onerous measures exist, the Commission should examine whether those measures are capable of addressing the concerns that justify its action, before adopting the more onerous approach. The joint proposals, which the Commission had published and had therefore initially dealt with its concerns, would have been less onerous than a complete prohibition. The Commission is free to make commitments that have been offered binding only in part or to a particular extent. The Commission cannot lawfully propose, and so should not accept, commitments which go further than a prohibition decision that it could have adopted under Article 7 of Reg. 1/2003. A permanent prohibition on transactions between the companies could not have been proportional. Only exceptional circumstances, not suggested in this case, could justify a permanent and complete prohibition. The object of Article 82 is not to prohibit or weaken dominant positions but only to stop abuses, so the Commission cannot prohibit a dominant company from maintaining or strengthening its position, as long as it does not infringe competition rules. In this case, the Commission had intended to weaken the position of De Beers, and to force Alrosa, a company not directly concerned with proceedings under Article 82, to work towards a change in the structure of the market. The Commission has no power to do this. Sales between Alrosa and De Beers in open auctions would not be contrary to competition rules. So the Commission's decision should be annulled on the ground of proportionality alone.

On the right to be heard, the Court said that Alrosa was not a mere interested third party, but was the party contracting with De Beers in a long-lasting relationship that the decision would end. Alrosa had been involved in the administrative proceedings. It should therefore have been treated as an "undertaking concerned". Observance of the right to be heard is a fundamental principle of Community law in all proceedings liable to end in a measure adversely affecting the person in question. Since the Commission had changed its mind, after having published draft commitments that it had been ready to accept, it had a duty to hear the parties' comments on the observations of third parties, and the facts justifying its new conclusion. The Commission could change its mind only if the facts had altered or its initial assessment was based on incorrect information. Alrosa had a right to be heard on the additional commitment offered by De Beers, and it had not been given that right fully.

Alrosa judgment – comments

The *Alrosa* judgment is subject to appeal to the Court of Justice, and my law firm represents Alrosa. So my comments on the judgment must be very prudent.

The judgment deals with several issues in connection with proportionality : the Commission's obligation, as the Court saw it, to make an economic analysis sufficient to make judicial review possible, the extent of judicial review, the application of the proportionality principle to decisions under Article 9, the adequacy of the less onerous solutions available, and the parallel between the powers of the Commission under Article 9 and its powers when adopting prohibition decisions under Article 7. The Court clearly concluded that the Commission had tried to adopt a quasi-regulatory solution which went beyond what the Commission could justify under competition law. This last point is important, since consideration of commitments will often appear to provide opportunities to bring about changes in the market that go further than merely ending the presumed infringement that was the subject of the Commission's preliminary assessment or statement of objections. It is also important that the Commission has a duty to assess for itself whether commitments that have been offered go further than is necessary to deal with the Commission's concerns. Even if the Commission had been able to say that it had carried out an economic analysis, the Court would still have disagreed with the conclusion, if the same conclusion had been reached.

So the judgment, although at first sight concerned with a relatively simple set of facts, is important on a series of substantive issues, subject of course to what the Court of Justice may ultimately decide.

On procedural issues, the judgment seems less important, because similar facts are not likely to occur again, and if they do, the Commission will presumably be careful to give the second company the right to be heard if its interests are affected by the commitment proposed by the dominant company. If Alrosa had merely been one of several companies dealing with De Beers, it might not have been specifically and individually affected by the commitment. It is important that Alrosa had a right to be heard although its own freedom to buy and sell was not formally restricted, because its possibilities of selling to its most important traditional buyer was being taken away. Apparently the Commission had not considered the effect of the commitment on Alrosa.

As the case law develops, practising lawyers should remember that there is another part of the Commission that also has regularly to consider whether to accept what are in effect commitments when they are offered, in anti-dumping cases. The Community Courts are likely to see similarities.

The Court clearly considers that when the Commission has taken one position or reached one conclusion, even a provisional conclusion in a procedural step, the Commission must be able to justify its new position if it changes its mind. A situation in this respect similar to the *Alrosa* case occurred in *Impala* [17] where the Commission was criticised by the Court of First Instance for being unable to explain why it had changed the position set out in its

[17] Case T-464/04, *Impala v. Commission*, July 13, 2006. The Court has accepted that the Commission can change its mind if new facts have come to its notice. Presumably the Commission is entitled, if it thinks it appropriate to do so, to make further enquiries to see if its initial conclusions are justified. This may be the reason for the Commission's recent enquiries into the competitive effects of ordering airlines to surrender slots at busy airports. If the Commission gets additional evidence suggesting that it should change its mind, it will be obliged to give the companies in question an opportunity to comment on it, to defend their interests.

statement of objections. It follows that the Commission ought not formally to publish draft commitments unless it is reasonably satisfied that they are in fact sufficient to solve the competition problems. It should not publish them merely to obtain comments, unless it makes that very clear. The view of the Court is reasonable, but it is hoped that it will not make the Commission even more reluctant to change its mind than it sometimes has been.

Alrosa – procedural implications in other kinds of commitment cases

It is not clear, because the issue did not arise, how far, if at all, De Beers itself would have been able to challenge the decision as being contrary to the principle of proportionality. De Beers offered the commitment as it was finally accepted, but the Commission had a duty, the Court said, to see if the offer went further than was necessary. That duty presumably was owed to De Beers, as well as to Alrosa, although Alrosa was in a much stronger position because it had not agreed to the final version of the commitment, it was not in a dominant position, and it was nevertheless deprived of access to an important and long-standing trading partner. As the Court said that the Commission could have chosen to accept the commitment only in part, in certain respects, or only for a limited period of time, the judgment implies that the Commission must apply and respect the principle of proportionality even if it is dealing only with the enterprise that offered the commitment.

This seems correct, although it may seem surprising at first sight. It is possible to imagine situations, not like that in the *Alrosa* case, in which the dominant company would offer commitments *e.g.*, not to discriminate on price or not to offer selective price reductions, that would be unjustifiably anticompetitive, and which would discourage the dominant enterprise from competing legitimately. A dominant enterprise might in some circumstances be pleased to have an excuse for not competing on price or for not offering selective discounts. In such circumstances a commitment that at first sight might seem to constrain only the interests of the dominant enterprise might in reality harm the interests of its customers. As the Community law rules on price reductions by dominant companies are unfortunately very unclear and are liable to have regulatory or even anticompetitive effects,[18] it is particularly important that the Commission must consider very carefully to see if what appears to be a dutiful proposal by a law-abiding company might in reality, whether intentionally or not, have unjustifiable and anticompetitive consequences. In such circumstances, of course, the dominant company would not criticise its own proposal. But it would be extremely important, in the interests of consumers, that the Commission should do so. The *Alrosa* judgment implies that the Commission would have a duty to do this.

In such a situation, procedurally a customer of the dominant company might have an interest in challenging the commitment decision long after it had been adopted, even if it had not criticised it at the time. Indeed, it might be difficult for even an already-established customer to describe convincingly how it might be harmed by an innocent-sounding commitment not to discriminate. But from a procedural viewpoint it might not be easy to raise the issue later, and certainly it might be hard to raise it with retroactive effect. A commitment decision after all protects the dominant company after the decision comes into force, if the company carries out the commitment. The protection must extend to claims by private plaintiffs, as well as action by competition authorities (although private plaintiffs may still claim that the company's conduct <u>before</u> it was modified by the commitment was illegal).

Because in a commitment decision the Commission makes no finding about whether an infringement has been committed in the past, decisions under Article 9 are not likely to lead to claims for compensation. That is in fact one of the advantages of such decisions for the companies offering the commitments.

Alrosa – substantive implications

As a substantive issue, commitments not to discriminate should be looked at by the Commission extremely carefully. An obligation not to discriminate is (among other things) a duty not to apply dis-

[18] Temple Lang and O'Donoghue, "Defining legitimate competition: How to clarify pricing abuses under Article 82 EC", 26 *Fordham International Law Journal* (2002) 83-162; O'Donoghue and Padilla, *The law and economics of Article 82 EC* (Hart, 2006) ch. 7.

similar conditions to equivalent transactions. But a dominant company in a complex industry might be able to negotiate in such a way that the transactions did not appear to be "equivalent". The customer or other company discriminated against is not likely to know the terms given to its competitors, and may have no way of knowing (or no way of proving) that it was being discriminated against. One way (in practice one of the few reasonably convenient ways) in which an obligation not to discriminate can be monitored is by arranging for the dominant company's auditors to certify that they have looked at every transaction of the kind in question to see if it involved discrimination. But auditors may overlook aspects of transactions, since verifying non-discrimination obligations is not a well-developed part of their activities, and (more importantly) because the elements giving rise to discrimination would be different in every industry, and could not be identified with confidence by normal audit disciplines.

In this context, attention should be paid to the judgment of the Court of Justice in *Laboratoires Boiron*,[19] in which the Court said that national courts have a duty under Article 10 EC to order disclosure of evidence, even from third parties, if that is necessary to enable a claimant to make its claim. The Commission has called attention to this important case in the staff paper published with the "White Paper" on claims for damages.[20]

These issues are important because it is already clear that commitment decisions are likely to be adopted in circumstances in which the solution or remedy for the supposed abuse or anticompetitive practice is relatively complicated (even when the industry itself is not). Great care and considerable foresight and judgement on the part of the Commission are therefore needed to ensure that a commitment is both effective (in the sense of doing what it was intended to do) and is not going to produce undesirable and unnecessary anticompetitive effects.

These issues are also important because commitment cases are likely to encourage or tempt the Commission to envisage measures that are essentially regulatory rather than based on competition

[19] Case C-526/04, [2006] ECR I-??? Sept. 7, 2006, paras. 55, 57.

[20] Commission, *White Paper on Damages Actions for Breach of EC Antitrust Rules*, COM (2008) 165 final, April 2, 2008; *Commission Staff Working Document accompanying the White Paper*, SEC (2008) 404.

law.[21] (The difference is, in essence, that competition law allows competition authorities only to prevent or to put an end to identified illegal conduct that restricts competition, but does not empower the authorities to take steps to make a legal market more competitive, however desirable that might seem). The *Alrosa* judgment makes it clear, subject to the views of the Court of Justice, that the Commission cannot make a commitment binding unless the resulting obligations could have been imposed in a prohibition decision based on the Statement of Objections or preliminary assessment in the case in question. This finding is unlikely to be altered by the Court of Justice, since it is analogous to what that Court said in the context of interim measures in the first *Ford-Werke* case.[22]

So the Commission, although the Court recognised in the *Alrosa* judgment that it might suggest possible commitments to the dominant enterprise, must resist the temptation to suggest regulatory measures. This has two kinds of implications. First, the Commission must not suggest or make binding a commitment that is not limited to solving the competition concerns identified by the Commission in its preliminary assessment in the specific case. Second, however broad those concerns may have been or however they may have been expressed, the Commission must not make binding commitments that could not be imposed at all under competition law, such as the commitment in the *Alrosa* case which the Court found was designed to weaken the dominant position of De Beers, and to lead to restructuring the industry. The Commission has no power under competition law to weaken or take away a dominant position, except perhaps to the extent to which it has been illegally obtained. In addition, the commitments made binding must not be disproportionate in the strict sense, that is, they must not be more burdensome than necessary to deal with the concerns stated by the Commission.

This means that commitment decisions under Article 9 of Regulation 1/2003 are subject to constraints which do not apply to commitments offered by companies during the first phases of procedures under the Merger Regulation. The Remedies Notice[23] makes

---

[21] Temple Lang, *op. cit., supra*, 2005 Fordham Corporate Law Institute (2006), at pp. 316-320.

[22] Cases 228 and 229/82, *Ford Werke* [1984] ECR 3091.

[23] *OJ* No. C-6/3, [2001] para. 11.

it clear that commitments in the first phase must be sufficient to clearly rule out "serious doubts" about the merger. At that stage the Commission is not in a position to judge exactly what remedies it could insist on, and is entitled to accept any proposal that clearly solves any possible problem. Under Article 9 neither the Commission nor the companies involved are under time pressure, so they can work out how far a commitment can legitimately go.

It is important that the Court in *Alrosa* insisted that a dominant company must be allowed to trade freely, even if the result is to maintain or strengthen its dominance, provided only that it respects competition rules. This means that if for example in any case the Commission were to suggest commitments the effect of which was to constrain the freedom of a dominant enterprise to compete on price, the commitments would be unjustified and inconsistent with Community competition law. In this context it should be remembered that the Court said in the *Atlantic Container Line* case[24] that the "special responsibility" of a dominant company merely means that it is subject to Article 82, and that non-dominant companies are not. The "special responsibility" is not a basis for imposing obligations to help competitors or to restrict the ability of the dominant company to compete, if the dominant company has not committed any identifiable abuse. Nor is there any basis for imposing regulatory obligations in commitment decisions in Article 81 cases.

The Court's comments about the effects *erga omnes* of commitment decisions seem to confirm that third parties who are beneficiaries of commitments (*e.g.*, commitments not to discriminate) have the right to rely on the decisions before national courts and national competition authorities, whenever appropriate.

As already mentioned, the Commission was apparently surprised, when Reg. 1/2003 came into force, that more commitment cases arose than had been expected. The *Alrosa* judgment does nothing to make commitments less acceptable to the companies involved. But it seems likely to make the commitment procedure under Article 9 less convenient for the Commission, and certainly means that commitment decisions can be used less widely, and for more limited purposes, than the Commission apparently assumed.

[24] Case T-191/98, [2003] ECR II-3275, para. 1460.

The Commission will have to use commitment decision more carefully in future.

Different types of commitments cases

Some distinctions should be drawn between different categories of commitments cases.

In some cases, such as the football television case, the enterprises involved are already legitimately regulating their affairs, and the Commission is involved, in effect, only to ensure that they are regulated in a non-restrictive way. In other cases, such as *Alrosa*, in which the facts are commercial or industrial, the regulatory pressure comes from the Commission (on the initiative of a complainant, in the *Alrosa* case), and it is in these cases that the Commission must ensure that it does not go further than competition law, properly so called, allows. This is so also for a second reason. Where the enterprises are obliged to regulate their affairs in order to arrange football competitions for television rights, there is no obvious reason why the Commission's intervention should result in more complicated arrangements. However, in the commercial and industrial cases, the commitments add considerably to the complexity of the situation. That in itself may be undesirable, unless it is really necessary, but it also increases the likelihood that the Commission will be asked to agree to revised commitments, because of changed circumstances.

The collecting Societies cases are in an intermediate category, because the existing agreements restrict competition under Article 81, and the competition issues that arise need to be assessed under Article 81(3) as well as Article 81(1) itself.

The airline cases are in yet another category, for which there are precedents in the past practice of the Commission. In previous cases the Commission, when dealing with agreements for cooperation between the only two airlines flying on a given route between two cities, has said in effect that the agreement cannot be approved under Article 81 in existing circumstances, but could be approved if market entry was made possible. In the past, market entry could be made possible only through the action of the State concerned, and the States usually made entry possible, to enable the airlines to cooperate. Today, market entry often needs to be made possible by making slots available, and the commitments in the *Austrian Airlines* and *Skyteam* cases envisage that. The effect, in the previous cases, was to bring about a degree of liberalisation which had not been generally achieved, and in that sense the effect was regulatory, although the Commission's position was proper. In the recent cases, in which the airlines were willing and able to make slots of their own available for the purpose of solving the competition concerns expressed by the Commission, the solutions envisaged appear to be within the powers of the Commission under Reg. 1/2003.

All the types of cases just mentioned involve more than one enterprise, so any arrangements that the Commission could not impose can if necessary be made by contract between them. Difficulties would arise only if one or more of the parties was not willing to agree to some element of the overall arrangements, and the Commission had no power to impose the key feature.

The scope of Remedies

If commitment decisions cannot go further than prohibition decisions to provide remedies for infringement, it becomes necessary to clarify how far prohibition decisions can go. The usual answer is that they can do everything necessary to put an end to the infringement. However, it is not clear whether a prohibition decision can go further and take away some or all of the market power or advantages illegally obtained by the companies in question. This is important in particular in the case of exclusionary abuses,[25] in particular if as a result of the abuses the markets has "tipped" in favour of the companies that have acted illegally. Merely stopping the infringement for the future may not do enough to make the market fully competitive again.

Competitors that have suffered from the exclusionary abuse, while they may be able to recover compensation, are unlikely to get a remedy from a national court that goes further than the Commission has gone. If measures are to be taken to restore or

---

[25] Exploitative abuses can more often be remedied by awarding compensation.

recreate competitive conditions that have been weakened or eliminated by unlawful conduct, those measures should be general measures taken in the public interest by a competition authority, and not in private litigation for the benefit of an individual competitor.

Points of comparison with US consent decrees

The Commission's commitment decisions do not require judicial approval. In the USA, consent decrees must be accepted by a court. The US practice is to try to ensure that the remedy negotiated will be timely, balanced and capable of being administered. A US court would not be likely to accept a draft consent decree that left issues unresolved, or made it necessary to add to or renegotiate the decree if circumstances changed in a probable way. The *Alrosa* judgment makes it clear that commitment decisions may be looked at critically by the Community Courts, and that the Commission should not assume that anything that the enterprise proposes may be accepted, if the Commission wishes to accept it, without serious scrutiny. The *Alrosa* judgment has brought Community practice much closer to the situation in the USA.

The *Alrosa* judgment, by insisting that the Commission cannot make binding an obligation that it could not have imposed in a prohibition decision, means that the Commission cannot use Article 9 to oblige a company to pay compensation, as is possible under US practice ("disgorgement"). On the other hand, Reg. 1/2003 allows both structural and behavioural remedies, so both are possible, in principle, under commitment decisions, subject always to the proportionality requirement, which is explicitly stated in Article 7(1).

Conclusions

The *Alrosa* judgment has made it clear, unless the Court of Justice says otherwise, that the Commission should not make a commitment binding unless the Commission could have adopted a prohibition decision in the same terms, dealing with an identified competition infringement[26] sufficiently indicated in a Statement of Objections or preliminary assessment, and unless the commitment is proportional to the infringement or concerns. The Commission cannot base a commitment decision on a preliminary assessment that merely says, in effect, that there is not much competition in the market and it would be better if there was more. A preliminary assessment obliges the Commission to say clearly what it believes that the infringement may be.

It is clear that commitment decisions are a useful tool which enables the Commission to deal with cases that it either could not otherwise deal with, satisfactorily or at all, or which would otherwise necessitate an amount of time and effort that the Commission could not provide.

Commitment decisions are particularly useful in cases in which the remedy needed is complicated. The Commission has always been unimaginative as far as remedies are concerned, and its already slow procedures are not likely to produce effective remedies in complex cases. The Commission usually does not, in the first Statement of Objections in any individual case, envisage detailed remedies. A complex case therefore is likely to necessitate a second Statement of Objections, adding greatly to the total length of the whole procedure. If the case is complicated because the industry is a high-technology industry, the result is very likely to be that the remedy that finally results is too late, obsolete, or ineffective. Commitment decisions offer one possible way of avoiding such unsatisfactory situations.

However, the inherent limitations of commitment decisions must be recognised. The Commission cannot use them in cases in which it considers that a fine is necessary. More seriously, it can only use them in cases in which the enterprise involved is ultimately willing to offer a commitment, so that unless the Commission is firm, the enterprise is in a position to influence the situation. Companies are well aware that the Commission is reluctant to start any big complicated cases, no matter how serious the infringement or how important the industry. Companies may therefore hope ultimately

---

[26] See TEMPLE LANG, "European Competition Law and Compulsory Licensing of Intellectual Property Rights – A Comprehensive Principle", 4 *Europarättslig Tidskrift* (2004) 558-588 (explaining that a compulsory licence can only be ordered to end an identified abuse).

to be allowed to offer inadequate remedies in cases which the Commission is unable or unwilling to deal with effectively. A determined company may believe that it need not offer even an inadequate commitment if the Commission is reluctant to open an investigation at all.

Another inherent limitation of commitment decisions is illustrated by the *CISAC* case. In brief, in that case the Commission has no power under competition law to impose a satisfactory solution on all the performing rights Societies, at least without further very complicated, lengthy and time-consuming procedures. Any completely satisfactory solution would need the agreement and the participation of all of the Societies. So such a solution can be blocked by the most obstinate or most aggressive Society, unless the Commission can use its competition law powers in such a way that those Societies will ultimately realise that they need to assent to a reasonable industry-wide result. It remains to be seen whether the Commission will try to bring this about.

Another feature of commitment decisions should be pointed out. The Commission still seems to have no clear practical concept of exclusionary abuse.[27] This means that the Commission finds it difficult to analyse and deal with cases in which the infringement does not fall into recognised categories of illegal behaviour (and may reach the wrong result even in cases of well-recognised kinds of conduct). This may mean that the Commission will ultimately accept commitments that are not satisfactory, either in practice or intellectually. However it may also mean that the Commission is led to deal pragmatically with novel or complex cases which it is unlikely to be able to deal with satisfactorily. In such cases an inadequate or unsatisfactory remedy, by accepting a commitment, may be better than nothing, or may be accepted by the Commission to save face because it is not in a position to do any better. In general, commitment decisions provide the Commission with the possibility of avoiding dealing fully and correctly with difficult or complex cases.

[27] See *e.g.*, Temple Lang, *Anticompetitive Non-pricing Abuses under European and National Antitrust Law*, in Hawk (ed.), 2003 Fordham Corporate Law Institute (2004) 235-340; generally O'Donoghue & Padilla, *The Law and Economics of Article 82 EC* (Hart, 2006).

Accepting commitments is therefore not necessarily a sign of success for the Commission. It may also be a sign of weakness, whether procedural or analytical. The Commission will not avoid this kind of difficulty until it has a clear and practical concept of exclusionary abuse. Unfortunately the Commission seems unlikely to reach such a concept in the near future. The Commission will not overcome its procedural weaknesses either, unless it is willing to contemplate some form of administrative law judge who could be more decisive and more experienced than Commission case teams.

But it is important to recognise that the Court in the *Alrosa* judgment has provided an intellectual framework or set of principles for dealing with commitments in Article 81-82 cases which did not exist previously, and which the Commission must follow carefully.

A national competition authority dealing with a case of unilateral behaviour is not constrained by Article 7, because Article 3 of Reg. 1/2003 allows national laws to be stricter than Article 82. It should of course be constrained by the limits of the national law rule. But the risk of requiring commitments that would have unforeseen or anticompetitive consequences is probably greater for national authorities than for the Commission, particularly if they are not sufficiently aware of the fact that the principles stated in the *Alrosa* judgment also apply, by analogy, to them.

PART III.

Transversal Issues

ALTERNATIVE ENFORCEMENT TECHNIQUES – THE UK EXPERIENCE

BY

CHRISTOPHER BROWN[1]

BARRISTER, MATRIX CHAMBERS, LONDON
FORMERLY REFERENDAIRE, UK COMPETITION APPEAL TRIBUNAL

I. – INTRODUCTION

This paper surveys the position in the UK with regard to "alternative enforcement" of competition law. It will be readily apparent that the explosion of alternative enforcement techniques ("AETs") has been more than mirrored at domestic level in the UK. The UK authorities[2] already have some or substantial experience in relation to commitments, settlements and studies/investigations of markets.[3] Away from public enforcement, the UK courts have seen a number of damages and other actions brought by private parties, either piggy-backing on an infringement decision at EU or domestic

---

[1] This paper attempts to state the law and practice as it stood on 31 July 2008. My thanks to David Bailey for his comments on an earlier draft of this paper. The usual disclaimer applies.

[2] In the UK there are various authorities competent to apply and enforce UK competition law. **The Office of Fair Trading** ("OFT") is the principal competition authority. It is entrusted with the task of enforcement of the prohibitions contained in Chapters I and II of the Competition Act 1998 ("the 1998 Act"), which are the UK equivalents of Articles 81(1) and 82 EC respectively; it is the first-phase body in relation to merger control, assessing whether "merger situations" need to be referred to the **Competition Commission** ("CC") for in-depth review; and it is more generally entrusted with ensuring that markets work well : to that end, it may carry out "market studies" and consider whether markets ought to be referred to the CC for investigation of whether features of them restrict, distort etc competition. The OFT exercises concurrent jurisdiction with the **sectoral regulators** – the Office of Communications ("Ofcom"), The Gas and Electricity Markets Authority ("Ofgem"), The Office for the Regulation of Electricity and Gas (Northern Ireland) ("Ofreg"), The Water Services Regulation Authority ("Ofwat"), the Office of Rail Regulation ("ORR") and the Civil Aviation Authority ("CAA") – to enforce the Chapter I and II prohibitions and (with the exception of the CAA) to make market investigation references. (For simplicity, this paper refers only to the OFT in the context of market studies and investigations.) The CC conducts, among other things, in-depth investigations into mergers and markets referred to it by the OFT.

[3] The OFT has also issued two draft "opinions" on the compatibility with Article 81/the Chapter I prohibition of the current system of distribution for newspapers and magazines. These are not covered in this paper. See http://www.oft.gov.uk/news/press/2008/36-08.

level or as a stand-alone proceeding.[4] The OFT has published certain *Recommendations to Government* on the topic of damages actions.[5] Private enforcement is not, however covered in this paper.

This paper takes the following form. It surveys each of the various AETs at the authorities' disposal, paying particular attention to market investigation references ("MIRs"), and looks at some of the decisional practice and a few of the interesting issues to emerge.

II. – Commitments

Legislative framework

The OFT's power to accept commitments was granted to it by the Competition Act and other Enactments (Amendment) Regulations 2004,[6] which amended the 1998 Act so as to include *inter alia* section 31A :

"31A Commitments

(1) Subsection (2) applies in a case where the OFT has begun an investigation under section 25 but has not made a decision (within the meaning given by section 31(2)).

(2) For the purposes of addressing the competition concerns it has identified, the OFT may accept from such person (or persons) concerned as it considers appropriate commitments to take such action (or refrain from taking such action) as it considers appropriate.

(3) At any time when commitments are in force the OFT may accept from the person (or persons) who gave the commitments –

(a) a variation of them if it is satisfied that the commitments as varied will address its current competition concerns;

(b) commitments in substitution for them if it is satisfied that the new commitments will address its current competition concerns.

(4) Commitments under this section –

(a) shall come into force when accepted; and

(b) may be released by the OFT where –

[4] There are several sets of private follow-on actions currently pending before the Competition Appeal Tribunal ("CAT"), including, most recently, Case 1098/5/7/08, *BCL Old Co et al v BASF* and Case 1077/5/7/07, *Emerson Electric et al v Morgan Crucible*. Note that the first, and so far only, award of damages for breach of competition law made by a court in the UK was the interim award granted by the CAT in *Healthcare at Home v Genzyme*, [2006] *CAT* 29. All CAT judgments are available on its website : www.catribunal.org.uk.

[5] OFT 916 resp, November 2007 : http://www.oft.gov.uk/shared_oft/reports/comp_policy/oft916resp.pdf.

[6] SI 2004/1261.

(i) it is requested to do so by the person (or persons) who gave the commitments; or

(ii)it has reasonable grounds for believing that the competition concerns referred to in subsection (2) or (3) no longer arise.

..."

Section 31B provides that where it accepts commitments the OFT shall not continue the investigation or make a decision as to whether an infringement has taken place. Section 31E provides the OFT with the power to seek the enforcement of commitments by a court.

The OFT's *Enforcement* guidance [7] elucidates the OFT's approach to commitments. Among other things :

- It is likely to consider commitments to be appropriate only where the competition concerns are readily identifiable, the concerns are fully addressed by the party's proposal, and the commitments can be implemented effectively and, if necessary, quickly. [8]
- Absent exceptional circumstances it will not accept commitments in cartel cases, nor in cases "involving serious abuse of a dominant position". [9]
- Nor will it accept commitments where compliance would be hard to discern or where not to complete the investigation and make a decision would undermine deterrence. [10]

The guidance also deals with matters such as variation and release of commitments and the procedure to be adopted. It is noted that the OFT is unlikely to be receptive to a commitments proposal following receipt of representations in response to a statement of objections ("SO"). [11]

Decisions in relation to commitments are susceptible to appeal to the CAT. Note that such appeals are on "judicial review" grounds only, rather than "on the merits". [12]

[7] OFT 407, Dec. 2004 : http://www.oft.gov.uk/shared_oft/business_leaflets/ca98_guidelines/oft407.pdf.

[8] *Ibid.*, para. 4.3.

[9] *Ibid.*, para. 4.4, fn. 16 to which clarifies that predatory pricing would generally be regarded as a serious abuse.

[10] *Ibid.*, para. 4.5.

[11] *Ibid.*, para. 4.16.

[12] Sch. 8 to the 1998 Act, para. 3A.

Decisional practice

Thus far, there have been just three commitments decisions under the 1998 Act, and none for over two years.

In *TV Eye* [13] the OFT accepted commitments from a company, owned by the major commercial television broadcasters in the UK, which provided credit risk assessment and credit security administration services to its shareholders and other broadcasters. The OFT had identified concerns related to the effect of TV Eye's arrangements on the terms and conditions offered to media agencies by member broadcasters, namely the facilitating of a collective boycott of media agencies that refused to put in place certain credit security arrangements. Among other things, the commitments ensured, in the OFT's view, that TV Eye would only distribute to its members details about that member's credit risk, rather than details of other members' arrangements with media agencies. [14]

Associated Newspapers [15] concerned long-term exclusivity arrangements entered into by the owner of *Metro* ("AN"), the free London-wide morning newspaper, with various transport operators. The OFT suspected that AN's conduct in entering into the arrangements was contrary to the Chapter II prohibition, foreclosing the market for the supply of advertising space in London-wide newspapers (and thereby the London-wide newspaper readership market). [16] AN offered commitments pursuant to which it was *inter alia* to release its exclusive rights relating to the afternoon and evening slots (which hitherto had remained unexploited) and allow third party access to its distribution racks on (in essence) FRAND terms. [17]

Interestingly, since the commitments were accepted the market has witnessed an important development. In September 2006 two free afternoon newspapers were launched : *thelondonpaper* (pub-

---

[13] CA98/03/2005.

[14] In March 2006 the OFT released TV Eye from certain commitments on the basis that it was no longer engaged in certain activities covered by them : http://www.oft.gov.uk/news/press/2006/58-06.

[15] CA98/02/2006.

[16] At the relevant time, vertical and land agreements were exempted from application of the Chapter I prohibition; vertical agreements are however now subject to the Chapter I prohibition.

[17] See para. 27. Note that the OFT did not seek (nor did it have the power to seek) commitments from other parties, such as London Underground and Network Rail (which owns the mainline railway stations concerned), who in any event were not party to the investigation : it therefore did not compel the transport operators to re-tender the afternoon and evening rights.

lished by News International) and *London Lite* (published by AN). Both are distributed by "street merchandisers", a method viewed with some suspicion by the OFT in its commitments decision.[18] Time will tell whether the "bloodbath" predicted by some[19] materialises: as at the end of July 2008, both are still very much in business.

Lastly, in *Sp Manweb*[20] Ofgem accepted commitments from a supplier of non-contestable electricity connection services whom it suspected of engaging in discriminatory behaviour in favour of an affiliate company contrary to the Chapter II prohibition: various practices appeared to hinder independent connections providers ("ICPs") in bidding for and performing connections work and so put them at a competitive disadvantage. The commitments were designed to ensure that SP Manweb did not discriminate between its affiliate and ICPs; Ofgem was given a mechanism for monitoring performance in this respect.

Observations

There are too few cases to draw any general conclusions, but the relatively limited use of the commitments procedure is in itself an interesting phenomenon. This may be due to the fact that the OFT is concentrating its competition enforcement resources on its "priority" work – in particular cartels – and so is opening very few "effects" cases. In any event, the suggestion raised by some that some parties might seek to use the commitments route to obtain an exemption decision by the backdoor has presumably not materialised or, if it has, has unsurprisingly fallen on deaf ears at the OFT.

---

[18] See para. 46: "Street merchandising is logistically more complex, requiring 300 to 400 merchandisers daily, handing out newspapers, to achieve the critical mass circulation. This makes it a more expensive option than using racks and would be unsustainable as a long-term distribution method. ..."

[19] See eg *The Guardian*, "London Lite risks newspaper 'bloodbath'" 17 August 2006, available at www.guardian.co.uk/media/2006/aug/17/business.pressandpublishing.

[20] Www.ofgem.gov.uk/About%20us/enforcement/Investigations/ClosedInvest/Documents1/55.pdf.

III. – Settlements

In the UK, the competition agencies have, perhaps unwittingly at first, become EU pioneers in the use of settlements. The OFT has now resolved, or is in the process of resolving, four cases by such means and the ORR has settled an abuse of dominance investigation in this way, too.[21] The OFT has innovated further in its approach to a sixth investigation, into suspected widespread bid rigging in the construction sector, by offering those under investigation a take-it-or-leave-it "accelerated procedure".[22]

Rather than embark on a formal policy formulation exercise, the OFT appears to be "learning by doing". As mentioned above, thus far it has settled with cartel participants in four cases and has offered an "accelerated procedure" in a fifth. At the time of writing, a formal decision had been published in only one of the cases (*Independent Schools*); in respect of the others, the OFT has so far only issued press releases.

Decisional practice

1. *Independent Schools*[23]

During the period from March 2001 to June 2003, 50 fee-paying independent schools infringed the Chapter I prohibition. As part of a settlement negotiated with the OFT, the schools each admitted that they had participated in the exchange of information in relation to future fee increases and that in so doing they had committed an infringement of the Chapter I prohibition. Each school agreed to pay a nominal fine of £10,000 and make an *ex-gratia* payment to fund a £3 million educational trust (for the benefit of pupils attending the schools during the years of infringement). The OFT undoubtedly took into account the fact that the schools were non-profit making charities when agreeing to the low levels of

[21] *English, Welsh and Scottish Railway Limited*, decision of the Office of Rail Regulation, November 17, 2006 (*available at* http://www.oft.gov.uk/shared_oft/ca98_public_register/decisions/EWSrail.pdf).

[22] See Press Release "OFT closes door on cartel leniency in construction bid rigging cases in England" March 22, 2007 (http://www.oft.gov.uk/news/press/2007/50-07).

[23] Www.oft.gov.uk/advice_and_resources/resource_base/ca98/decisions/schools.

fines.[24] Furthermore, the OFT's decision made no finding as to the actual effect of the exchange of information on fee levels.

2. *BA/Virgin*[25]

In May 2004, British Airways ("BA") introduced a passenger fuel surcharge ("the surcharge") of £5 per return ticket in response to rising oil prices. Between May 2004 and September 2005 the surcharge was increased five times, reaching £60. On four of these occasions there was collusion between BA and Virgin Atlantic ("Virgin") in the form of telephone calls and emails between employees at the two companies, unbeknownst to their superiors.

In June 2006, Virgin approached the OFT, admitted its part in the collusion and successfully applied for immunity under the OFT's leniency policy. It also obtained "no action" letters immunizing its employees against prosecution under the so-called "cartel offence" (pursuant to which dishonest horizontal price-fixing is a criminal offence punishable by a fine and/or a custodial sentence of up to 5 years).[26]

BA fully co-operated with the OFT's investigation, and this co-operation was rewarded with a reduction in the eventual fine under the OFT's leniency policy. On 1 August 2007 the OFT announced that BA had admitted to colluding with Virgin, in breach of UK competition law, and had agreed to pay a fine amounting to £121.5 million. This figure includes a further reduction on account of the settlement.[27]

It is currently unclear how great the percentage reduction reflecting the settlement was; nor is it yet known how much BA has achieved in terms of "damage limitation" in the formal decision (eg findings by the OFT as to the effect of the collusion on prices). However, it is likely at a minimum that BA will have insisted on

[24] It also noted the parties' voluntary admission of infringement; the trust fund payments; and the fact that the parties immediately ceased the conduct upon becoming aware of the fact that it was unlawful: see OFT Decision, para. 1425 *et seq*.

[25] Http://www.oft.gov.uk/news/press/2007/113-07.

[26] See ss 188 *et seq* of the 2002 Act.

[27] A parallel announcement was made on the same day by the US Department of Justice in relation to its own investigation of the same conduct: see http://www.usdoj.gov/atr/public/press_releases/2007/224928.htm.

there being no findings as to the cartel's effects, mindful of the likelihood of follow-on private suits by victims.[28]

3. *Dairy products*[29]

On 7 December 2007 the OFT announced that it had concluded "early resolution agreements" with several supermarket retailers and dairy processors pursuant to which the parties admitted their involvement in collusion over the retail price of certain dairy products and agreed to pay a fine. The OFT's press release stated that each settling party would receive a "significant reduction" in the fine that would otherwise have been imposed, subject to providing ongoing cooperation. On 15 February 2008 it was announced that a further dairy processor had also settled with the OFT.

Two supermarkets have not settled, and the OFT's investigation into them is ongoing. The *Dairy products* case is thus the first "hybrid" settlement case that the OFT has dealt with.

4. *Tobacco products*[30]

On 11 July 2008 the OFT announced that it had reached a settlement with six out of twelve firms under investigation for alleged price coordination in relation to tobacco products in the UK. The *Tobacco products* case is the second "hybrid" case the OFT is dealing with. All six admitted liability in respect of all of the alleged infringements and would, according to the press release issued by the OFT, all receive "a significant reduction" in the fine. The total penalties imposed on the six firms amounts to £132.3 million, as opposed to £173.3 million before the application of discounts for leniency and settlement.

5. *Construction industry bid rigging*[31]

The OFT has, since 2005, been investigating a large number of firms in the construction industry whom it suspects of having

---

[28] Indeed, since the settlement was announced there has been a settlement of a private class action in the US whose terms encompass victims in the UK. Under the deal, which is to cover some 8 million passengers, around 5 million UK customers have until 2012 to apply for $144.4 million in refunds from BA and Virgin. Each passenger may claim £10 per single trip.

[29] Http://www.oft.gov.uk/news/press/2007/170-07; http://www.oft.gov.uk/news/press/2008/22-08.

[30] Http://www.oft.gov.uk/news/press/2008/82-08.

[31] Http://www.oft.gov.uk/news/press/2007/49-07.

engaged in bid rigging in relation to thousands of tenders. Some 37 firms applied for leniency. On 22 March 2007 the OFT announced that it would no longer accept any further applications for leniency; however, it did make an offer of reduced financial penalties to all those firms under investigation which had not applied for leniency. To qualify, the firms in question would be expected to admit to participation in bid rigging and make "certain ancillary promises", which is taken to mean the waiving of certain procedural rights and, possibly, undertakings as to their future conduct.

The OFT stated that the reductions in penalty would not be as large as those available to firms that had applied for leniency, but would nonetheless be "significant".

Once again details are sketchy, but it would appear that this so-called "accelerated sanctions" procedure differs from settlements in certain significant ways:

- There will be little if any scope for "bargaining" with the OFT: the authority will advertise publicly the "take-it-or-leave-it" terms on which it is prepared to grant "amnesty" to those implicated; it will then be for the firms to accept or decline the offer.
- Firms will have increased certainty compared to the settlements process, in that they will benefit from the offer so long as they satisfy the conditions set out by the OFT. Settlement procedures, by contrast, carry no certainty of success; to the contrary, the agency retains full discretion as to whether to enter into such discussions at all and, if it does, it remains free to withdraw at any time (as, of course, do the parties).

On 17 April 2008 the OFT issued an SO to 112 firms in the construction sector; according to the OFT's press release, over 40 of these firms took advantage of the OFT's accelerated sanctions offer. [32]

Broad indications emerging from the early UK case-law

Given that only one "settlement" decision has been formally adopted and published thus far, it is difficult to draw concrete conclusions as to emerging OFT policy at this stage. However, the OFT's practice thus far has been decidedly less formalistic than the

[32] Http://www.oft.gov.uk/news/press/2008/52-08.

approach advocated by the European Commission's proposals. This is to be welcomed. Moreover, the following is relatively clear from public statements (including speeches by OFT officials):

- The incentive for the OFT to settle will be greatest when faced with a large number of defendants. Investigations into one or just a few firms routinely take at least two or three years; enforcement action against dozens of firms, each of whose liability is potentially different from the others, will inevitably take a lot longer to execute.
- That said, the *BA/Virgin* case shows that even where the number of cartel participants is low, the OFT will be open to settlement discussions in appropriate cases.
- The OFT will not expect a formal written settlement submission akin to that of the European Commission. It has not adopted such a rigid stance in the first cases, and officials have recognised the disbenefits of the Commission's more rigid proposed approach. Instead, the parties will be expected to sign an "early resolution agreement", the sole copy of which would presumably be kept by the OFT. That, from the perspective of the parties concerned, would be a welcome policy feature, and it ought to encourage firms to settle.
- The OFT is receptive to settlement in "hybrid" cases, ie cases where some but not all parties indicate a willingness to settle (eg *Dairy products*), and it has indicated that it would also be prepared to contemplate "partial" settlements (ie settling certain charges against a firm but not others). However, it is likely to proceed with considerably greater caution in such instances, given the loss of resource savings that such cases would entail.
- The OFT recognises the need for a genuine "carrot" encouraging firms to consider settling, in the form of significant reductions in the size of the penalty. In *Independent Schools* the settlement involved each school paying a fine of £10,000. That the fines were very low was due in part to the fact the schools concerned were all not-for-profit charities: a requirement to pay sizeable penalties would have been to the detriment of current pupils and their parents, in terms of diverting resources away from the provision of education and/or higher fees. The OFT did not, however, state in its decision what the fine for each school would have been in the absence of settlement, and so at present it is impossible for outsiders to discern the OFT's attitude to what the size of the reduc-

tion should be. OFT officials have said that there will be no fixed maximum percentage discount – in this respect its approach differs from the Commission's proposed approach. There will in addition be no requirement on the parties to indicate their view as to the maximum fine that might be imposed.

- The press release in *BA/Virgin* suggests that reductions in fines arising out of the OFT's leniency and settlements policies will be cumulative. This is important, as otherwise there would be a risk of undermining the leniency regime. That said, the OFT will be alive to the risks of excessively large reductions (and the consequent potential dissuasive effect on immunity applicants) and the "coercive" effect such potential discounts might have.
- It appears that the OFT does not consider it necessary to have issued a statement of objections, or at least a detailed statement, before entering into a settlement agreement[33] (although an official recently suggested that first discussions will usually take place around the time of the issue of the SO, save where the arguments are relatively clear-cut, in part to avoid the risk of "false positives"). In common with the EC system, however, it is a procedural requirement that the OFT issue a SO prior to issuing a decision, and one can foresee the OFT adopting a similar approach in this regard to the Commission's draft policy: the SO will include the party's admission but may not, at least in non-hybrid cases, go much further than that.
- The OFT may be more likely to be receptive to settlement where the party or parties include in the settlement proposals an offer to compensate victims of the cartel in some way, particularly where there would otherwise be little incentive for the victims to sue. In *Independent Schools*, for example, the offer to make *ex gratia* payments to (which ultimately totalled £3 million) to an educational trust fund designed to benefit pupils who had attended the schools during the period of infringement was a central feature of the settlement. However, the OFT is unlikely to entertain a compensation fund which involves it expending a lot of its own resources in administration. The OFT is more likely to be interested if the parties themselves are prepared to underwrite the

[33] It would appear that the settlement in BA/Virgin occurred prior to the issue of a statement of objections.

operational costs (including the remuneration of the fund's trustees). Furthermore, officials have recently cast doubt on the relevance of redress mechanisms in the OFT's consideration of whether to settle, which suggests that *Independent Schools* might have been an exceptional case.

- It appears unlikely that, in "hybrid" cases, the OFT will publish formal decisions in relation to parties that have agreed to settle separately from its decision in relation to parties who do not settle. This should at least avoid the risk that settling parties will be exposed to "follow-on" litigation under sections 47A or 47B of the Competition Act 1998 prior to non-settling firms' exposure – a risk that would undoubtedly make the settlements regime considerably less attractive.
- As part of an administrative settlement, the UK agencies appear content to refrain from opining on the effects of a cartel on prices. As part of the *Independent Schools* investigation the OFT agreed not to make any finding on this point. The ORR, albeit in the context of an abuse of dominance case, also agreed as part of the early resolution not to make any finding as to the damage that may have been suffered by competitors whose access to the market had been foreclosed by the abusive conduct in question. The agencies' stance in this regard is unsurprising : first, it is one of the obvious "carrots" with which it can tempt parties to settle; and secondly, it is in any event rare for the OFT to engage in such complex exercises when it is irrelevant for the purposes of proving liability in cartel cases.

Areas of uncertainty in UK policy

Certain aspects of the OFT's emerging practice are less clear, however – in particular :

- The extent to which the OFT will be prepared to negotiate the terms of the settlement. It is unlikely that the OFT will ever admit publicly that settlements involve an element of "horse-trading" with firms and their advisors, but in reality that is precisely what happens. In every case it is likely that parties will, at a minimum, have to admit liability and agree to a truncated procedure, which is likely to encompass a short reply to the statement of objections (which, if it has not already been issued, may well be shorter than usual), limited to correcting factual errors, and an agreement not to request an oral hearing at which further submissions could be made. However, there should be some scope for negotiation around issues such as the duration of the infringement and restitutionary measures. It is unclear to what extent the OFT will be willing to enter into negotiation around the size of the reduction of the penalty.

- The extent to which the OFT will have regard to the likelihood of "follow-on" damages actions by victims when deciding whether to exercise its discretion to enter into settlement discussions. It is clear that the OFT considers the encouragement of private enforcement to be a desirable policy objective; and it has been suggested by the OFT's Chairman that the OFT is more likely to consider settlements to be appropriate where victims, taken individually, have suffered relatively small loss (even if, taken in aggregate, the loss is very substantial), and where, therefore, private enforcement is perhaps less likely[34].

  Yet the recent representative follow-on action brought by the Consumers Association against JJB Sports in respect of loss suffered by consumers as a result of the *Replica Football Shirts* cartel, together with the class action brought against BA and Virgin on behalf of UK and US customers and recently settled in the US, suggests that subsequent private litigation even in cases where individual loss is small may be becoming more prevalent now in the UK than had been predicted.
- The extent to which the OFT will be keen to eschew settlements in favour of establishing a "track record" of effective penalty setting. Clearly the OFT will be mindful of the deterrent effect of imposing significant penalties, but where the settling party's turnover is substantial, large penalties will still result even through a settlement procedure, as *BA* shows.

Further observations

Arguably, the incentives for the OFT to settle are *higher* than in other jurisdictions due to the structure of the appeals system in the UK. Appeals to the CAT against infringement decisions of the OFT

[34] *See* Philip Collins, "Public and private enforcement : challenges and opportunities", 6 June 2006, available at http://www.oft.gov.uk/shared_oft/speeches/0306.pdf.

are to be determined "on the merits". They are full re-hearings in which parties may challenge both substantive and procedural aspects of the decision and may call and cross-examine factual and expert witnesses. Two cartel appeals before the CAT – *JJB Sports et al v OFT*[35] and *Argos et al v OFT*[36] – have involved substantial witness evidence. This is to be contrasted with the more limited "judicial review" jurisdiction afforded to the CAT under the Enterprise Act 2002 ("the 2002 Act") in merger cases and the intensity of review engaged in by the CFI under Article 230 EC.

The UK's more intensive review mechanism has two consequences:

- first, defending appeals is, all things being equal, a more expensive exercise (there being, in addition, no guarantee that the OFT will recover (all of) its costs even if it prevails);
- secondly, the risk of an appeal being successful is inevitably greater than where the appeal is restricted to "judicial review".

This may help explain the differences between the Commission's approach and that of the OFT. In any event, it is suggested that the OFT's more flexible and pragmatic approach is more likely to result in the desired outcome: a more effective antitrust enforcement system.

IV. – Market studies and investigations[37]

1. – *Overview*

Competition is commonly said to be about a process of rivalry in the marketplace. It might be said that market studies and, especially, MIRs are focussed on creating or increasing rivalry, where it is found wanting.[38]

Part 4 of the 2002 Act provides the statutory framework for the investigation of markets. Such inquiries are not new, however.

---

[35] [2004] *CAT* 17.

[36] [2004] *CAT* 24.

[37] See, generally, Whish *Competition Law* (6th ed., forthcoming 2008), ch. 11, which contains very useful tables of all market studies and MIRs conducted or made to March 2008.

[38] To that effect, see Peter Freeman, "Investigating Markets and Promoting Competition: The Competition Commission's Role in UK Competition Enforcement", Beesley Lecture Series, 18 October 2007, p. 2 (available at www.competition-commission.org.uk/our_role/speeches/index.htm).

From the middle of the 20th century the CC, and its predecessor bodies (successively the Monopolies and Restrictive Practices Commission, Monopolies Commission and Mergers and Monopolies Commission ("MMC")), have been entrusted with examining markets. Previously, the remit was to examine (in essence) whether a "monopoly situation" existed, and, if it did, to examine whether the situation acted contrary to the public interest.[39] The 2002 Act modified the CC's remit by moving away from a focus on "monopoly situations" and the public interest, concentrating instead on whether "features" of markets result in an "adverse effect on competition" ("AEC"). Moreover, the process was largely de-politicised : hitherto, the MMC was confined to making recommendations to the Secretary of State (which were often followed, but not in every case), whereas the 2002 Act granted the CC wide-ranging remedial powers and almost entirely removed the Secretary of State from the process.[40] The 2002 Act also introduced specialist judicial control, in the form of the CAT. These reforms largely mirror those adopted in relation to the UK merger control regime.

Section 5 of the 2002 Act provides the statutory basis for the conduct of "market studies" by the OFT. It is to market studies that we turn first.

2. – *Market studies*

A noticeable trend since the 2002 Act came into force is the sheer number of market studies that the OFT has conducted. This may be contrasted with the relatively limited amount of "standard" enforcement work it has been carrying out.[41] It is certainly consistent, however, with the OFT's desire to take a holistic approach to markets : its mission is to "make markets work well for consumers".[42]

---

[39] See Fair Trading Act 1973, ss. 6-11 and 48-49.

[40] He retains a role in certain limited circumstances, such as where national security issues arise (ss. 139 and 153) and where he is not satisfied with a decision of the OFT not to refer (s. 132). To date, the SoS has not made use of any of his MIR powers.

[41] The OFT has not published a decision on the question of infringement of Articles 81/82 or Chapters I and II of the 1998 Act since 20 November 2006. That said, there are several investigations in the public domain that are ongoing, some of which have been referred to in section III above; others include *Cigarettes* (Chapter I), *Household products* (Chapter I) and *Cardiff buses* (Chapter II).

[42] See eg OFT Annual Plan 2008-09, p. 9 : http://www.oft.gov.uk/shared_oft/about_oft/ap09/ap09.pdf.

Statutory basis

Section 5 of the 2002 Act gives the OFT the power to acquire information "about matters relating to the carrying out of its functions". The studies themselves are published pursuant to the OFT's power to "prepare... reports in respect of matters relating to any of its functions".[43]

The OFT has a broad range of functions, including the enforcement of consumer regulations, the promotion of consumer information and education, competition law enforcement and the making of MIRs. This needs to be borne in mind when considering the 28 market studies the OFT has conducted (or is in the process of conducting) thus far: certain studies are primarily concerned with the OFT's consumer protection function,[44] some are clearly concerned with both consumer and competition law issues;[45] and others with purely competition-related issues.[46]

Such studies may arise in different ways, including as a result of:

- a "super-complaint" by a designated consumer body;[47]
- complaints under competition law;
- suggestions made by other authorities or interested parties (businesses, trade associations etc);
- the OFT's consumer/competition work; and
- internal OFT research.[48]

Market studies can be "short" or "full" and their duration can last from just a few months to a year or more. Whether the study should be "short" or "full" will depend on factors such as the

[43] S. 4(4); see *Market Studies: Guidance on the OFT approach ("Market Studies Guidance")*, OFT 519, November 2004, para. 3.15.

[44] Eg. *Ticket agents*: www.oft.gov.uk/shared_oft/reports/consumer_protection/oft762.pdf (January 2005) (*inter alia* addressing potentially unfair terms in consumer contracts and recommending that the Society of Ticket Agents and Retailers produce model terms for its members).

[45] Eg. *New car warranties*: www.oft.gov.uk/shared_oft/reports/consumer_protection/oft683.pdf (December 2003) (addressing servicing restrictions in new car warranties and inadequate advice to consumers on their servicing options).

[46] Eg. *CUPI*: www.oft.gov.uk/shared_oft/reports/consumer_protection/oft861.pdf (December 2006) (addressing provision of public sector information to commercial re-users, particularly in circumstances where the public sector body is also active on the downstream market).

[47] See s. 11 of the 2002 Act. Thus far, 8 bodies have been designated as super-complainants (three of which have recently been amalgamated). The OFT is obliged to respond within 90 days explaining what action, if any, it intends to adopt: this can include a market study and an MIR. Thus far, there have been 9 super-complaints, 4 of which have resulted in a market study and 3, directly or indirectly, in an MIR: see table in Whish, *op. cit.*

[48] See *Market Studies Guidance*, para. 2.1.

nature of the market in question; the complexity of the issues; the amount of information already available; the scale of consultation and research to be conducted; and the potential outcome.[49] A short study may be a precursor to deciding whether to refer a market to the CC.

The OFT's information gathering powers, however, are limited. Significantly, whilst it may request information pursuant to section 5 of the 2002 Act it does not have the power to compel the provision of that information, and so recipients are at least theoretically able to refuse to cooperate. The only exception is where the OFT is considering making an MIR : in such circumstances the OFT has the power to compel a person to give it information, and it is a criminal offence intentionally and without reasonable excuse not to comply with such a request.[50]

Market studies can result in a range of possible outcomes, amongst which :

- an MIR (or undertakings in lieu) (the result of 5 market studies[51]);
- competition or consumer enforcement action (no studies, although threatened in *New car warranties*);
- recommendations to Government, particularly where the market failure is due at least in part to restrictions imposed by legislation) (11 market studies);
- encouraging voluntary action by market participants (6 market studies);
- itself publishing information to assist consumers (none so far); and
- giving the market a clean bill of health (4 market studies).

As of the end of July 2008 the OFT had published 26 market study reports; three further studies were ongoing.[52] In addition, the ORR has conducted one study, into *Rolling Stock*,[53] and OFGEM

[49] *Market Studies Guidance*, para. 3.1-3.2.

[50] See ss. 174 and 175 of the 2002 Act.

[51] One of which, *Extended warranties for electrical goods*, was a reference under the old "complex monopoly provisions" contained in the 1973 Act.

[52] The OFT's website has a section dedicated to market studies : see http://www.oft.gov.uk/advice_and_resources/resource_base/market-studies/.

[53] Http://www.rail-reg.gov.uk/upload/pdf/325.pdf (The study resulted in an MIR to the CC, which is pending).

has recently launched a market study into energy supply markets.[54]

Observations

Observations worth making include the following.

- The possibility of conducting market studies is an extremely useful tool in the OFT's armour. It allows the OFT to inquire into markets without the need to make an MIR reference, which would be onerous for all concerned. Although they are a soft form of enforcement, market studies have undoubtedly led to important reforms in a number of sectors. For example, as a result of the OFT's *New car warranties* study, manufacturers voluntarily dispensed with restrictions that tied the warranty to servicing at franchised garages (which are, in general, significantly more expensive than independent garages); this led to consumer and business savings of £120m to £170m over two years, according to an evaluation study commissioned by the OFT.[55] On the other hand, there is a risk, particularly with recommendations to Government, that no action will be taken.[56]
- Although they are called "market studies", that does not fully convey the nature of the OFT's work in this area. A quick glance at the studies conducted thus far shows that the issues the subject of the studies varies enormously and include studies into the *Financial Services and Markets Act*,[57] *Public procurement*,[58] *Public subsidies*,[59] the *Pharmaceutical Price Regulation Scheme*,[60] and *Internet Shopping*.[61]
- Market studies are undoubtedly a flexible tool in other senses, too. As mentioned above, studies can be "short" or "full"; another facet of their flexibility can be seen in the range of "out-

[54] Press release R/6, 21.2.08 : http://www.ofgem.gov.uk/Media/PressRel/Documents1/ProbeFINAL.pdf.

[55] *Evaluating the impact of the car warranties market study*, Report by Europe Economics, OFT 852, June 2006 (www.oft.gov.uk/shared_oft/about_oft/oft852.pdf).

[56] In *Pharmacies* (www.oft.gov.uk/shared_oft/reports/comp_policy/oft609.pdf) the OFT recommended Government action to liberalise entry to the community pharmacy market; the recommendations were not, however, acted upon.

[57] Http://www.oft.gov.uk/shared_oft/reports/financial_products/oft757.pdf.

[58] Http://www.oft.gov.uk/shared_oft/reports/comp_policy/oft841.pdf.

[59] Http://www.oft.gov.uk/shared_oft/reports/comp_policy/oft750.pdf.

[60] Http://www.oft.gov.uk/shared_oft/reports/comp_policy/oft885.pdf.

[61] Http://www.oft.gov.uk/shared_oft/reports/consumer_protection/oft921.pdf.

comes" that result and in other knock-on effects, such as the "sunshine regulation" effect that these studies undoubtedly have.[62]

– Market studies are the closest domestic equivalent to European Commission sector inquiries. Their greater flexibility, both in terms of process and outcomes, allied to the (unspoken) threat of referring markets to the CC for in-depth investigation, arguably make it a more useful tool than the European Commission's sector inquiry powers; perhaps for that reason, among others, it has been utilised much more intensively.

3. – *Market investigations*

General observations

The market investigation regime is the only one of its kind in Europe. Whilst certain other Member States have developed mechanisms for inquiring into markets,[63] none has such a wide-ranging and potentially intrusive regime. Interestingly, the CC currently has only one ongoing merger investigation on its books[64] compared to three pending MIR cases (and the implementation of remedies in two other MIR cases). For those reasons, if for no other, it is worth dwelling on MIRs.

The CC's task is to conduct an in-depth inquiry, lasting up to two years, into one or more features of a market referred to it by the OFT.

Statutory framework

The central planks of the MIR regime are contained in sections 131 and 134 of the 2002 Act.

---

[62] Eg. *Private dentistry* (Government published an action plan to implement the OFT's proposals, which had been aimed at voluntary action by the profession); *Commercial use of public information* (the OFT's study has been cited in various further studies connected to the re-use of public sector information and in the context of the European Commission's impending review of Directive 2003/98 on the re-use of public sector information, *OJ*, 2003 L345/90).

[63] See FREEMAN, "Market Investigations", Second Annual Chatham House Competition Conference, who notes (at p. 5) less extensive regimes in Germany, Ireland and Italy.

[64] *Anticipated acquisition by BOC Limited of the packaged chlorine business and assets carried on by Ineos Chlor Limited*, referred on 29 May 2008 : see http://www.oft.gov.uk/news/press/2008/68-08.

(i) *Section 131 – the OFT stage*

Section 131(1) provides as follows:

> "The OFT may... make a reference to the [CC] if the OFT has reasonable grounds for suspecting that any feature, or combination of features, of a market in the United Kingdom for goods or services prevents, restricts or distorts competition in connection with the supply or acquisition of any goods or services in the United Kingdom or a part of the United Kingdom."

A number of comments may immediately be made.

– *"Make a reference"*

It is for the OFT (or sectoral regulator) to refer a market to the CC: the CC has no original jurisdiction. The OFT is required to include certain elements in its reference, *inter alia* a description of the goods and services to which the "feature" relates (s 133(1)(c)). It must also give reasons for its decision to refer (s 172).[65] The reference may confine the CC's investigation to goods/services supplied in a particular place, or to or from particular persons (s 133(2) and (3)).[66] References may be varied, however, and no limitation is placed on the persons who may request such a variation.[67]

Prior to making a reference, the OFT must consult on its intended course of action: this seems to be sensible, bearing in mind the consequences for the parties (and the CC) of a reference, although it does have the effect of elongating the procedure.[68]

– *"Reasonable grounds for suspecting"*

It will readily be apparent that the threshold for referring ("reasonable grounds for *suspecting*") is low. The OFT need not have reasonable grounds for *believing* there to be features distortive of competition. In *Association of Convenience Stores v OFT*[69] the CAT

[65] Reference decisions range from short to very long (152 pages in *BAA*).

[66] See the OFT's reference decision in *BAA* (limiting the reference to the supply of airport services by BAA): www.oft.gov.uk/shared_oft/reports/transport/oft912.pdf.

[67] To date, there have been variations in two MIRs: *Store Cards* (variation requested by CC) and *Domestic LPG* (variation requested by undertakings present in the market). The CC must, where it does not request the variation, be consulted: s. 135(2).

[68] Take the recent *Groceries* MIR, for example: more than six months elapsed from the date of the OFT's agreeing to reconsider the Association of Convenience Stores' request to its actually referring the market. In *BAA*, the consultation process added more than three months to the process.

[69] [2005] *CAT* 36, para. 7.

confirmed that the hurdle is a low one.[70] Note, however, that the OFT has no *duty* to refer a market in such circumstances – merely the power to do so.[71] The OFT has published guidance containing further factors bearing on its decision whether to refer a market to the CC. It will consider whether[72]:

– it would be more appropriate to proceed with competition enforcement under the 1998 Act (Articles 81 and 82 EC and/or domestic counterparts);[73]

– it would be more appropriate to accept undertakings in lieu of a reference ("UIL");[74]

– a reference would be a proportionate response to the scale of the suspected problem;[75]

– there is a reasonable chance that appropriate remedies will be available.[76]

---

[70] Note also the CAT's comments that the OFT should not unduly delay a decision as to whether to refer – to do so may itself be vulnerable to challenge under judicial review principles: para. 12.

[71] This contrasts with the 2-stage process under the 2002 Act for the control of mergers: once the OFT believes that it is or may be the case that a merger may result in a significant lessening of competition ("SLC"), it is (subject to one or two exceptions) under a duty to refer the merger to the CC for in-depth investigation: see ss. 22 (completed mergers) and 33 (anticipated mergers). On the interpretation of the OFT's duty, see *Office of Fair Trading v IBA Health*, [2004] *EWCA Civ* 142.

[72] See *Market Investigation References*, OFT Guidance, February 2006 *("OFT MIR Guidance")*, para 2.1 *et seq* (http://www.oft.gov.uk/shared_oft/business_leaflets/enterprise_act/oft511.pdf).

[73] The OFT has said that MIRs are likely to focus on problems arising from uncoordinated parallel conduct or industry-wide features of a market where it does not suspect anti-competitive collusion: *OFT MIR Guidance*, para. 2.4. In addition, and importantly, the OFT is willing to consider referring oligopolistic markets showing signs of tacit collusion, stating that whilst the concept of collective dominance may be applicable the case law does not cover all coordinated parallel conduct that may have an AEC: *ibid.*, para. 2.5. Markets displaying networks of vertical agreements preventing the entry of new competitors may also be suitable for an MIR; single firm conduct (absent other "features") is, however, unlikely to be the subject of an MIR: *ibid.*, para. 2.6-2.7.

[74] The *OFT MIR Guidance* suggests that UIL is unlikely to be common, particularly as the OFT will in most cases not have a sufficiently detailed understanding of the problem to be able to tell whether UIL would achieve "as comprehensive a solution as is reasonable and practicable" (section 154(3) of the 2002 Act): para 2.20. There have been 2 UIL cases so far: *BT* (http://www.ofcom.org.uk/media/news/2005/09/nr_20050922) (Ofcom) and *Postal Franking Machines* (http://www.oft.gov.uk/shared_oft/monopolies/franking.pdf) (OFT).

[75] Factors the OFT will take into account include the size of the market; the proportion of the market affected by the 'feature' said to give rise to an AEC; and the persistence of the feature: *ibid.*, para. 2.28.

[76] For example because the market is global in scope and so any remedy for the UK would have little discernible impact on the market's operation in the UK: *OFT MIR Guidance*, para. 2.30.

– *"Feature or combination of features"*

Section 131 is drawn in deliberately broad terms, allowing the investigation of a wide range of aspects of a market, whether taken individually or in combination with others.[77] Features include (s 131(2)):

- the structure of the market concerned (or any aspect of the structure);[78] and
- the conduct of suppliers (whether or not on that market) and customers, including failure to act and any (other) unintentional conduct.

Examples of conduct offered by the *OFT MIR Guidance*[79] include: the conduct of oligopolies (where (i) there is evidence of market features enabling tacit collusion to take place and (ii) the OFT reasonably suspects that "the oligopolists are not competing effectively with consequences that are likely to be detrimental to their customers"[80]); "facilitating practices"; "custom and practice" (such as the practice of manufacturers' RRPs, where these are generally followed by retailers); and networks of vertical agreements.[81]

As for customers' conduct being a "feature", the OFT refers to high search costs, which can blunt competition among sellers, although it adds that customers' conduct on its own is unlikely to be sufficient to justify an MIR.[82]

(ii) *Section 134 – the CC stage*

Section 134 provides in material part as follows:

> "(1) The Commission shall, on a market investigation reference, decide whether any feature, or combination of features, of each relevant market prevents, restricts or distorts competition in connection with the supply or acquisition of any goods or services in the United Kingdom or a part of the United Kingdom."

---

[77] In this respect, see Freeman, "Market Investigations in the United Kingdom: The Story So Far", in Monti *et al* (eds), *Economic Law and Justice in Times of Globalisation: Festschrift for Carl Baudenbacher,* (Nomos, 2007) 352, 360.

[78] The *OFT MIR Guidance* cites the following potential structural issues: market concentration; vertical integration; conditions of entry, exit and expansion; government regulations and policy; informational asymmetries; switching costs; and countervailing buyer power: section 5.

[79] Section 6.

[80] Para. 6.6.

[81] For an example under the *ancien régime*, see *The Supply of Beer* Cm 651 (http://www.competition-commission.gov.uk/rep_pub/reports/1989/245beer.htm#full).

[82] *Ibid.*, para. 7.10.

If so, then there is an AEC : section 134(2).

If the CC finds an AEC it must consider the issue of remedies – specifically :

- whether it should take action itself to remove the AEC or its detrimental effect on customers,[83] (or recommend that others take action); and if so
- what action should be taken (s 134(4)), bearing in mind (i) the need to achieve as comprehensive a solution as reasonable and (ii) any relevant customer benefits (s 134(6) and (7)).

Remedial action may therefore deal with the *source* of the problem (the AEC) and/or with its *consequences* (the detrimental effect).[84] The CC will have regard to costs, proportionality and effectiveness of potential remedies.[85] The social and environmental costs of any remedies are not, however, for the CC to take into account.[86]

Types and forms of remedy

As with the term "features" the remedies stage is meant to provide the CC with the flexibility to take account of the circumstances of the case. Subject to the requirements set out above, the CC is free to choose the remedy or remedies most suitable to the AEC it has found. The *CC MIR Guidance* suggests six types of remedy :[87]

- Structural (divestment);
- Reducing entry barriers or switching costs;
- Recommendations for changes to regulations;
- Directions to firms to discontinue certain behaviour;
- Price caps;
- Monitoring mechanisms.

See further the remedies diagram in the Annex to this paper.

[83] The phrase "detrimental effect on customers" is defined as (a) higher prices, lower quality or less choice of goods or services in any market in the United Kingdom or (b) less innovation in relation to such goods or services : s. 134(5).

[84] See further *CC MIR Guidance*, para. 4.6, which notes that the CC will in practice try to tackle both.

[85] *Ibid.*, para. 4.9 *et seq.*

[86] *Ibid.*, para. 4.11; see also *Groceries*, para. 2.13.

[87] Para. 4.18.

Note, however, that the CC does *not* have the power to sanction past behaviour, nor does it have the power to levy financial penalties : remedies are purely forward-looking.

Remedies will take the form of orders or undertakings. The CC anticipates orders being more common than undertakings, particularly where numerous parties are involved.[88]

The Government has committed to responding publicly within 90 days of any report recommending that it take action.[89]

Process and information gathering

The CC's process is a transparent one, and compares favourably to those of other competition agencies. All market investigations follow a particular pattern, which is set out in a chart annexed to this paper. All of the principal documents issued by the CC, including working papers, results of surveys etc., together with submissions and papers provided by interested parties, are all placed on the CC's website.

The CC's approach is an inquisitorial one. This, coupled with there not being any possibility of the CC imposing financial penalties,[90] may mean that the CC is able to develop a fuller, more balanced understanding of the mechanics of a market than authorities might be able to do under a prohibition-based system.[91]

The CC's powers to seek information are greater than those enjoyed by the OFT in relation to market studies. It may require persons to provide documents and give evidence; it may also ask "persons carrying on a business" to provide estimates, forecasts, returns or other information.[92] The CC may impose penalties in the event of non-compliance.[93] It does not, however, have the power to

[88] *CC MIR Guidance*, para 4.44.

[89] "A Wold Class Competition Regime", DTI White Paper, July 2001, para. 4.15.

[90] Note, however, that the CC may recommend enforcement action by the OFT or bring certain matters to its attention which trigger an investigation : see, most recently, press reports that the CC has provided the OFT with certain information, in the form of emails it had received in the context of its *Groceries* market investigation (see App. 9.1 to the Final Report, para. 10 *et seq*), in connection with the OFT's recently commenced investigation into suspected price-fixing in relation to food and toiletries : eg. *Daily Telegraph*, "Walmart was whistleblower in OFT's supermarket investigation", 27 April 2008 (http://www.telegraph.co.uk/money/main.jhtml?xml=/money/2008/05/04/cnoft104.xml).

[91] See FREEMAN, "The Story So Far", *op. cit.*, 367.

[92] S. 176(1)(a), referring to s. 109.

[93] S. 176(1)(b), referring to s. 110; the penalties are set out in s. 111.

conduct "dawn raids" (in contrast to the European Commission's sector inquiry powers[94]).

Appeals to the CAT

The 2002 Act introduced the right of any "aggrieved person" to apply for judicial review any decision of the CC on an MIR.[95]

MIRs to date

To date there have been nine MIRs, of which eight were made by the OFT and one by the ORR. In chronological order they are as follows:

- Store Card Credit Services;
- Domestic LPG;
- Home Credit;
- Classified Directory Advertising Services;
- Northern Ireland Banking;
- Groceries;
- Payment Protection Insurance;
- BAA Airports;
- Rolling Stock.

The OFT is currently considering at least one further request.[96]

Observations

Whilst the regime is still, to an extent, in its infancy, certain observations may already be made:

First, the correct selection of markets for reference is a difficult challenge, but it is critical to the effectiveness of the MIR regime.[97]

[94] See Regulation 1/2003, Article 17(1).

[95] Section 179; note that decisions of the OFT as to whether to refer markets are also susceptible to judicial review. There have been two applications to the CAT under s. 179 thus far, both of which in relation to the groceries market. The first was in respect of the OFT's decision not to refer the groceries market to the CC: see *Association of Convenience Stores v OFT*, *op. cit.* The second was brought in respect of the certain of the CC's findings and remedies in its *Groceries* report: see Case 1104/6/8/08, *Tesco PLC v Competition Commission* (pending).

[96] See http://www.oft.gov.uk/news/press/2007/37-07 (newspaper and magazine distribution).

[97] See eg. FREEMAN, "The Story So Far", *op. cit.*, 358: "If the CC's resources are dissipated on cases which are neither of sufficient importance to the operation of the UK economy nor raise issues of more general applicability, it is hard to se the MIR contributing to usefully to competition enforcement".

The OFT must be careful not to refer too many markets : the CC has a limited budget and can only realistically handle a certain number of cases per year, and the burden on parties is significant too. The referring body must therefore seek to ensure that it refers those markets displaying complex problems (which are possibly intractable in the absence of intervention) leading to potentially high consumer detriment – ie those cases where CC action may be expected to have a significant impact. [98]

Secondly, and related, the length of market investigations is confined to two years. That may sound like a long time, but it is relatively short compared to many investigations under Articles 81 and 82, and, given the breadth of issues under consideration and the potentially large number of interested parties, can place the CC under considerable strain. [99] There is an obvious tension between the need for rigour and transparency, on the one hand, and speed, on the other; striking the right balance is key to the achievement of the CC's task.

Thirdly, it is noticeable that AEC has been found in every market referred to the CC thus far, albeit on occasion on narrower grounds than those identified by the referring body. [100] Contrast that with the proportion of mergers it has found to result in SLC. [101] Whilst the headline statistic might be eye-catching, on reflection it is probably not so surprising :

- Markets are usually referred only after the referring authority has spent a good deal of time probing the market itself, often on the back of considerable prior knowledge (especially on the part of the sectoral regulators). In relation to mergers, the OFT has only a limited period within which to come to a referral decision, may not have any detailed knowledge of the sector concerned and may

[98] The Chairman of the CC, writing at the start of 2007, said that "[a]fter a possibly uncertain start, the selection of cases appears to be improving", *ibid.*, 358.

[99] One only need look at the recent *Groceries* investigation to appreciate the scale of the task with which the CC was confronted : among other things, it received over 700 submissions from interested parties and held 81 hearings across the UK.

[100] For example, in *Store Cards* the OFT was concerned about both the upstream and downstream markets but CC "cleared" the upstream market (supply of store card services to retailers), finding AEC only in relation to the downstream market (supply to consumers). Likewise, in *Northern Ireland Banking* the CC did not find the market to be characterised by coordinated effects, contrary to the OFT's initial concerns.

[101] Approximately one-third of mergers referred to the CC thus far have been found to result in SLC; note, however, that another one-third of referred mergers have not resulted in a decision by the CC due to the parties pulling out.

feel a good deal less certain about the future operation of the market, were a merger permitted to proceed.

- The OFT has no *duty* to refer markets to the CC; with mergers, on the other hand, it does have a duty (once it believes that it is or may be the case that the merger may be expected to result in SLC), subject to certain limited exceptions.
- The test is widely drawn and permits the CC to identify a very broad range of "features" which may have an AEC. In practice, many if not all markets have elements of "failure" (information asymmetries, switching costs etc.) about them, and many can be expected to "benefit" from measures taken to dissipate information asymmetries or reduce switching costs.

Fourthly, in terms of "features" the CC has found to result in AEC it is not easy to discern any trend, but the focus has often been on switching costs and information asymmetry. In several of the markets, such as *Home Credit*, *Store Cards* and *Domestic LPG*, one detects a strong emphasis on consumer protection : in each of those markets the CC found that consumers were unable to exercise choice, because of restrictive contract terms, a lack of information or the complexity of comparing different suppliers' offerings.

Fifthly, it is similarly difficult to point to any particular trend in the remedies imposed by the CC, save that, thus far at least, they have not been particularly intrusive.[102] This is perhaps unsurprising, given the duty on the CC not to impose disproportionate remedies. It appears that estimates of customer detriment help to inform CC's approach to remedies, as this will be relevant to the question of proportionality.[103]

Perhaps the most important observation related to features and remedies is that several of the markets addressed thus far by the CC did not display conduct capable of being addressed under the prohibition-based regime. In cases such as *LPG* and *Home Credit* there was no evidence of (tacit) collusion or joint or single dominance. In other words, absent the MIR regime such markets would not have been susceptible to intervention by the competition authorities despite evidence of a lack of competition in them. That, it is sub-

---

[102] The CC has, however, hinted at structural remedies in its "Emerging Thinking", in *BAA* : see http://www.competition-commission.gov.uk/inquiries/ref2007/airports/emerging_thinking.htm.

[103] See FREEMAN, "Investigating Markets...", *op. cit.*, p. 16.

mitted, is one of the most powerful arguments in favour of the MIR regime: to coin the famous Heineken advert, it can refresh certain markets that prohibition-based regimes cannot reach. Moreover, MIRs can be used to attack the underlying *causes* of particular agreements or abusive conduct – features such as barriers to entry are clearly capable of sustaining such behaviour.[104] Whilst it is true to say that the authorities cannot compel firms to compete, they can at least improve the *incentives* for competitors and/or customers to create or insist upon more vigorous competition.

Sixthly, there is the interesting question of the relationship between MIRs and EC competition law. Article 3(2) of Regulation 1/2003 provides as follows:

> "The application of national competition law may not lead to the prohibition of agreements, decisions by associations of undertakings or concerted practices which may affect trade between Member States but which do not restrict competition within the meaning of Article 81(1) of the Treaty, or which fulfil the conditions of Article 81(3) of the Treaty or which are covered by a Regulation for the application of Article 81(3) of the Treaty. Member States shall not under this Regulation be precluded from adopting and applying on their territory stricter national laws which prohibit or sanction unilateral conduct engaged in by undertakings."

Where the CC identifies features having an AEC such as industry-standard supply agreements whose terms and conditions do not provide customers with sufficiently clear information, thus resulting in information asymmetries, is it precluded from imposing remedies in circumstances where those agreements would not be in breach of Article 81?[105]

The answer would seem to be no, on the basis that the CC would not be prevented from imposing remedies falling short of outright prohibition (such as a requirement to provide adequate information to customers); furthermore, this is unlikely to be a practical concern in many cases – in most cases where one or more agreements are under scrutiny, application of the tests contained in the MIR regime and Article 81 would presumably arrive at the same result,

---

[104] See, in this respect, GEROSKI, "The UK Market Inquiry Regime", Paper presented to the Fordham Corporate Law Institute 31st Annual International Antitrust Law and Policy Conference, 7-8 October 2004, p. 4.

[105] See *OFT MIR Guidance*, *op. cit.*, para 2.12 (noting that Art. 3(2) does not prevent investigation but may affect the remedies that can be imposed). See also *CC MIR Guidance*, para. 1.12 *et seq.* In *Store Cards*, at para. 10.9, the CC referred in general terms to its having taken Regulation 1/2003 into account when considering remedies.

given that the tests both concentrate on the restriction of competition.[106]

Perhaps of more concern is that the CC is not a designated NCA for the purpose of applying Articles 81 and 82 EC. In circumstances where it identifies features restrictive of competition and suspects the same to be in breach of Articles 81 and/or 82 (for example, a *Delimitis*-style network of parallel agreements) the CC is barred from deciding on the latter but must instead refer the matter to the OFT, which, if it decides to investigate at all, will need to decide whether to do so in parallel with the CC or subsequently. This is arguably an unsatisfactory state of affairs, and one which might in due course need to be reformed.[107]

Finally, one might wonder whether the undoubtedly substantial costs of the MIR regime – both to parties active in markets under investigation and to the CC (and indirectly the taxpayer) – are outweighed by the benefits. Is Sir Jeremy Lever's comment on the pre-2002 Act regime that "[one] seriously [has] to question whether... the task is sufficiently well defined and valuable to justify the use of the public and private resources required"[108] – a fair one now (regardless of whether it was at the time)?

Whilst it may be too early to conduct a cost/benefit analysis at this stage, the CC provides estimates of consumer detriment in its decisions, and in July 2007 it issued a summary of the "[e]stimated costs to consumers of mergers and market outcomes against which the CC took action between April 2006 and March 2007".[109] In that latter document, the CC estimated that the total annual cost to UK consumers of the AECs found in *Domestic LPG*, *Home Credit* and *Classified Directory Advertising Services* was approximately £103.5 million. Whilst estimating consumer detriment is fraught with difficulty, these figures give some idea of the potential benefits of the MIR regime.

[106] Note also that the *OFT MIR Guidance* states that the OFT is unlikely to refer markets where Article 81 is applicable to an agreement or agreements: *ibid.*, para. 2.14.

[107] A further interesting issue concerns the status of CC MIR decisions in private actions: should relevant findings of fact contained in them be binding on the parties in subsequent cases concerning the same or substantially the same subject-matter? Cf. the status of findings of fact made by the OFT in the course of an investigation under the 1998 Act: see s. 58.

[108] Lever, "UK economic regulation: use and abuse of the law", [1992] *ECLR* 55, 62.

[109] Http://www.competition-commission.gov.uk/our_role/analysis/estimated_costs_06_07.pdf.

V. – Tentative conclusions

All of the AETs available to the UK competition authorities are relatively new tools. It is too early to say how effective they will turn out to be. However, there are already signs that the OFT's settlements regime is bedding down as an effective tool in the OFT's armoury, and the OFT and CC have emphasised the benefits for consumers of market studies and MIRs that have been shown by evaluations of their work. Whilst there may need to be some further reform in due course, it will most likely be in the British way : evolution, not revolution.

ANNEX

1. Enforcement routes open to OFT (1) – general

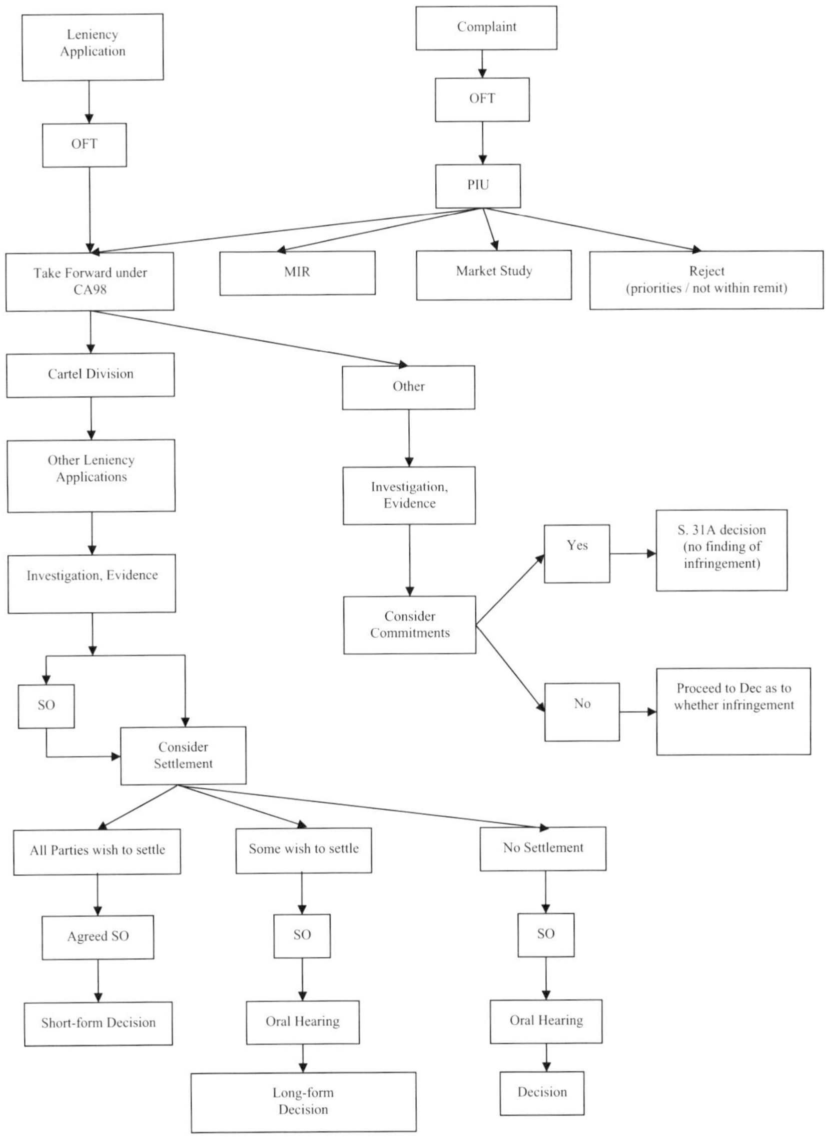

2. Enforcement routes open to OFT (2) – Market Study/MIR

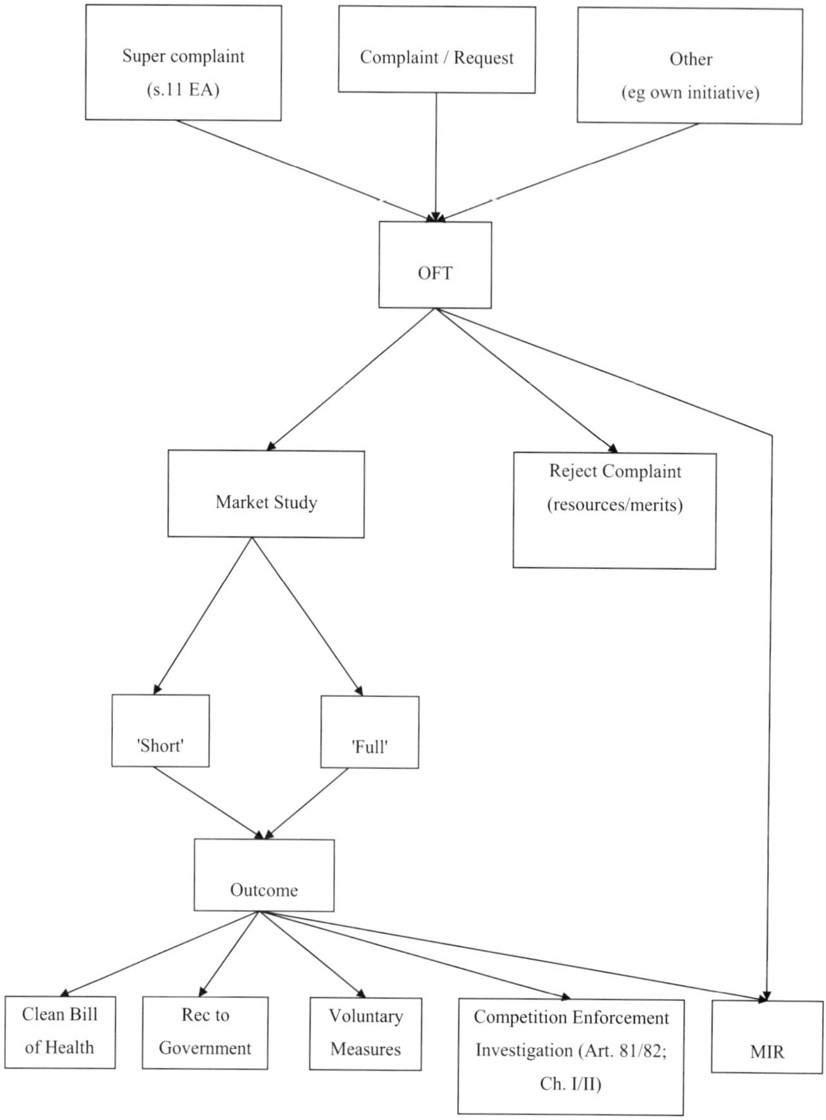

3. Market Studies – Range of Outcomes

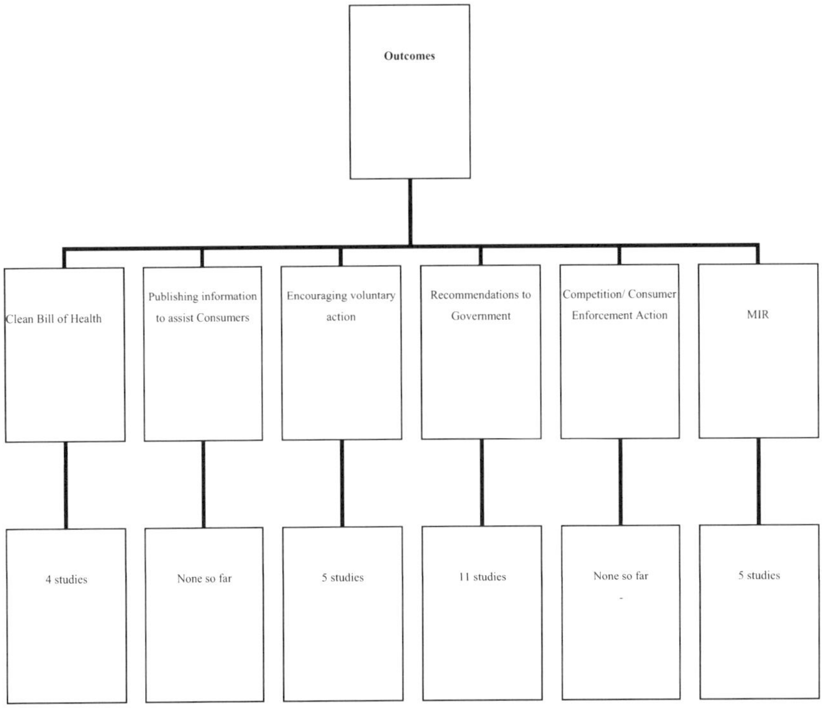

4. MIRs – Process

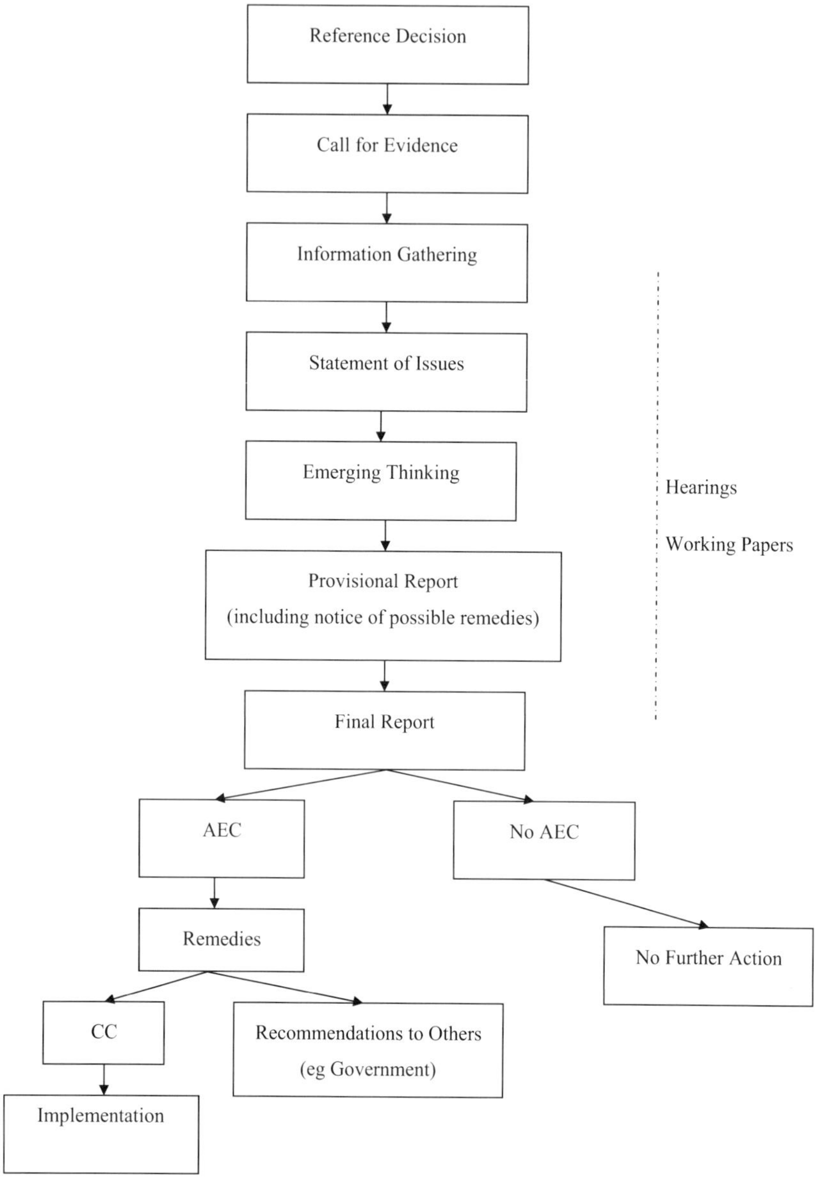

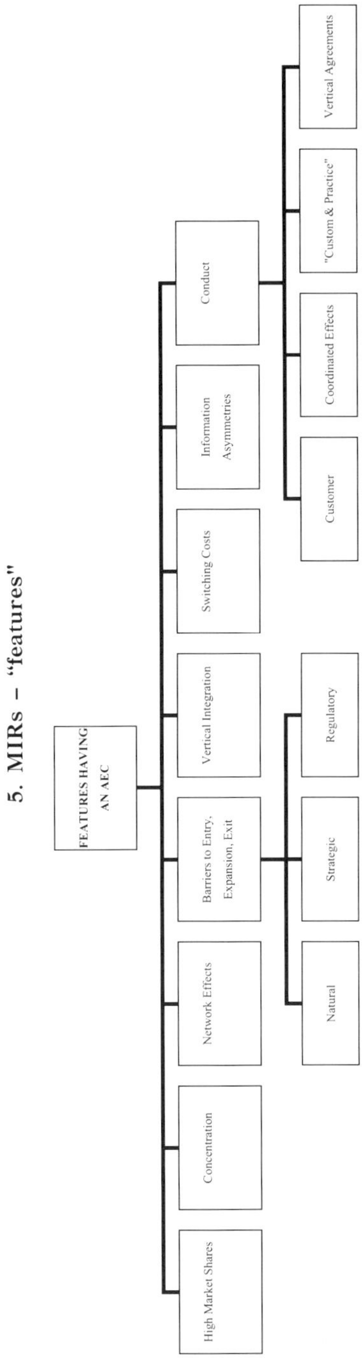
5. MIRs – "features"
FEATURES HAVING AN AEC
High Market Shares
Concentration
Network Effects
Barriers to Entry, Expansion, Exit
Natural
Strategic
Regulatory
Vertical Integration
Switching Costs
Information Asymmetries
Conduct
Customer
Coordinated Effects
"Custom & Practice"
Vertical Agreements

6. MIRs – remedies

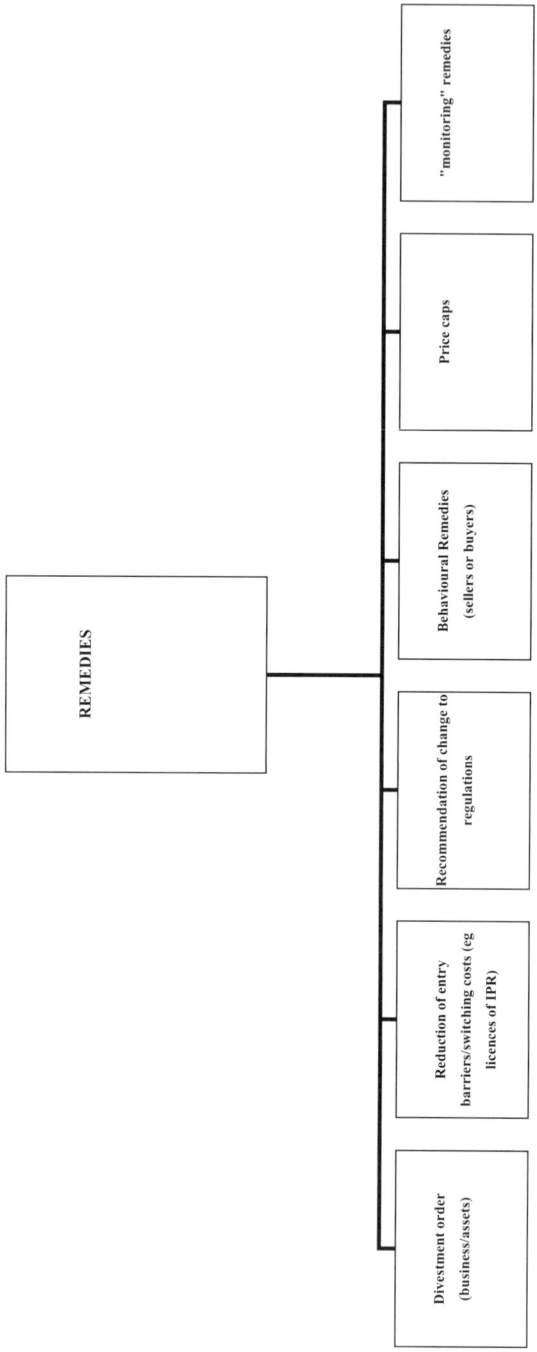

FROM HARD TO SOFT ENFORCEMENT OF EC COMPETITION LAW – A BESTIARY OF "SUNSHINE" ENFORCEMENT INSTRUMENTS

BY

NICOLAS PETIT[1]

LECTURER (*CHARGÉ DE COURS*), UNIVERSITY OF LIÈGE
CO-DIRECTOR OF IEJE
AND ASSOCIATE, HOWREY LLP

AND

MIGUEL RATO[2]

SENIOR ASSOCIATE, HOWREY LLP

INTRODUCTION

For a number of reasons – notably its limited administrative resources – the European Commission ("the Commission") seems to be relying increasingly on methods of competition law enforcement based on informal pronouncements (press releases, oral statements, etc.) and soft law instruments.[3] Surprisingly, and in stark contrast with the extensive body of literature devoted to the Commission's more muscular enforcement initiatives[4] under Articles 81 and 82

[1] Nicolas.Petit@ulg.ac.be.

[2] RatoM@howrey.com. The views expressed in this paper cannot be attributed to Howrey LLP or any of its clients. The authors thank E. Fegatilli, M. Heim, E. Provost and T. Soames for their helpful comments.

[3] Despite the fact that the very idea that sunshine enforcement techniques are on the rise when compared to traditional competition law enforcement mechanisms can be disputed. Indeed, a number of observers have noted that the Commission's formal enforcement powers have increased with the adoption of Regulation 1/2003. See generally, on soft law instruments, U. MORTH, "Soft Law in Governance and Regulation : An Interdisciplinary Analysis", *Edward Elgar Pub*, 2004, pp. 37-38.

[4] In particular through the steep increase in the fines imposed in cartel cases and through the numerous Article 82 EC procedures opened lately.

EC and the EC Merger Regulation ("the ECMR"),[5] the pervasive use of soft law and informal legal instruments in European Community ("EC") competition policy has gone relatively unnoticed.[6]

In our view, these alternative mechanisms of competition law enforcement raise many important legal questions – not only theoretical but also of very significant practical relevance. For instance, is compliance with such instruments mandatory? Are they amenable to judicial review? Can they introduce new legal standards that depart from established case-law? To what extent can they be relied upon as a reference for competitive assessments, etc.?

The aim of this article is therefore to provide a broad picture of the various formal and informal instruments through which the Commission carries out the soft enforcement of EC competition rules. We refer to them as "sunshine" enforcement instruments and explain the reasons behind this label in Section I. We then provide a typology of those various instruments in Section II. Finally, we explore their advantages and drawbacks in Sections III and IV respectively. Section V concludes.

I. – "Sunshine" enforcement and its relevance for EC competition law

At the end of the XIXth century, in the United States, the railway regulator devised a method of intervention based on the belief that if it disclosed to the public information about any excessive pricing (or profits) by railway companies – in particular through the release of informal statements, reports, studies, etc. – those operators would have no choice but to slash their

---

[5] See Council Regulation (EC) No 139/2004 of 20 January 2004 on the control of concentrations between undertakings, *OJ* L 24, 29.01.2004, pp. 1-22.

[6] To date, only a limited number of studies have dealt with this issue. See for instance, H.A. Cosma and R. Whish, "Soft Law in the Field of EU Competition Policy", (2003) *European Business Law Review* 25; In the field of State aid, see M. Cini, "The soft law approach: Commission rule-making in the EU's state aid regime", *Journal of European Public Policy*, 8:2, 2001, pp. 193-196. More generally, see G Falkner, O. Treib, M. Hartlapp and S. Leiber, "Complying with Europe: EU harmonisation and soft law in the member states", (2005) *Cambridge University Press*, pp. 221-227, Linda A.J. Senden, "Soft law and its implications for institutional balance in the EC", *Utrecht Law Review*, http://www.utrechtlawreview.org/, Volume 1, Issue 2 (December) 2005.

prices.[7] In other words, through the disclosure of information to a large audience (including the customers, suppliers and competitors of railway companies as well as the general public), the railway regulator shone a bright light on the behaviour it wished to influence, thereby giving rise to the expression "sunshine regulation".[8]

Recent trends in the enforcement of EC competition law lead us to believe that sunshine regulation is making its appearance in Europe over a century after its inception. In this paper we use the expression sunshine enforcement loosely to refer to methods of enforcement which aim to reveal to the public not only (i) the anticompetitive behaviour of specific firms, but also (ii) abstract categories of anticompetitive practices through the adoption of general soft law instruments.[9]

First, it appears that the Commission is becoming increasingly vocal in the context of its enforcement of Articles 81 and 82 EC. This is borne out by the "growing" number of press releases, informal statements, academic articles, papers, etc. issued by the Commission itself or authored by Commission officials. Whilst the majority of these public interventions are in theory of a purely informative nature, they have, in practice a variety of other functions.[10] For instance, following the Court of First Instance's ("CFI") dismissal of the appeal brought by Microsoft against the Commission's decision of 2004, Commissioner Kroes made the following statement :

> "The Court has upheld a landmark Commission decision to give consumers more choice in software markets. That decision set an important precedent in terms of the obligations of dominant companies to allow competition, in particular in high tech industries".[11]

---

[7] See P.C. Carstensen, "Law and Economics Through History : McCraw's prophet of regulation", (1984) *Harvard University Press*, pp. 885-886; See also C. Henry, "Public service and competition in the European Union", (1997) *International Advances in Economic Research*, Vol. 3, pp. 265-267.

[8] See H. Dumez et A. Jeunemaître, "Les institutions de la régulation des marchés : Etude de quelques modèles de référence", (1999) 1 *Revue Internationale de Droit Economique* 11, p. 20.

[9] See F. Wilckmans, F. Tuytschaever and A. Vanderelst, *Vertical Agreements in EC Competition Law*, Oxford University Press, 2006, pp. 36-41 (*title* : "Hard and Soft EC competition law").

[10] See G. Majone, "Regulation in Comparative Perspective", *Journal of Comparative Policy Analysis : Research and Practice*, 1999, pp. 309-324.

[11] See Commission Press Release, Commission welcomes CFI ruling upholding Commission's decision on Microsoft's abuse of dominant market position, MEMO/07/359 of 17 September 2007.

Shortly thereafter, the Commission created on DG Competition's website a page highlighting its enforcement activities in the Information and Communications Technologies ("ICT") sector, thereby sending a message not only to firms in that sector, but also to the public that it intended to "closely monitor the information industry, consumer electronics and internet sectors in order to ensure compliance of market players with EU competition law".[12]

Second, the Commission seems to be making increasing use of soft law instruments to provide legal guidance to firms (but also to the National Competition Authorities ("NCAs") and courts of EU Member States) through a diverse array of curiously named documents, such as staff discussion papers, position papers, non-papers, consultation papers, notices, guidelines, communications, opinions.[13] Whilst we recognize that theses types of instruments are generally designed to assist firms in complying voluntarily with EC competition law (thereby achieving a form of "sunshine" enforcement),[14] our analysis also suggests that they serve another related "sunshine" enforcement purpose : their wide dissemination may increasingly allow suppliers, customers, competitors, or contractual partners of firms whose conduct breaches Articles 81 and 82 EC to detect such breaches and to assist competition authorities in bringing them to an end through follow-on actions on the basis of conventional enforcement mechanisms.[15]

While its advantages are obvious, sunshine enforcement may however be a double-edged sword for competition authorities. It is a well-established general principle of EC law that the Commission, in adopting measures that define its future conduct or that interpret the law, places a limit on the enforcement discretion it enjoys.[16]

---

[12] See http://ec.europa.eu/comm/competition/sectors/ICT/overview_en.html.

[13] From a purely normative standpoint, these soft law instruments are closer to the concept of regulation rather than enforcement in so far as they are general in scope and do not apply the provisions of the EC Treaty *ex post* or contemporaneously to the infringing conduct. In our view, however, they represent a different type of competition law enforcement that takes place *ex ante*. By contrast to traditional forms of regulation, these instruments (i) are not adopted following a formal legislative procedure; (ii) do not give rise to the same rights and obligations; and (iii) are primarily designed to assist competition authorities and courts in applying the competition rules and private parties in complying with them. See, similarly, H.A. Cosma and R. Whish, *supra* at p. 28.

[14] Of course, our interpretation of the concept of "enforcement" could be criticized, if only because firms complying with the soft law instruments are in principle insulated from formal enforcement actions.

[15] Such as complaints to competition authorities or proceedings brought before national courts.

II. – A review of the various "sunshine" enforcement instruments

As noted above, the Commission has so far relied on a myriad of "sunshine" enforcement instruments which differ in scope (general v. individual), author (the Commission itself, DG Competition, individual Commission officials, third parties, etc.), purpose (publicity, guidance, etc.) form (written or oral),[17] and binding effect.[18] For this reason, it is difficult to propose a homogeneous typology of "sunshine" enforcement measures based on clear distinguishing features and with bright-line boundaries. We therefore try to group them according to certain obvious common characteristics and order them, where possible, from least to most formal. Based on this subjective classification, we (i) briefly describe each type of legal instrument identified; (ii) examine the goals usually pursued with its adoption; and (iii) consider whether it has binding legal effects on the Commission and/or on third parties.

A. – *Oral statements*

In a world driven by information, Competition Commissioners, individual DG Competition officials and spokespersons often convey enforcement messages to the general public through oral statements. Speeches given at international symposiums, interviews and press conferences offer convenient opportunities to announce new enforcement actions, provide insider explanations of the Commission's analysis in specific cases, and send warnings to firms suspected of a violation of EC competition law. Whilst over the past twelve years, the three successive Competition Commissioners appear to have been equally vocal – we have found no evidence of an increase in the number of speeches delivered by Competition Commissioners – the content and implications of their public pronouncements seem to be, however, a question of individual person-

[16] On the basis of the principles of legitimate expectations, "estoppel", legal certainty and "*patere legem quam ipse fecisti*".

[17] Oral statements are by their very nature less likely to prove authoritative than written acts, which may be circulated more widely.

[18] We do not examine other less orthodox – but by no means less effective – forms of intervention such as information purposefully leaked to the press by regulators, etc. See, for a good account of this phenomenon, M. Heim, "The Impact of the Media on EU Merger Decisions", (2003) 2 *European Competition Law Review* 49.

ality. Commissioners such as Karel Van Miert or Neelie Kroes are well-known for their powerful – and often controversial – statements.[19]

Commission officials cannot, in principle, divulge information or express opinions on the Commission's activities.[20] The statements made by individuals employed by the Commission are, however, not all covered by the same rules. First, Commissioners are not civil servants within the meaning of the Staff regulations and enjoy a legal mandate to represent the Commission in public. Second, the Commission's spokespersons, who are called upon to discuss the Commission's activities before the media, enjoy a general authorization, within the meaning of Article 17 of the Staff regulations, to make public statements that convey information received in the line of duty not otherwise available to the public. All other civil servants must obtain the authorization to disclose information on the Commission's enforcement activities. This being said, Commission officials regularly comment in public on ongoing investigations or decisions adopted. In practice, only the highest ranking civil servants – such as Directors General, Deputy Directors General, Directors, Heads of Unit and cabinet members – make such statements. In this context, Commission officials usually take extreme care to ensure that they speak "in a personal capacity", and that "the views expressed [by them] are not an official position of the European Commission".

Although the topic has not generated a great deal of interest from legal scholars – perhaps due to the mistaken belief that such oral statements are devoid of legal content or effect – the question whether oral statements have legal implications seems to have been settled by the Community courts. First, in *Air France v. Commission* the CFI confirmed that an oral statement by the Commission's spokesman was a legal act in so far as it produced legal effects and,

[19] For instance, a few months ago, Commissioner Kroes publicly rebuked the United States' Assistant Attorney General for Antitrust for his "totally unacceptable" criticism of the CFI ruling in the *Microsoft* case. See T. Buck, "Kroes rebuffs US on Microsoft ruling", *Financial Times*, 19 September 2007.

[20] Articles 17(1) and 17a(1) of the Staff Regulations provide as follows: "An official shall refrain from any unauthorised disclosure of information received in the line of duty, unless that information has already been made public or is accessible to the public"; "An official has the right to freedom of expression, with due respect to the principles of loyalty and impartiality". See Staff Regulations of Officials of the European Communities, available at http://ec.europa.eu/civil_service/docs/toc100_en.pdf.

as such, could be the object of a direct challenge by individual applicants.[21] In that case, the spokesman had announced that a proposed concentration between two companies fell outside the scope of the ECMR because it did not have a Community dimension.[22] Subsequent case-law confirms that formal oral pronouncements by Commission officials are likely to constitute legal acts.[23] By contrast, "off-the-record" statements are immune from judicial scrutiny.[24]

Second, oral statements may limit the enforcement discretion of the Commission and, as a result, be relied upon by affected parties to challenge a formal Commission decision. In *Roberts and Roberts v. Commission*, the CFI reviewed the substance of a public speech given by a Commission official on specific aspects of the application of competition law to pub contracts.[25] The Court sought to determine whether the legal standard applied in a subsequent formal decision adopted by the Commission was consistent with the legal test outlined in the speech. Whilst the Court found no discrepancy between the content of the speech and the decision, the mere fact that it embarked on such an assessment implies that oral statements may be considered as representing the Commission's official policy, and as a result can create legitimate expectations for third parties.

It is therefore clear that oral statements can give rise to a legal duty, on the part of the Commission (and, conversely, to rights ben-

---

[21] See Case T-3/93, *Air France v. Commission*, [1994] E.C.R. II-121 at §§46-48.

[22] A Commission spokesman had stated publicly that a proposed concentration between British Airways and Dan Air did not meet the turnover thresholds for the application of the ECMR. The statement followed non-binding letters (i) from a Director of the Commission disclaiming that he did not represent the Commission's views and (ii) from the Commissioner for competition. Air France, a competitor, challenged the statement. The CFI considered that the statement could be the subject of judicial review under Article 230 EC. The statement had legal effects on the Member States (it confirmed the jurisdiction of the Member States to review the transaction) and on the firms (which were no longer subject to the requirement of prior notification).

[23] See Case T-52/96 R, *Sogecable v. Commission*, [1996] E.C.R. II-797, where the Court noted that informal comments of the spokesman (confirming a formal Commission decision) were not reviewable. The wording of the case is however, ambiguous. See J. FAULL, "The Spokesman and the Law", in *European Integration and International Co-ordination – Studies in Transnational Economic Law in Honour of Claus-Dieter Ehlermann*, Kluwer Law International, 2002 at p. 164.

[24] *Idem*.

[25] See Case T-25/99, *Roberts & Roberts v. Commission*, [2001] E.C.R. II-1881. See also, Case T-133/95 and T-204/95, *IEEC v. Commission*, [2001] E.C.R. I-3875, in which the Court examined whether speeches delivered by two Commissioners had created legitimate expectations, which would have been subsequently breached as a result of the adoption of a formal Commission decision.

efiting individuals), to abide by its pronouncements in subsequent enforcement initiatives, under pain of being found in breach of general principles of EC law.

Furthermore, in *Volkswagen AG v. Commission*, the CFI considered that an interview given by Commissioner Van Miert in which he revealed that Volkswagen would soon be the subject of an infringement decision and incur a large fine constituted a breach of EC law principles (such as the duty of good administration and the presumption of innocence).[26] Although this breach was not sufficient for the Court to annul the decision itself (because it would not have altered the substance of the Commission's findings),[27] the ruling suggests that such violations are capable of giving rise to a right to claim damages pursuant to Article 288 EC.[28]

B. – *Articles written by Commission officials*

Commission officials routinely address issues relating to the enforcement of EC competition law in articles published in generalist[29] and scientific reviews, academic treatises,[30] etc. In contrast with oral statements – which mainly focus on public policy issues – written articles typically relate to technical and/or case-specific issues of EC competition enforcement. Very often, those articles clarify aspects of the Commission's reasoning underlying particular investigations and decisions that might otherwise have remained unknown. They constitute therefore a useful source of guidance for legal practitioners, who frequently rely upon them to provide advice to their clients.[31]

As noted above, in principle Commission officials write in a personal capacity. Most competition law scholars and practitioners are certainly familiar with the archetypal disclaimer that "the views

[26] See Case T-62/98, *Volkswagen AG v. Commission,* [2000] E.C.R. II-2707.

[27] *Idem.* at §283.

[28] *Id.* at §282 The Court stated : "Moreover, in causing such sensitive aspects of the matters under deliberation to be disclosed to the press, the Commission acted in a manner injurious to the interests of good administration at the Community level precisely inasmuch as it enabled the public at large to have access, during the process of investigation and deliberation, to such information, internal to the administration".

[29] See, for instance, See M. Petite, "EU Commitment to free competition remains unchanged", *Financial Times*, 27 June 2007.

[30] See, for instance, the competition law treatise edited by J. Faull and A. Nikpay, *The EC Law of Competition*, Oxford University Press, 2007.

[31] See H.A. Cosma and R. Whish, *supra*, p. 50.

expressed by the author do not necessarily reflect the official position of the European Communities" and that "responsibility for the information and views expressed lies entirely with the author". As a result, their written opinions are not an expression of the Commission's enforcement policy and therefore should not limit the Commission's discretion.

This being said, whilst it is certainly true that articles written by Commission officials in a personal capacity and published in law reviews, for example, do not have legal implications for the Commission,[32] in our view a different solution presumably applies to articles that appear in official publications of the Commission. This is because such official publications, by their very nature and regardless of the presence of the customary disclaimers, appear to be endorsed by the institution. For instance, articles published in the widely disseminated *EC Competition Policy Newsletter* (published by the Commission) may create legitimate expectations for firms and their counsels.[33]

C. – *Expert reports and third parties studies*

The Commission relies increasingly on reports and studies authored by third parties. In commissioning such reports, the Commission typically seeks expert advice that will allow it to gather data on particular economic sectors or commercial practices,[34] to determine the feasibility/desirability of proposed policy reforms,[35] to assess the outcome of past enforcement actions in certain fields/sectors,[36] or simply to promote the emergence and

[32] Although, in practice, and as noted above they convey indications on the views of Commission officials in respect of certain commercial practices, economic sectors or perhaps more controversially ongoing investigations.

[33] The *EC competition policy newsletter* is published three times a year and is made widely available on the Internet. See http://ec.europa.eu/comm/competition/publications/cpn.

[34] See *Economic impact of regulation in the field of liberal professions in different Member States*, I. Paterson, M. Fink, A. Ogus *et al.*, Study for the European Commission, DG Competition, January 2003 available at http://ec.europa.eu/comm/competition/publications/prof_services/executive_en.pdf.

[35] See *Study on the conditions of claims for damages in case of infringement of EC competition rules*, Comparative report prepared by D. Waelbroeck, D. Slater and G. Even-Shoshan, 31 August 2004 available at http://ec.europa.eu/comm/competition/antitrust/actionsdamages/study.html.

[36] See, in the field of maritime transport, *The application of competition rules to liner shipping*, Final report, Global Insight *et al.*, 26 October 2005, available at http://ec.europa.eu/comm/competition/antitrust/others/maritime/shipping_report_26102005.pdf.

discussion of innovative ideas on intricate issues of EC competition policy.[37]

Those expert reports are generally drafted by third parties (including law firms, academics and research centres, economic and business consultancies) and are thus neither binding on the Commission nor amenable to judicial review.[38] They usually contain the following disclaimer: "The study represents its authors' views on the subject matter; views which have not been adopted or in any way approved by the Commission and which should not be relied upon as a statement of the Commission's or its services views".[39]

In practice, however, several confusing developments in the Commission's practice tend to elevate such expert reports to the rank of authoritative sources of EC competition policy. First, the reports are made widely available to the public, being published by the Office for Official Publications of the European Communities and posted on the Commission's Internet website.

Second, and more importantly, the terms of reference and questions defined by the Commission – which delineate the experts' mandate – often conceal a pre-determined enforcement choice. For instance, in the field of State aid, the Commission regularly seeks expert advice at advanced stages of its formal investigations to refine its economic understanding of a case.[40] Similarly, the Commission was arguably already persuaded of the virtues of private

---

[37] See *The Economics of Unilateral Effects*, M. Ivaldi, B. Jullien, P. Rey, P. Seabright, J. Tirole, IDEI, Toulouse November 2003, Interim Report for DG Competition, European Commission, available at http://ec.europa.eu/comm/competition/mergers/studies_reports/the_economics_of_unilateral_effects_en.pdf; *Information Exchange among Firms and their Impact on Competition*, Office for Official Publications of the European Community, Luxemburg, 1995, K.U. Kühn and X. Vives; *New Industrial Economics and Experiences from European Merger Control – New lessons about collective dominance?*, Study commissioned by the European Commission, Office for Official Publications of the European Communities, Luxemburg, 1995, E. Kantzenbach, E. Kottmann and R. Krüger; *Minority Share Acquisition : The Impact upon Competition*, Office for Official Publications of the European Communities, Luxemburg, 1986, S. Meadowcroft and D. Thompson.

[38] Pursuant to Article 230 EC, only acts that emanate from European institutions can be challenged through annulment proceedings before the European courts.

[39] In addition, it is often provided that: "The European Commission does not guarantee the accuracy of the data included in the report, nor does it accept responsibility for any use made thereof".

[40] See COMP/2008/F3/003 : Appel d'offres relatif à la réalisation d'une étude sur la garantie illimitée de la République française à La Poste; COMP/2008/F3/001 : Study to benchmark the cost and profit accounting of certain services provided by Deutsche Post AG (DPAG).

enforcement of EC competition law when it commissioned the extensive Ashurst Study.[41]

Third, with the emergence of new institutional models, the dividing line between third-party expert reports and the Commission's own views on EC competition law enforcement is becoming increasingly blurred,. The Commission has recently, created *sui generis* organs with permanent advisory duties to which high-profile experts have been appointed. For instance, it created in 2003 the Economic Advisory Group on Competition Policy ("EAGCP"), a discussion forum comprising prominent economists directly appointed by the Competition Commissioner[42] whose role is to "support DG Competition in improving the economic reasoning in competition policy analysis" and to deliver opinions on "issues of topical interest".[43]

In sum, the Commission's appropriation, in practice, of third-party reports may create an optical illusion as to their role as well as to the relevance of the policy orientations and legal interpretations contained therein. This also has the potential to exert a significant influence on firms' conduct (and counsels giving legal advice).

D. – *Press releases*

The Commission usually issues press releases following the adoption of a formal decision under Articles 81 and 82 EC or the ECMR (*e.g.* decisions finding an infringement and imposing fines, commit-

---

[41] See N. Kroes, SPEECH/05/533 of 22 September 2005, *Enhancing Actions for Damages for Breach of Competition Rules in Europe*, Dinner Speech at the Harvard Club New York, 22nd September 2005 : "Our debate in Europe is of rather a different nature. It is not about reducing the excesses of damages actions, not because there aren't any excesses, but simply because we hardly have any actions for damages at all. The recent Ashurst study found that this form of private action is totally underdeveloped in Europe. That is why the Commission – as I said, *convinced by the potential benefits of encouraging private enforcement of the competition rules* – wants to stimulate public debate in Europe on this topic (emphasis added)".

[42] Upon proposal of the Chief competition economist. See http://ec.europa.eu/dgs/competition/economist/eagcp.html.

[43] The EAGCP has *inter alia* issued opinions on "Non-horizontal merger guidelines" and on the "Economic approach to Article 82 EC". See http://ec.europa.eu/dgs/competition/economist/eagcp.html. Within the framework of the EAGCP, three sub-groups have been set up to work on issues related to anti-trust, mergers and state aid. The advisory groups meet 3-4 times a year in Brussels. Each of these meetings is a full day brainstorming session with typically one core competition policy issue being discussed. Each sub-group presents an "opinion" on a topic commissioned by the Chief Economist, the Director-General or the Commissioner.

ment decisions, decisions imposing remedies, etc.).[44] In addition, it occasionally adopts press releases to comment on or clarify certain developments in EC and national competition laws (often in the form of "Memos" or "Frequently Asked Questions").[45]

In recent years, the Commission's practice of issuing press releases has witnessed a dual evolution which, in our view, displays some features of sunshine enforcement. First, the number of press releases adopted by the Commission – in particular in the field of Articles 81 and 82 EC ("PR-AT") has steadily increased, as evidenced in the table below.[46]

---

[44] In particular, in respect of Decisions adopted pursuant to Articles 7 to 10 of Council Regulation 1/2003 of 16 December 2002 on the implementation of the rules on competition laid down in Articles 81 and 82 of the Treaty, (2003) *O.J.* L 1/1. See also, C. KERSE and N. KHAN, *EC Antitrust Procedure*, 5th ed., Thomson Sweet & Maxwell, 2005; L. ORTIZ BLANCO, *EC Competition Procedure*, 5th Ed., Thomson Sweet & Maxwell, London, 2005 at §6-050. The Commission's press releases (and other written information disclosed to the press) are issued by its Directorate-General for Press and Communication. This department is under the authority of the President of the Commission and is headed by a Director General and by the Spokesperson. The Spokesperson is assisted by more than twenty spokespersons responsible for specific portfolios, among which competition policy. See J. FAULL, *supra*, p. 160.

[45] The Commission increasingly adopts press releases to comment on judgments handed down by the Community courts (such press releases are common in the context of judgments under Article 234 EC) and on measures adopted by other bodies (EC legislation, decisions of NCAs, etc.). For instance, following the CFI's ruling in *Tetra Laval*, the Commission publicly expressed its disagreement with the standard of judicial review endorsed by the Court. See Commission Press Release, Commission appeals CFI ruling on Tetra Laval/Sidel to the European Court of Justice, IP/02/1952 of 20 December 2002. See, more generally, L. ORTIZ BLANCO, *supra*, §4.33. Press releases labelled "Memos" generally seek to clarify legal issues arising from certain cases (the Commission usually issues Memos in the context of settlements when it does not adopt a final decision). Memos describe briefly the facts of the case and the legal approach followed by the Commission, and sometimes provide answers to FAQs. During the *British Airways* proceedings, the Commission explained that its press releases are an important source of guidance for firms, as they convey its stance on certain practices. See Case T-219/99, *British Airways plc v. Commission*, [2003] E.C.R. II-5917 at §62 ("According to the press release on the principles concerning travel agents' commissions, issued on the same day that the contested decision was adopted, that decision constituted a first step in dealing with commissions paid by airlines to travel agents. The principles established in that press release also gave clear guidance for any other airline in a situation similar to that of BA, and the Commission stated that it would take all measures necessary to ensure that those principles were complied with by other airlines in equivalent situations"). In the *Austrian banks cartel* case, the CFI noted that the Commission, through the adoption of a press release, had clarified the state of the law with respect to agreements on bank interest rates. The Court accordingly rejected the allegation that the Commission had been ambiguous and had created legal uncertainty. See Cases T-259/02 to T-264/02 and T-271/02, *Raiffeisen Zentralbank Österreich AG and others v. Commission*, [2006] E.C.R. II-5169 at §507.

[46] Authors' calculation based on the press releases available on the Commission's Internet website.

TABLE 1

Number of press releases issued by the Commission (antitrust and mergers)

	2008 (Jan-May)	*2007*	*2006*	*2005*	*2004*	*2003*	*2002*	*2001*	*2000*	*1999*	*1998*	*1997*	*1996*	*1995*
PR-AT	38	101	99	77	65	75	58	79	55	41	45	28	25	34
PR-ECMR	60	193	169	150	85	78	82	103	130	139	95	82	34	59

Second, the Commission issues a growing number of press releases in mere procedural matters wholly unrelated to substantive legal issues.[47] The objectives pursued by the Commission in so doing are less clear. It may be the case that it simply seeks to inform the public. It may also be the case that such press releases pursue ulterior "sunshine" enforcement goals. For instance, the Commission may publish a press release related to an ongoing investigation with a view to inciting parties who may hold information of significance to the case to come forward (*i.e.* an information gathering purpose).[48] In addition, merely by bringing to the fore the fact that a firm is under investigation, such press releases can create the impression that the Commission has already reached a finding as to the existence of an infringement, and may induce that firm to modify its behaviour (*i.e.* a compliance inducement purpose).[49]

Despite a paucity of relevant judicial precedent, the question whether a press release may contain an indication of the Commission's likely conduct when assessing future cases – and thereby restrict its enforcement discretion – appears to be settled. In *Roberts and Roberts v. Commission*, the Court examined whether a press release issued by the Commission had created legitimate expectations for the applicants challenging a subsequent Commission decision.[50] After reviewing the content of the press release, the Court found that it had not created such expectations because the legal standard described in it – which the applicants claimed should have been applied in their case – did not apply to the relevant facts. This

[47] See C. Kerse and N. Khan, *supra* at §6-050.

[48] See C. Kerse and N. Khan, *supra* at §6-050.

[49] The Commission may for instance inform the public that it has taken the decision to open formal proceedings against a specific firm which it suspects of infringement of the competition rules, without, however, having a sufficiently strong case to adopt, at that stage, a Statement of Objections.

[50] See Case T-25/99, *Roberts and Roberts v. Commission*, *supra* at §§124 and 130.

being said, the fact that the Court examined whether the challenged decision was consistent with the orientations contained in the press release strongly suggests that such press releases can have a binding effect on the Commission and as a result limit its discretion in enforcing EC competition law.[51]

E. – *Commission papers (discussion papers, non-papers, etc.)*

Driven to a large extent by DG Competition, a new breed of "papers" dealing with specific legal issues (and/or economic sectors) has mushroomed in EC competition enforcement. Despite their heterogeneous nomenclature (discussion papers, non-papers, position papers, consultation papers, working papers, etc.), those papers share at least three common features. First, they are authored by services within DG Competition (generally, units or directorates), and as such are not necessarily reviewed by other Commission services (the legal service, for instance),[52] or by the Commissioners.[53]

---

[51] Other cases in which the applicants relied on a Commission press release either concerned different legal issues (such as whether a press release constitutes evidence) or did not result in a ruling on the substance. In *General Electric v. Commission*, for instance, the applicant sought to demonstrate that two press releases reporting an interview with the Competition Commissioner had given rise to the "legitimate expectation" that the Commission would clear a merger transaction in exchange for stronger remedies offered by the merging parties. The Court however dismissed the argument on procedural grounds. See Case T-210/01, *General electric v. Commission*, [2005] E.C.R. II-5575 at §53. In *TACA*, the applicants relied on a Commission press release (as well as on various "articles") as a source of evidence. It was alleged that the press release provided evidence that the Commission had – unlawfully – enforced Article 82 EC to bypass the legislative immunity enjoyed by liner conferences under Article 81 EC. The Court however refused to hold that the alleged circumvention of Article 81 EC was a breach of EC competition law. See Cases T-191/98 and T-212/98 to T-214/98, *Atlantic Container Line AB and others v. Commission*, [2003] E.C.R. II-3275 at §§453 and following. Finally, in *Royal Philips Electronics NV v. Commission*, the CFI held that the adoption of a press release would have given rise to a "duty to state reasons" pursuant to Article 253 EC only if it had contained "a decision which can be the subject of an application for annulment under Article 230 EC". Accordingly, press releases may encapsulate legal decisions having adverse effects on third parties (a referral decision under Article 9 of the ECMR, for instance). See Case, T-119/02, *Royal Philips Electronics NV v. Commission*, [2003] E.C.R. II-1433 at §392.

[52] This arguably explains why, for instance, in the DG Competition Paper Concerning Issues of Competition in Waste Management, it is explicitly acknowledged that "the views expressed in the present document are purely those of the Directorate General for Competition at the time of writing".

[53] This explains why they are often labeled "Staff papers". In addition the authors of these papers are not necessarily identified. Most of the time, the papers simply mention "Commission services documents". See, for instance, Consultation paper on the review of Council Regulation 4056/86 laying down detailed rules for the application of Articles 81 and 82 of the Treaty to maritime transport. Note, however, that the author of the paper is often indirectly identifiable as the addressee of the replies to the consultation process.

Second, such papers are generally adopted in the context of the "review" of specific enforcement policies (such as, for instance, the so-called "Article 82 EC review", which seeks to increase the role of economic analysis in abuse of dominance cases).[54] They are therefore, by their very nature, acts with a provisional status, setting out DG Competition's preliminary views on certain practice(s)/sector(s) and, in certain circumstances, posing questions to stakeholders.[55] Third, these papers are general in scope, and do not target individual market players.

In contrast with so-called "Green papers" and "White papers", which are formally adopted by the Commission and normally culminate in legislative action,[56] this other type of Commission paper is not necessarily followed-up by immediate, subsequent, action (*e.g.* adoption of guidelines, decisions, etc.). For instance, the Merger Remedies Study and,[57] perhaps more importantly, the Discussion Paper on the Application of Article 82 of the Treaty to Exclusionary Abuses remain in a state of administrative limbo, more than 2 years after their release.

Despite their lesser status, these heterogeneous papers may serve to better define the boundaries of anticompetitive behaviour, as well as the legal standards applicable. In addition, the wide consultation and discussion process that usually follows their publication can be expected to shed light on the legal issues addressed and make market players more sensitive to the potentially anticompetitive nature of certain business practices.[58]

---

[54] See Discussion Paper on the Application of Article 82 of the Treaty to Exclusionary Abuses, Brussels, December 2005, available at http://ec.europa.eu/comm/competition/antitrust/art82/discpaper2005.pdf. They may also follow expert reports issued by third parties. See, for instance, Consultation paper on the review of Council Regulation 4056/86 laying down detailed rules for the application of Articles 81 and 82 of the Treaty to maritime transport, 27 March 2003, available at http://ec.europa.eu/comm/competition/antitrust/legislation/maritime/en.pdf.

[55] See Consultation paper on the review of Council Regulation 4056/86 laying down detailed rules for the application of Articles 81 and 82 of the Treaty to maritime transport, *supra*.

[56] They usually give rise to a legislative proposal from the Commission to the Council (and possibly the Parliament).

[57] In October 2005, the Commission issued a self-evaluation document reviewing its policy on merger remedies (its goal was also to determine whether (and where) further improvements were needed). The study followed a process of consultation of firms involved in merger transactions having led to the adoption of remedies. See DG COMP In-House Merger Remedies Study, October 2005 available at http://ec.europa.eu/comm/competition/mergers/studies_reports/remedies_study.pdf.

[58] See F. Wijckmans, F. Tuytschaever and A. Vanderelst, *Vertical Agreements in EC Competition Law*, Oxford University Press, 2006, pp. 40-41.

As regards their legal status, it should be noted that the papers' authors always seek to shelter the Commission from subsequent legal consequences stemming from their content. For instance, in addition to the usual disclaimer that it "may not, in any circumstances be regarded as stating an official position of the European Commission", the Discussion Paper on Article 82 EC bluntly states that it "has no enforcement status".[59] In other words, the Commission wishes to remain free to deviate from the legal standards contained in its papers in the course of its enforcement activities. This caution is understandable : papers are provisional documents intended to stimulate debate, and should not fetter the Commission's discretion in subsequent enforcement action (for instance, through the creation of legitimate expectations).

To date, the Community courts have not ruled on the legal effects of this type of document.[60] In our experience, although the expectations they create may not rise to a level warranting legal protection, it is undeniable that, in practice, such discussion papers, non-papers and the like have a profound influence on the daily work of legal practitioners. This is all the more so in the – not so uncommon – instances where the state of the law is unclear or in a state of flux (*e.g.* the legal standards applicable to rebates granted by dominant firms).

F. – *Annual reports on competition policy*

Since 1971, the Commission has published an Annual Report on Competition Policy (the "annual report")[61] providing an overview of the main developments in EC competition policy and summarizing changes to EC competition rules that have occurred over the

---

[59] See Discussion Paper on the Application of Article 82 of the Treaty to Exclusionary Abuses, *supra* at p. 1.

[60] In *British Airways v. Commission*, Advocate General Kokott recalled that the Commission's Discussion Paper on Article 82 EC was bound to comply with the case-law of the Court of Justice (see Case C-95/04 P, Opinion of AG V. Kokott, *British Airways plc vs Commission*, [2007] E.C.R. I-2331 at §28). In *Cementbouw Handel & Industrie BV*, the CFI declined to enter into the debate over the interpretation of the Green Paper on the review of Regulation 4064/89. See Case T-282/02, *Cementbouw Handel & Industrie v. Commission* [2006] E.C.R. II-319. In Case T-312/02, *Meca-Medina and Majcen v. Commission*, [2004] E.C.R. II-3291, at §§46-47, the Court found support in a Commission working paper to conclude that rules regulating doping fell outside the purview of the economic activities covered by Articles 81 and 82 EC.

[61] The annual report on Competition Policy is published by the Commission in response to a request of the European Parliament contained in a resolution of 7 June 1971.

course of the previous year.[62] The annual report is adopted by the Commission as a whole, in the form of an official "Communication". It is usually preceded by a foreword from the Competition Commissioner.[63]

Importantly, annual reports show, through selected examples, how the EC competition rules are implemented. In addition, they are often supplemented by various sets of annexes (in the form of Staff working papers), which provide detailed case-specific information, methodological information, statistics, etc. Again, annual reports constitute a useful tool to instigate voluntary compliance with the law.

Whilst they are characterized by their strong policy-making content, annual reports are nonetheless capable of having legal effects. By virtue of their general scope, normative statements made in the context of annual reports have been judged by the Court as capable of having binding effects on the Commission. In the notorious *Hercules v. Commission* case (*Polypropylene*), the applicant alleged that a Commission decision applying Article 81 EC was not adequately reasoned, and thus infringed Article 253 EC (ex Article 190 EC).[64] In particular, the applicant argued that in adopting an infringement decision, the Commission must take account of the opinion of the hearing officer, even though it is not obliged to follow it. By failing to mention that the hearing officer had delivered his opinion, the Commission decision in question would have been inadequately reasoned. The applicant based its claim on the "decision taken by the Commission to institute the position of the hearing office and from the hearing officer's terms of reference", which had been appended to the Thirteenth report on competition policy. The Court cautiously avoided having to determine whether the hearing officer's terms of reference contained in the Report constituted a decision amenable to judicial review under Article 230 EC. However, the Court went on to consider whether the Commission had followed the procedure pertaining to the hearing officer's intervention as provided in the document annexed to the annual report and found that the Commission had not breached any fundamental

[62] The annual report is now published in conjunction with the General Report on the activities of the European Union.

[63] See, for instance, Report on Competition Policy 2006, 2006 COM(2007)358 final.

[64] Case T-7/89, *SA Hercules Chemicals NV v. Commission*, [1991] ECR II-711.

requirement contained therein (the Court held that according to the terms of reference, the hearing officer's report is not, for the purposes of Article 190 EC, an opinion which the Commission is required to obtain when taking an infringement decision). In so doing, the Court confirmed that, in a fashion similar to the obligations that may stem from oral statements and press releases, the Commission must abide by the rules it imposes on itself, under pain of breaching the principle of legal certainty.[65]

G. – *Sector inquiries*

Pursuant to Article 17 of Regulation 1/2003, the Commission can launch "investigations into sectors of the economy and into types of agreements". These wide-ranging investigations are usually referred to as sector inquiries. And the Commission is likely to launch them in particular where "the trend of trade between Member States, the rigidity of prices or other circumstances suggest that competition may be restricted or distorted within the common market".[66] In contrast with traditional investigations, the Commission does not need to rely on other reasons (such as a suspicion that anticompetitive conduct has occurred) when it decides to open a sector inquiry.[67] Yet, it holds similar powers and, in particular, the ability to send requests for information to firms and to carry out inspections of business premises.[68]

Importantly, the purpose of sector inquiries is not necessarily to trigger formal enforcement actions. Rather, Article 17 of Regulation 1/2003 provides that the Commission may "publish a report on the results of its inquiry into particular sectors of the economy or particular types of agreements across various sectors and invite comments from interested parties". In practice, only a fraction of all sector inquiries carried out to date (*i.e.* in the energy sector,[69]

---

[65] See also, for a similar interpretation, Case T-528/93, *Métropole Télévision v. Commission*, [1996] E.C.R. II-649 at §169: "In that case the Commission had in fact made known, through its annual report on competition policy, a number of rules which it had imposed on itself relating to access to the file in competition proceedings".

[66] See Article 17(1) of Regulation 1/2003, *supra*.

[67] See L. Ortiz Blanco, *supra*, §5.04.

[68] See Articles 18 and 20 of Regulation 1/2003, *supra*.

[69] See, on this, http://ec.europa.eu/comm/competition/sectors/energy/inquiry/index.html.

financial services,[70] local loop,[71] leased lines,[72] roaming,[73] 3G media content[74]) have led to formal enforcement action. In most cases, the Commission has published a detailed report identifying instances of market failures as well as raising questions on the existence of anticompetitive business behaviour in the sector investigated.

In the same way as traditional sunshine enforcement, the *mere initiation* of sector inquiries has allowed the Commission to bring about significant changes in firms' conduct. For instance, following the initiation of the so-called "leased line investigation", a number of telecoms operators decided to slash the prices of their services immediately.[75] Similarly, in the context of an informal sector inquiry relating to CD pricing in Germany, the music majors abandoned the practice of publishing minimum list prices.

In addition, the *final report* may cast light on potentially suspicious commercial practices or simply conclude that one or several firms active in the sector under investigation wield significant market power. This disclosure, coupled with the threat of follow-on enforcement actions (by competition authorities and courts),[76] legislative intervention,[77] or public opprobrium,[78] may in and of itself induce changes in the conduct of firms active in the economic sector examined by the Commission.

---

[70] See http://ec.europa.eu/comm/competition/sectors/financial_services/inquiries/index.html.

[71] See http://ec.europa.eu/comm/competition/sectors/telecommunications/archive/inquiries/local_loop/index.html.

[72] See http://ec.europa.eu/comm/competition/sectors/telecommunications/archive/inquiries/leased_lines/index.html.

[73] See http://ec.europa.eu/comm/competition/sectors/telecommunications/archive/inquiries/roaming/index.html.

[74] See http://ec.europa.eu/comm/competition/sectors/media/inquiries/3G_archive.html.

[75] See D. Choumelova and J. Delgado, "Monitoring Competition in the Telecommunications Sector: European Commission Sector Inquiries", in P.A. Buigues and P. Rey (Eds), *The Economics of Antitrust and Regulation in Telecommunications*, Edward Elgar, Cheltentham, 2004 at pp. 273-275.

[76] See D. Wood and N. Baverez, "Sector Inquiries under EU Competition Law", *Competition Law Insight*, at p. 4.

[77] In the context of its energy sector inquiry, the Commission has made reference to possible changes to the European regulatory framework for energy markets.

[78] In the context of its energy sector inquiry, the Commission clearly insisted, in its Final Report, on the fact that consumers and businesses were being harmed by inefficient and expensive gas and electricity markets. See, for a summary of these findings, http://ec.europa.eu/comm/competition/sectors/energy/inquiry/index.html.

H. – *Formal Commission Guidelines, Notices and Communications*

Over the past fifteen years, the Commission has issued an increasing number of Guidelines, Communications and Notices.[79] These instruments are adopted by the Commission as a whole and published in the *Official Journal of the European Union* ("*OJ*"). Examples of such Communications include the Guidelines on vertical restraints, the Guidelines on the applicability of Article 81 to horizontal co-operation agreements, the Commission Notice on the definition of the relevant market for the purposes of Community competition law, the Guidelines on the assessment of non-horizontal mergers under the Council Regulation on the control of concentrations between undertakings.[80]

Put simply, the main purpose of these formal instruments is to provide assistance to firms,[81] competitions authorities and national courts,[82] when engaging in complex competitive assessment.[83] They

---

[79] See D. GERADIN and N. PETIT, "Judicial Remedies under EC Competition Law : Complex Issues arising from the 'Modernisation' Process", (2005) *Fordham International Law Journal*, pp. 393-439. There is no significant difference between these instruments, which seem to be interchangeable (see, on this, H.A. COSMA and R. WHISH, *supra* at p. 51). In a nutshell, the proliferation of such guidelines, notices and communications is due to the recognition that economic operators need added guidance in light of (i) the requirement, introduced by the adoption of Regulation 1/2003, that firms themselves assess the legality of their business practices and (ii) the increased sophistication of substantive EC competition law resulting in part from the influence of micro-economic analysis.

[80] Although the Commission's website exhibits most notices, the Commission does not publish a full list of all those in force. However, a list of such notices has been published as an Annex to the Notice on co-operation between the Commission and National Courts. See Commission Notice on the co-operation between the Commission and the courts of the EU Member States in the application of Articles 81 and 82 EC, *OJ* C 101/54 of 27 April 2004. There are doubts as to whether this list is exhaustive given that a number of notices are not mentioned (sub-contracting, exclusive commercial agents, etc.). It has been suggested that the omitted instruments should now be presumed defunct. See C. COOK and N. KHAN, *supra* at § 1-026. For a full list, see VAN BAEL and BELLIS, *Competition Law of the European Community*, 4th Ed., Kluwer Law International, The Hague, 2005, at pp. 1146-1148.

[81] See Commission Notice – Guidelines on Vertical Restraints, *OJ* C 291/1 of 13 October 2000, at §3 : "By issuing these Guidelines the Commission aims to help companies to make their own assessment of vertical agreements under the EC competition rules".

[82] See Commission Notice on the co-operation between the Commission and the courts of the EU Member States in the application of Articles 81 and 82 EC, *supra* at §8 : "National courts may find guidance in Commission regulations and decisions which present elements that are similar to those in a case they are dealing with, as well as in Commission notices and guidelines relating to the application of Articles 81 and 82 EC and in the annual report on competition policy".

[83] To that end, they set out the views of the Commission (*i.e.* its interpretation of statutory and case law). In addition, the Commission often builds on the case-law of the EC Courts, where existing precedent is unclear or where it does not fully answer a specific question. See for instance, Commission Notice on agreements of minor importance which do not appreciably restrict competition under Article 81(1) of the Treaty establishing the European Community (*de minimis*), *OJ* C 368/13 of 22 December 2001.

thus pursue enforcement-related goals, *i.e.* they aim to induce firms to comply with EC competition law and to assist courts and competition authorities in applying it.

In addition, in our view, those Communications addressing substantive issues of competition law may also represent a form of sunshine enforcement.[84] In the decentralized enforcement system instituted by Regulation 1/2003 (and *a fortiori* within the realm of the private enforcement of competition law), competitors, suppliers, customers and governments play a key role in the detection of competition law infringements. It can be argued that the Guidelines, Notices and Communications adopted by the Commission increase the likelihood that those dealing with infringers' will be able to detect anticompetitive behaviour, and attempt to bring it to an end.

In that respect, the Guidelines on the application of Article 81(3) of the Treaty are a case in point. Despite their title – which suggests that they focus solely on the interpretation of the exception provided in Article 81(3) EC – the Guidelines deal at length with substantive issues underlying "the prohibition rule of Article 81(1) EC".[85] Similarly, the Guidelines on the applicability of Article 81 to horizontal co-operation agreements devote considerable space to categories – and examples – of unlawful agreements and practices, under the heading "assessment under Article 81(1)".[86]

From a purely legal standpoint, the most interesting issue raised by these Communications, Notices and Guidelines is perhaps whether they have a binding effect on the Commission.[87] Generally

[84] Most of these instruments concern substantive issues of EC competition law. More recently, the Commission has adopted such instruments with respect to procedural matters. See C. Cook and N. Khan, *supra* at §1-026.

[85] See L. Idot, "La qualification de la restriction de concurrence : à propos des lignes directrices de la Commission concernant l'application de l'article 81, §3", in *La Modernisation du droit de la concurrence* (G. Canivet), LGDJ, Paris, 2006 at p. 88.

[86] The Guidelines on Vertical Restraints contain similar provisions, under the heading "negative effects of vertical restraints». Commission notice – Guidelines on Vertical Restraints, *supra* at §103-114.

[87] By contrast, the related issue of whether these instruments are amenable to judicial review appears less significant. In *France v. Commission*, the ECJ held that a Commission Notice which aimed at formally interpreting a directive but which surreptitiously introduced new legal obligations could be the subject of an annulment action. See Case C-325/91, *France v. Commission*, [1993] E.C.R. I-3283. This being said, one may argue that challenging illegal guidelines through annulment proceedings is a trivial issue in practice. Guidelines are in themselves incapable of having *direct* adverse legal effects on firms (unless they are decisions in disguise). Only decisions enforcing Article 81 and 82 EC may have such effect. And, in such cases, the addressee of the

speaking, the likelihood that they will significantly constrain the Commission in an individual case is limited by the fact that such instruments are general in nature. The Commission may thus find an infringement in circumstances where an assessment under the Notice would seem to imply that no such infringement can be established.[88]

This being said, the Court has recognized that Guidelines, Communications and Notices can constrain the Commission's enforcement discretion through a form of "Estoppel".[89] This principle is encapsulated in the judgment handed down in *Dansk Rørindustri and others v. Commission* :

> "The Court has already held, in a judgment concerning internal measures adopted by the administration, that although those measures may not be regarded as rules of law which the administration is always bound to observe, they nevertheless form rules of practice from which the administration may not depart in an individual case without giving reasons that are compatible with the principle of equal treatment. Such measures therefore constitute a general act and the officials and other staff concerned may invoke their illegality in support of an action against the individual measures taken on the basis of the measures (see Case C-171/00, *P Libéros v Commission,* [2002] ECR I-451, paragraph 35).

decision can challenge that act directly before the CFI and, during the proceedings, call into question the validity of the guidelines. At any rate, there are doubts that firms can, in the current state of EC law, bring annulment actions against acts of a general nature, such as guidelines. In accordance with established case-law, individual applicants are unlikely to be affected "individually" by an act of a general nature that is not addressed to specific parties. This means that only privileged applicants (i.e. Member States and EU institutions) have legal standing to bring annulment proceedings against such general measures. This state of affairs is open to criticism for several reasons. First, putting aside State aid law, Notices adopted in the field of competition law are exclusively addressed to economic operators whose behaviour is covered by Articles 81 and 82 EC or by the ECMR. The likelihood that Member States or other EU institutions would appeal the adoption of these acts is therefore low. Consequently, there is a risk that these notices would be, *de facto*, shielded from legal review by the Community Courts with the attendant risk that the Commission could seek to take advantage of this vacuum to deliberately extend its powers.

[88] See M. Cini, "The soft law approach : Commission rule-making in the EU's state aid regime", *Journal of European Public Policy*, 8 :2, 2001, pp. 201-202.

[89] Put simply the Estoppel principle prevents a person from asserting or denying something in court that contradicts what has already been established as the truth. In the past, the Court followed a cautious approach when called to rule on the legal value of Communications. In the *Sugar* case, for instance, the Court accepted a claim that a particular infringement did not warrant a fine because the notice on commercial agents had created the impression that the conduct in question was not prohibited. See Cases 40/48, 50, 54/56, 111, 113 and 114/7, *Coöperatieve Vereniging "Suiker Unie" UA and others v. Commission*, [1975] E.C.R. 1663. In the *Hercules* case, *supra*, the Court considered that the Commission was bound by it pronouncements on access to the file. In Case C-251/98, *Spain v. Commission*, [2002] E.C.R, I-8031, the ECJ considered that the Commission was bound by its Communications on the interaction between the Commission and the Members States. For a more restrictive approach, see *Métropole Télévision*, *supra*.

That case-law applies a fortiori to rules of conduct designed to produce external effects, as is the case of the Guidelines, which are aimed at traders. *In adopting such rules of conduct and announcing by publishing them that they will henceforth apply to the cases to which they relate, the institution in question imposes a limit on the exercise of its discretion and cannot depart from those rules under pain of being found, where appropriate, to be in breach of the general principles of law, such as equal treatment or the protection of legitimate expectations*. It cannot therefore be precluded that, on certain conditions and depending on their content, such rules of conduct, which are of general application, may produce legal effects (emphasis added).[90]

Therefore, just as is the case with oral statements and press releases, a Commission decision that departs from principles or legal interpretations contained in existing Guidelines, Communications and Notices can be challenged on the grounds that it infringes general principles of EC law, such as the duty of good administration, protection of legitimate expectations or legal certainty.[91]

I. – *Guidance letters*

Recital 38 of the preamble to Regulation 1/2003 allows companies to seek the informal view of the Commission where the application of Article 81 or 82 EC to a given practice is uncertain (*e.g.* because the legal standard is unclear) or raises novel questions.[92] The Commission has specified in its "Notice on informal guidance relating to novel questions" the circumstances in which it would provide such guidance.[93]

Guidance letters have the potential to become a prime example of "sunshine" enforcement. They are aimed at a vast audience (the Notice states that "Guidance letters will be posted on the Commission's website"), and thus may be an effective tool to promote voluntary compliance with competition law and uncover types of anti-competitive behaviour that were hitherto not evident.[94]

[90] See Case, C-189/02 P, *Dansk Rørindustri and others v. Commission*, [2005] E.C.R. I-5425, at §§209-211.

[91] It would be perhaps more advisable, as a matter of judicial policy, to clearly recognize that the principles of Estoppel or *"patere legem quam ipse fecisti"* are general principles of EC law.

[92] This possibility was in fact created in response to concerns that, with the abolition of the requirement to notify agreements brought about by Regulation 1/2003, undertakings would no longer be able to clarify their legal position by subjecting a given agreement to Commission examination.

[93] See Commission Notice on informal guidance relating to novel questions concerning Articles 81 and 82 of the EC Treaty that arise in individual cases (guidance letters), *OJ* C 101/78 of 27 April 2004.

[94] *Idem* at §21.

Despite this potential, four years after their introduction, Guidance letters remain shrouded in mystery. Rather surprisingly, the Commission has never used them. If the role of such guidance letters is to clarify obscure or novel issues of competition law, it can perhaps be argued that the Commission is reluctant to crystallize a solution – that will bind it in the future[95] – in cases where a trial and error approach (through individual decisions) would be more advisable.

J. – *Inapplicability decisions*

Article 10 of Regulation 1/2003 allows the Commission to adopt *ex officio* decisions finding that Articles 81 and 82 are not applicable to certain practices.[96] Such inapplicability decisions adopted under Article 10 do not, strictly speaking, represent the *enforcement* of Articles 81 or 82 EC. This being said, we believe that Article 10 decisions constitute indirect enforcement decisions in so far as they define the boundary between lawful and unlawful behaviour.

Inapplicability decisions could prove useful "sunshine" regulation instruments (*i.e.* they can ensure voluntary compliance with EC competition law) as suggested by the language of Regulation 1/2003 itself, which provides that such decisions are "declaratory" in nature.[97]

Nevertheless, the Commission is yet to adopt its first inapplicability decision. Just as is the case with Guidance letters, the reasons for its unwillingness to do so are unclear. Perhaps, as noted above, it is due to a fear that they may limit not only the Commission's margin of discretion but also that of other competition authorities in formal enforcement cases.[98]

---

[95] Pursuant to the principles established by the ECJ in *Dansk Rørindustri and others v. Commission*, *supra* the Commission is arguably obliged to conform to orientations contained in its guidance letters when carrying out subsequent enforcement activities.

[96] Unlike Guidance letters which are requested by undertakings themselves.

[97] An act is regarded as "constitutive" when it modifies a legal situation. An act is considered as "declaratory" when it simply acknowledges a legal or factual situation. See G. Cornu, *Vocabulaire Juridique*, PUF, 3rd Ed., 2000.

[98] Findings of inapplicability are binding on national competition authorities and national courts in so far as Article 16 of Regulation 1/2003, which prohibits these bodies from taking decisions that conflict with the Commission's interpretation of EC law, also appears to cover these types of decisions. See Article 16 of Regulation 1/2003, *supra*.

III. – The virtues of sunshine enforcement instruments

A. – *Providing guidance*

In the debates preceding the adoption of Regulation 1/2003, many scholars and practitioners expressed fears that the abolition of the system of mandatory notification of agreements to the Commission would deprive firms of a significant source of guidance, represented by comfort letters and Article 81(3) EC decisions.[99]

It can be argued that the Commission's increasing reliance on the wide array of sunshine regulation instruments described in the previous sections has contributed to dispelling many of those concerns. These instruments have indeed provided useful guidance on substantive aspects of EC competition law to firms facing the intricacies inherent in the competitive assessment of their own behaviour. For instance, our experience suggests that the Discussion paper on Article 82 EC has proved invaluable in helping firms with significant market power and their advisors devise business strategies compliant with EC competition law in fields where the applicable legal standard is far from clear (such as rebates and tying).

In addition, due to the time required to expunge confidential information from formal infringement decisions – and very often to translate them – a number of years often passes between the date of adoption of such decisions and their publication in the *OJ*. In many instances, the Commission can compensate for these shortcomings by issuing detailed press releases or by summarizing the most salient aspects of its decisions in a variety of instruments (*e.g.* articles, annual reports on competition policy, etc.). By resorting to such sunshine instruments the Commission is able to clarify its interpretation of EC competition law in a timely fashion.

---

[99] See *e.g.* F. Montag and T. Janssens, "Article 81(3) in the context of modernisation – a lawyer's view", in D. Geradin (Ed.), *Modernisation and enlargement : two major challenges for EC competition law*, Intersentia : Antwerp, Oxford, 2004; H. Bourgeois, "The impact of modernization on companies and their counsels", in D. Geradin (Ed.), *ibid.*; V. Power, "Representing clients after the modernisation of EC competition law", (2003) *I.C.C.L.R.* 335; H.M. Gilliams, "Modernisation : from policy to practice", (2003) 28 *European Law Review*, 451.

B. – *Improving detection of anticompetitive behaviour*

By increasing the awareness and understanding of the role of EC competition law, "sunshine" enforcement instruments play a key role in the detection of anticompetitive conduct.[100] Although those effects are difficult to quantify, it is likely that the multiplication of public pronouncements on various competition law topics has allowed private economic actors to identify specific instances of anticompetitive conduct and take action against them before such infringements are detected by competition authorities.

For instance, one can speculate about the extent to which the flurry of press releases, speeches, statements and articles that followed the Commission's 2004 Microsoft decision,[101] contributed to the recrudescence of complaints alleging abuses in other markets not only against Microsoft, but also against other large firms active in dynamic markets.[102]

C. – *Reducing the Commission's administrative burden*

The Commission has often stated that it has limited administrative resources to deal with the workload imposed by its ever-increasing attributions. The adoption of Regulation 1/2003 represented the most far reaching attempt to alleviate that burden and

[100] See G.S. Becker, "A theory of competition among pressure groups and political influence", (1983) *The Quarterly Journal Of Economics*, Vol. 98, pp. 371-400.

[101] See the 24 Commission Press Releases published on the European Union website from 10 February 2000 to 27 February 2008, at http://ec.europa.eu/comm/competition/antitrust/cases/index/by_nr_75.html. See, also, N. Kroes, *Press conference on imposing penalty payments on Microsoft – introductory remarks*, European Commission, Brussels, 12th July 2006; N. Kroes, *Introductory remarks on CFI ruling on Microsoft's abuse of dominant market position*, Press conference, Brussels, 17th September 2007; N. Kroes, *Introductory remarks on Microsoft's compliance with March 2004 antitrust decision*, Press conference, Brussels, 22nd October 2007; N. Kroes, *Decision to impose € 899 million penalty on Microsoft for non-compliance*, Introductory remarks at press conference, Brussels, 27th February 2008. See *e.g.* N. Banasevic, J. Huby, M. Pena Castellot, O. Sitar and H. Piffaut, Commission adopts Decision in the Microsoft case, *EC Competition Policy Newsletter*, 2004, 2, pp. 44-48; C. Madero, N. Banasevic, C. Hermes, J. Huby and T. Kramler, The Court of First Instance rejects Microsoft's request for interim measures concerning the Commission's decision of 24 March 2004, *EC Competition Policy Newsletter*, 2005, 1, pp. 53-58; N. Banasevic, A. Barberá Del Rosal, C. Hermes, T. Kramler, I. Taylor and F. Verzelen, Commission imposes a penalty payment pursuant to Article 24(2) of Regulation 1/2003 on Microsoft, *EC Competition Policy Newsletter*, 2006, 3, pp. 27-29; T. Kramler, C.-C. Buhr and D. Wyns, The judgment of the Court of First Instance in the Microsoft case, *EC Competition Policy Newsletter*, 2007, 3, pp. 39-44. See *e.g.* European Commission, *EU competition policy and the consumer – a new brochure describing the basic concepts of European competition policy*, 2004.

[102] See B. Vesterdorf, "Article 82 EC: Where do we stand after the *Microsoft* judgement?", available at http://www.icc.qmul.ac.uk/GAR/Vesterdorf.pdf.

allow the Commission to focus on the most serious infringements of competition law. With the increased reliance on a number of instruments identified in this paper, the Commission could achieve similar goals. In so far as "sunshine" enforcement instruments encourage firms voluntarily to comply with the law and assist NCAs and courts in properly applying Articles 81 and 82 EC, they have the potential to diminish the number of cases before the Commission. In this respect, Notices, Guidelines, Communications, Guidance letters, Articles, Papers are particularly relevant.

D. – *Decision-making efficiency*

The adoption of "sunshine" enforcement instruments is much less cumbersome than that of legislative measures. As a result, they allow the Commission to be much more nimble in the course of its enforcement duties. The swift and timely regulation they are able to provide increases the efficiency of the Communities decision-making process and stands in stark contrast with the arcane and time-consuming traditional legislative procedure (see table below). Notwithstanding this, several sunshine enforcement instruments seem to suffer from the same shortcomings (*e.g.* the Discussion paper on Article 82 EC which is still to result in the adoption of guidelines on the application of Article 82 EC). [103]

TABLE 2

Timeframe for the adoption of general soft law instruments

Type of instrument	*Date of Commission draft (equivalent to legislative proposal)*	*Date of effective adoption*	*Duration*
Guidelines on non horizontal mergers	May 2007	28 November 2007	5 months
Guidelines on horizontal mergers	11 December 2002	16 December 2003	1 year
Guidelines on article 81(3) EC	3 October 2003	27 April 2004	6 months
Guidelines on technology transfer agreements	3 October 2003	7 April 2004	6 months

[103] See *Global Competition Policy*, Apr-08 (2) and, in particular, L. LOVDAHL-GORMSEN, "Will There Be Article 82 Guidelines and What Are the Implications?"; Cani FERNÁNDEZ and Albert PEREDA, "Will There Be Guidelines On Article 82 of the EC Treaty?"; D. GERARD, "The Commission on Velvet: Why it will probably not issue Article 82 guidelines any time soon".

E. – *Enhancing competition advocacy*

Competition Commissioners and in particular Commissioner Kroes have regularly emphasized the importance of developing a strong competition culture in the EC.[104] The proliferation of soft law instruments which are then extensively disseminated to the public increases the visibility of competition policy for the general public and thus contributes to its effectiveness (through possible follow-on actions). In addition, such wider understanding of the role and virtues of competition law by the public does not serve a mere informative purpose : it can be expected to increase the legitimacy of a field of the law where enforcement entails the imposition of quasi-criminal penalties and where the Commission's action is routinely met with virulent criticism at Member State level.

IV. – The vices of sunshine enforcement instruments

A. – *Poor substantive quality*

Very often, the substantive quality of soft law instruments leaves much to be desired. Their language may not be ideal, the legal standards and reasoning murky, the terminology inconsistent with previous practice, etc. These shortcomings negate many of the benefits expected from them.[105] For instance, Guidelines, Notices and Communications, are not always useful. Their degree of authority depends on a number of elements : outcome of the consultation process, wording, formal clarity, etc. Furthermore, those soft law instruments that are general in nature and designed to cover abstract categories of anticompetitive conduct are sometimes difficult to apply to a particular case.[106] In that respect the Guidelines

---

[104] See *e.g.*, Report prepared by the Advocacy Working Group, *Advocacy and Competition Policy,* ICN's Conference Naples, Italy, 2002; N. Kroes, *The Competition Principle as a Guideline for Legislation and State Action – the Responsibility of Politicians and the Role of Competition Authorities*, 12th International Conference on Competition, Bonn, 6th June 2005; P. Lowe, "Preserving and Promoting Competition : a European Response", Speech, St Gallen Competition Law Forum, 11 May 2006; N. Kroes, *Competitiveness – The common goal of competition and industrial policies*, SPEECH/08/207 of 18th April 2008.

[105] See European Consumer Law Group, "Soft Law and the Consumer Interest", ECLG/071/2001, March 2001, pp. 12-21.

[106] See C. Cook and N. Khan, *supra*, at §1-026. To address these problems, some guidelines provide examples to clarify the analysis of particular cases.

on Article 81(3) EC, which suggest that companies perform a burdensome and complex economic analysis to determine whether the agreements they concluded are lawful (balancing pro-competitive benefits with anticompetitive effects), are a case in point.[107]

B. – *Decision-making opacity*

The increased efficiency in the decision-making process allowed by sunshine enforcement instruments is also their Achilles heel. As a result of their simplified adoption process, a number of such instruments (in particular, guidelines and other general instruments) are not subject to the scrutiny of the other Community institutions. This may be a cause of concern where these measures not only frame the margin of discretion enjoyed by the Commission in the implementation of competition policy, but also lead to the imposition of new legal obligations on firms, thereby concealing quasi-legislative choices (*e.g.* the guidelines on corrective measures which clearly favour structural remedies over behavioural ones). Moreover, although the release of a Commission draft document is usually followed by a wide consultation process (involving different stakeholders such as consumer and trade associations, legal experts) guaranteeing a certain degree of accountability, the Commission is under no duty to justify its policy choices or give reasons where it ignores the views volunteered by third parties.

C. – *Regulatory mess/inconsistencies*

The proliferation of sunshine enforcement instruments leads to a fragmentation of legal sources which complicates the task of those practising EC competition law. To address this issue, the Commission has recently sought to aggregate various Notices and similar Communications dealing with related subjects into single "consolidated" notice(s).[108]

[107] See Communication from the Commission – Notice – Guidelines on the application of Article 81(3) of the Treaty, *OJ*, C 101, 27.04.2004, pp. 97-118.

[108] See Commission Consolidated Jurisdictional Notice under Council Regulation (EC) N° 139/2004 on the control of concentrations between undertakings of 10 July 2007, which replaces (i) the Notice on the concept of concentration; (ii) the Notice on the concept of full-function joint ventures; (iii) the Notice on the concept of undertakings concerned; and (iv) the Notice on calculation of turnover.

In addition, two (or more) different sunshine enforcement instruments may contain inconsistent legal standards or positions. For instance, the press release issued following the adoption of the Commission 2004 infringement Decision against Microsoft states that the Commission assessed Microsoft's behaviour under the "rule of reason".[109] As noted by different commentators, this statement is not in line with the views formally expressed by the Commission in its Guidelines on the application of Article 81(3), which suggest that such a "rule of reason" tests does not exist in EC competition law.[110] Such inconsistencies are in all likelihood due to the fact that different instruments are drafted by different individuals and often not subject to wide-ranging internal consultation or reviewed by an overarching organ that would attempt to ensure coherence.

D. – *Avoid judicial review*

The question whether sunshine enforcement instruments are amenable to judicial review is of critical importance. The conventional view, which may be shared by the Commission, is that since only formal enforcement decisions taken at the "end of the chain" actually affect the rights and obligations of individual companies directly, accountability would be sufficiently ensured via judicial review of these formal, final decisions (*i.e.* infringement decisions, etc.).[111]

Certain authors, such as Larouche and De Vijser, have criticized this view, contending that it ignores the practical realities of economic regulation. Soft law instruments and other forms of informal action influence the scope and exercise of the powers of a number or public authorities such as national courts, NCAs and national regulatory authorities ("NRAs"). A Commission Communication interpreting the substance of EC competition law will, for instance, influence the enforcement activities – and in particular, the content of the decisions – adopted by the NCAs. It can therefore be argued that the rule of law would be better served if those acts were sub-

---

[109] See *Microsoft – Questions and Answers on Commission Decision*, MEMO/04/70 of 24 March 2004.

[110] See Van Bael & Bellis, *supra* at note 205, p. 82.

[111] This issue is explained at length by Larouche and De Vijser in a paper concerning electronic communications regulation. See P. Larouche and M. De Visser, "The triangular relationship between the Commission, NRAs and National Courts Revisited", *Communications & Strategies*, 10 January 2006.

ject to a certain degree of judicial scrutiny and the Commission held accountable for them.[112]

E. – *Increase legal uncertainty or promote controversial legal standards*

In certain instances, the Commission will be tempted to offer guidance on the application of Articles 81 and 82 EC that finds little support in the legal standards established by the Community courts' case-law. These novel interpretations will very often not give rise to criticism as regards the substantive solutions they entail because, for instance, the case-law is no longer considered sound in light of contemporary economic analysis.

This being said, the guidance thus offered will by definition create legal uncertainty. At least for this reason, these sunshine enforcement instruments are controversial. For instance, in the opinion delivered in *British Airways*, AG Kokott dismissed a novel legal standard relating to the assessment of rebates granted by dominant firms proposed by the Commission in the Discussion Paper on Article 82 EC and recalled that the applicable test remains the one defined by the Community Courts.[113] Subsequently, the Commission and its officials appear however to have either tried to reconcile the existing case-law with the pronouncements contained in the Discussion Paper or applied a new market foreclosure test suggested in the Discussion Paper.[114] Whichever the case may be, the Commission has sought to justify its choices through a variety of press releases and articles published in academic reviews and in the EC com-

---

[112] By contrast, however, we do not share the pessimism of these authors, when they consider that recommendations, guidelines and other soft-law instruments are immune from judicial scrutiny. The current state of the case-law allows, to a certain extent, to initiate annulment proceedings against soft law instruments. The fact that Article 230 EC does not expressly mention those acts does not, as confirmed by the Court in the landmark *ERTA* case, insulate them from judicial scrutiny. See Case C 22/70, *Commission v. Council*, [1971] E.C.R. I-263 at §42 ("all acts adopted by the institutions, whatever their nature or form, which are intended to have legal effects"). As a matter of principle, informal pronouncements and soft law instruments can be brought to justice, if they (i) are definitive (and not preparatory); (ii) have been adopted by a Community institution (in the present case, the Commission); and (iii) produce legal effects on a person's situation and affect that person in an adverse manner. See also Case C 294/83, *Les Verts v. Parliament*, [1986] E.C.R. 1339 at §24 which states that those acts "intended to have legal effects vis-à-vis third parties" can be challenged on the basis of Article 230 EC.

[113] See *supra*.

[114] See *Prokent-Tomra*, Commission decision of 29 March 2006, Case COMP/E-1/38.113, not yet published.

petition policy newsletter.[115] One such article in particular, concerning a specific infringement decision, stated as follows :

> "[the case] was analysed following the previous case law of the European Court of Justice, in addition to being based and supported by economic analysis in the spirit of the recently publicised DG Competition Discussion paper on the application of Article 82 to exclusionary abuses. The case can be considered an important step towards the envisaged reform of the application of Article 82 EC Treaty".[116]

To complicate matters further, a leading competition economist has forcefully argued that it is doubtful that the Commission applied, in that specific case, an effects-based approach analysis and in particular, the foreclosure test suggested in the Discussion Paper as claimed.[117] In sum, despite the Commission's guidance, some of the principles applicable to the analysis of Article 82 EC cases remain as nebulous as ever.

F. – *Discipline market players without taking a formal decision*

In a world driven by information, investors, customers, suppliers, etc. tend to react vigorously to any signal that may affect the market, no matter how insignificant it may be. In that respect, the mere announcement that a firm is being investigated by the Commission – from which no inference can be drawn that the firm in question committed an infringement – can potentially have a whole host of negative and unintended consequences.

For instance, the Commission's increasing practice of disclosing information on steps of a mere procedural nature taken in the context of its enforcement activities can prove extremely harmful to the firms under investigation. In particular, the public announcement that the Commission has opened formal proceedings against a firm will often be misconstrued as signifying that the adoption of a Statement of Objections – setting out the Commission's preliminary view that an infringement has occurred – is

---

[115] See Commission Press Release, *Commission imposes € 24 million fine on Tomra group for abuse of dominant position*, IP/06/398 of 29 March 2006; See F.P. Maier-Rigaud, "Article 82 Rebates : Four Common Fallacies", mimeo, available on www.ssrn.com;

[116] F. Maier-Rigaud and D. Vaigauskaite, "Prokent/Tomra, a textbook case? Abuse of dominance under perfect information", *EC Competition Policy Newsletter*, 2, 2006, p. 19.

[117] See D. Ridyard, "The Tomra decision – A disappointing start to the effects-based era of Article 82 enforcement", *Competition Law Insight*, 13 February 2007.

imminent.[118] The Commission seems to be fully aware of this potential for mischief and is therefore careful to explain that the initiation of formal proceedings means only that the Commission will pursue its investigation "as a matter of priority" and does not in any way prejudge the final outcome of the analysis.[119] This notwithstanding, this practice will often harm significantly many firms investigated by the Commission. A recent study by G. Langus and M. Motta shows, for instance, that the announcement to the market of a dawn raid has a strong and statistically significant effect on the firm's share price, with its cumulative average abnormal return being approximately – 2 %. One cannot exclude that the heightened public attention, market focus and pressure brought to bear by investors may, in many cases, induce a firm under investigation to commit to amend its behaviour in order for a competition authority to close even incipient proceedings. This may be an area of real concern where any change in a firm's behaviour is unwarranted given that a full investigation would in all likelihood have found no evidence of infringement.

In light of the risks identified above, it is clear that competition authorities should exercise the utmost caution when making such public announcements. In that respect, the record of the British NCA, the Office of Fair Trading ("OFT"), is worth mentioning. In a 2007 public announcement, the OFT erroneously suggested in a press release that a firm had committed several infringements of UK competition law.[120] The firm initiated defamation proceedings. In April 2008, the OFT acknowledged that its press release con-

---

[118] Until recently the Commission initiated formal proceedings simultaneously with the adoption of a Statement of Objections. A new trend seems to be emerging whereby the initiation of formal proceedings precedes and is therefore decoupled from the adoption of a Statement of Objections. In such cases, the initiation of formal proceedings constitutes a mere procedural measure which does not imply – and for that reason should not suggest – that a Statement of Objections will be adopted.

[119] See Commission Press Release, *Antitrust : Commission initiates formal proceedings against Qualcomm*, MEMO/07/389 of 1st October 2007.

[120] See OFT Press Release, *Wm Morrison Supermarkets plc : an apology*, 54/08 of 23 April 2008. The OFT issued a press release at the same time as a Statement of Objections against a number of large supermarkets and dairy processors, among which Morrisons. However, the press release incorrectly suggested that Morrisons was the subject of a provisional OFT finding of infringement in relation to milk, cheese and butter over a two year period (2002 and 2003), and that Morrisons had previously been warned by the OFT against anti-competitive behaviour. In fact, the OFT has not made any provisional finding of infringement against Morrisons in relation to the supply of butter and cheese. Nor had Morrisons been accused of any price fixing activity after 2002. The only allegation involving Morrisons related to liquid milk products in 2002.

tained "serious errors". It issued a new press release expressing its sincere apologies for the publication of erroneous, defamatory allegations and agreed to pay £100,000 in settlement of the defamation action.

G. – *"Buying" time*

Finally, the adoption of sunshine enforcement instruments may, in certain instances, be perceived as merely allowing the Commission to buy time. For instance, the Commission is under a legal duty (as guardian of the Treaty) to apply competition law and to act in a timely fashion in the interests of "good administration". In cases where its actions have been less than immediate, it may be tempted to defuse any criticism by issuing a press release of a merely procedural nature. Similarly, the publication of a consultation paper in an area where a clarification of competition policy appears long overdue may allow the Commission to devote more time to a thorough examination of the topic in question.

V. – Conclusion

The proliferation of sunshine enforcement instruments has pros and cons, supporters and detractors. Whilst its virtues in providing much needed guidance in certain nebulous areas of EC competition law as well as its contribution to the effectiveness of the Commission's enforcement activities are apparent and should not be called into question, its pitfalls are less well-known.

In our view, the Community courts bear significant responsibility in ensuring not only that the Commission does not abuse the wide margin of discretion it enjoys, but also that the Commission's reliance on soft law instruments does not prove inconsistent with higher sources of Community law.

ANNEX. – TYPOLOGY OF SUNSHINE ENFORCEMENT INSTRUMENTS

	Author	*General/ Individual (G/I)*	*Content*		*Publication*			*Binding nature*		*Possibility to bring annulment proceedings under Article 230 EC*		*Possibility to bring damages claims under article 288 EC*
			Policy	*Technical*	*Official Journal*	*Others*	*Not published*	*Binding on the Commission*	*ECJ/CFI precedent*	*Is the measure a challengeable act?*	*ECJ/CFI precedent*	
Oral statements	Commissioner; Commission spokespersons; Commission officials	G/I	x	x		x		x (If the author represents the Commission)	x CFI T-25/99, *Roberts and Roberts v. Commission*; CFI T-133/95 and T-204/95, *IEEC v. Commission*	x Depends on whether the statement is a formal pronouncement or an "off-the-record" statement CFI T-52/96 R, *Sogecable v. Commission*	x CFI T-3/93, *Air France v. Commission* CFI T-62/98, *Volkswagen AG v. Commission*	x CFI T-62/98, *Volkswagen AG v. Commission*
Articles written by Commission officials	Commission officials	G/I	x	x		x		x Arguably yes, where such articles seem to be endorsed by the Commission (*e.g.* articles published in the *EC Competition Policy Newsletter*).	No	Unlikely	No	Unclear

	Author	*General/ Individual (G/I)*	*Content*		*Publication*			*Binding nature*		*Possibility to bring annulment proceedings under Article 230 EC*		*Possibility to bring damages claims under article 288 EC*
			Policy	*Technical*	*Official Journal*	*Others*	*Not published*	*Binding on the Commission*	*ECJ/CFI precedent*	*Is the measure a challengeable act?*	*ECJ/CFI precedent*	
Expert reports and third party studies	Third parties	G/I	x	x		x	x	Unclear	No	Unclear	No	No
Press releases	Commission	G/I	x	x		x		x	x CFI T-25/99, *Roberts and Roberts v. Commission*	x A press release may nonetheless be challengeable if, in fact, it constitutes a decision in disguise	x CFI T-119/02, *Royal Philips Electronics NV v. Commission*	Yes
Commission papers (discussion papers, non-papers, etc.)	Units or Directorates within DG COMP	G	x	x		x		Yes	No	Unclear	No	No

	Author	*General/ Individual (G/I)*	*Content*		*Publication*			*Binding nature*		*Possibility to bring annulment proceedings under Article 230 EC*		*Possibility to bring damages claims under article 288 EC*
			Policy	*Technical*	*Official Journal*	*Others*	*Not published*	*Binding on the Commission*	*ECJ/CFI precedent*	*Is the measure a challengeable act?*	*ECJ/CFI precedent*	
Annual reports on competition policy	Commission	G/I	x	x		x		x	x CFI T-7/89, *Hercules v. Commission*; T-528/93, *Métropole Télévision v. Commission*	Unclear	No	Unclear
Final report following sector inquiries	Commission	G/I	x	x		x		Yes	No	Unclear	No	Unclear
Formal Commission Guidelines, Notices and Communications	Commission	G	x	x	x			x	x ECJ 40/48, 50, 54/56, 111, 113, 114/7, *"Suiker Unie" and Others v. Commission*, ECJ C-251/98, *Spain v. Commission*, ECJ C-189/02, *P Dansk Rørindustri and others v. Commission*	x	x ECJ C-325/91, *France v. Commission*	Yes

	Author	*General/ Individual (G/I)*	*Content*		*Publication*			*Binding nature*		*Possibility to bring annulment proceedings under Article 230 EC*		*Possibility to bring damages claims under article 288 EC*
			Policy	*Technical*	*Official Journal*	*Others*	*Not published*	*Binding on the Commission*	*ECJ/CFI precedent*	*Is the measure a challengeable act?*	*ECJ/CFI precedent*	
Guidance letters	Commis-sion	G/I		x		x		Yes	No	Likely	No	Likely
Inapplica-bility decisions	Commis-sion	I		x	x			Yes	No	Likely	No	Likely

THE DEVELOPMENT OF A NEW "SETTLEMENT CULTURE" IN COMPETITION CASES

What is left to the Courts?

BY

Denis WAELBROECK[1]

Partner at Ashurst
Professor at the Free University of Brussels
and at the College of Europe, Bruges

Since the adoption of the so-called "*modernisation package*" of EC competition law, the Commission has favoured the development of alternative enforcement techniques in the application of Articles 81 and 82 of the Treaty in the form essentially of "*negotiated solutions*". Thus :

- apart from the purely repressive decisions adopted under Article 7, the only decisions the European Commission appears to still be willing to adopt are decisions recording the adoption of "*commitments*" under Article 9 of Regulation 1/2003. More positive decisions such as inapplicability decisions under Article 10 of the Regulation or "*guidance letters*" under its 2004/C101/06 Notice have not been used to date and the Commission itself indicated its intention of using them parsimoniously in the future;[2]
- even within the purely repressive area, the so-called "*leniency*" policy enables undertakings – in return for a full confession – to avoid all fines or benefit from a substantial reduction of the latter;

[1] The author wishes to thank Mr Amar Benafla for his assistance in writing this article as well as Mr Christophe Lemaire for his precious comments. Thanks go also to Anna Duron for preparing the English version of this paper.

[2] See *inter alia* Recital 14 of the Preamble of Regulation 1/2003 stating that decisions taken under Article 10 have to be adopted "*in exceptional cases where the public interest of the Community so requires*".

– lastly, the new possibility for the Commission to offer, *via* a "*direct settlement*", a "*bonus*" to undertakings which do not defend themselves or do not contest the objections is a step in the same direction.

In all cases, since the parties have "*agreed*" to the commitments, they can normally not challenge such decisions in court.

The same trend can be observed in the field of mergers where the Commission settles most problematic cases *via* "*corrective measures*" or "*remedies*" proposed by undertakings and which cannot normally be challenged either in court.

Admittedly this new approach of "*negotiated solutions*" presents numerous advantages for the authority. Given DG COMP's limited resources – with approximately 750 officials – such solutions enable it to focus the majority of its resources on priority tasks and thereby avoid heavy procedures (as well as risks pertaining to judicial proceedings). Moreover, also undertakings may clearly prefer amicable resolutions to long and costly procedures.

In this regard, it should be kept in mind also that "*negotiated solutions*" are not specific to competition law but are practices frequently used by the State administration in other areas of law such as tax, road traffic offences, etc... (bearing in mind that in the area of criminal law, it is only exceptionally and within well determined limits that settlements are allowed for minor offences; see *infra*, Section C(2)(a)(ii)).

However, in so far as it leads ultimately to "*short-circuiting*" the rights of the defence and the right to a judge, this approach raises also a number of questions. As Ivo Van Bael aptly wrote at the time, setting aside procedural safeguards "*simply (by) embarking on a settlement course*" may create "*an alternative body of jurisprudence, surrounded by a cloak of mystery*".[3] The risk must be avoided therefore that proceedings be used to develop a parallel competition policy outside all judicial review without minimal procedural guarantees.

Indeed, negotiating with the Commission takes place with an authority which has the power to impose sanctions. It would therefore be easy for it to "*impose*" commitments or settlements which

[3] I. Van Bael, "Comments on the EEC Commission's Antitrust Settlement Practice", Swiss Review of International Competition Law Act, October 1984, p. 67.

may ultimately be considered unjustified, unless proper guarantees are built in.

This is particularly important as, by resorting to the settlement instrument, the Commission is *avoiding multiple procedural requirements and in particular the burden of judicial proceedings* to which it would otherwise be subject, with all the risks that this might potentially entail.[4]

Moreover, an additional difficulty in the EU context arises from the fact that the Commission is in the unique position of acting simultaneously as the "*investigator*", "*prosecutor*" and "*judge*" in any given case. In the long run – as we have written elsewhere[5] – we are convinced that a strict separation of the prosecution and decision making powers, granting the latter to an independent judge, would provide the healthiest decision making system.[6]

But even if the new introduction of a settlement system were reconcilable with the current system, it seems essential – when it comes to the development of a parallel policy based on settlements – to ensure at least that more important procedural "*safeguards*" are maintained than those currently in place.

---

[4] As is well-known Article 6 (1) of the European Convention on Human Rights and Fundamental Freedoms grants everyone "*in the determination of his civil rights and obligations or of any criminal charge against him*" the right to "*a fair trial*" before "*an independent and impartial tribunal established by law*". There are numerous examples of marginalisation of the judge in the Commission's practice but we will only mention amongst the most recent and publicized cases, the *Microsoft* case where the Commission did not hesitate to impose huge daily penalties in the event that *Microsoft* refused to give up (once and forever) its know-how to competitors, and this prior to the intervention of any judge. (See our reservations in this regard in D. WAELBROECK, "Microsoft Round 12 – Is the Commission now trying to pre-empt the judges?", *Competition Law Insights*, 2007. It seems that the pressure exerted by the Commission had as a consequence that a company such as Microsoft had no choice but to accept *inter alia* the "*pricing principles*" in spite of the controversial and questionable nature of the obligations imposed).

[5] See *inter alia* D. WAELBROECK & D. FOSSELARD, "Should the decision making power in EC Antitrust Procedures be left to an Independent Judge?", *Y.E.L.*, 1994, pp. 111 et seq.; D. WAELBROECK and M. GRIFFITH, "Note on the TGV Nord and Pont de Normandie case of the French Cour de Cassation of 5 October 1999", *CML Rev.*, 2000, p. 1465; D. WAELBROECK, *Twelve feet all dangling down and six necks exceeding long – the EU network of competition authorities and the European Convention of Fundamental Rights*, in The EU Network of Competition Authorities Hart Publishing, 2005, p. 465 and D. WAELBROECK & C. SMITS "Le droit de la concurrence et les droits fondamentaux", in *Les droits de l'homme dans les politiques de l'Union européenne*, Larcier, 2006, p. 135.

[6] The European Community is indeed probably one of the last legal systems in the world where this is not the case (and this although we have seen a spectacular increase in the amount of fines imposed).

Finally, compared to the classical system of formal decisions, settlements are also problematic in so far as they deprive *lawyers of clear precedents guiding them in the application of the law*. Indeed, since a settlement decision is generally extremely short, and moreover generally adopted without concluding whether or not there is an infringement, it is difficult to know the significance it has or should be granted.

Admittedly, a brief summary of the agreement is generally published. However, for a better understanding of the law by the legal community at large and irrespective of the broader issues relating to the right to a judge mentioned above, there are, in our view, good reasons to believe that the Commission should in a number of cases either resort again more widely to formal decisions, or at least use a more transparent policy than the one currently in use with respect to "*negotiated solutions*".[7]

Hereafter, we propose to assess successively the various aspects of this new settlement policy, i.e. :

- "*commitment decisions*" under Article 9 of Regulation 1/2003;
- the "*leniency*" and "*non-contestation of facts*" policies;
- the recent introduction of a "*direct settlement*" policy in horizontal cartel cases.

A. – Commitment decisions under Article 9 of Regulation 1/2003

1. – *Origins of the system*

Before discussing their legal framework, it should be remembered that negotiated solutions have existed long before the adoption of Regulation 1/2003.[8] In its *Fifth Report on Competition Policy* (p. 9), the Commission stated that "*although this procedure is less well known*", it had enabled some cases to come to a close with a minimum of administrative intervention. A few years later, it reported in reply to an *MEP* question that, in practice, only one case out of

[7] See also I. Van Bael, mentioned *supra*, p. 68 and from the same author "EEC Antitrust Enforcement and Adjudication as seen from the Defence Council", Swiss Review of International Competition Law, 1979, p. 9.

[8] Council Regulation N° 1/2003 of 16 December 2002 on the implementation of the rules on competition laid down in Article 81 and 82 of the Treaty.

thirty was closed with a formal decision, all others being informally settled. [9]

Although originally, the practice of negotiated solutions found no legal basis in the procedural Regulation itself, Article 9 of Regulation 1/2003 [10] henceforth allows expressly the Commission to take a decision making the commitments binding on the undertakings concerned. Article 9 of the Regulation specifies that a settlement is conceivable if the Commission considers that the commitments offered by an undertaking meet the competition concerns identified by it in a "*preliminary assessment*" or to use its own words:

> "*1. Where the Commission intends to adopt a decision requiring that an infringement be brought to an end and the undertakings concerned offer commitments to meet the concerns expressed to them by the Commission in its preliminary assessment, the Commission may by decision make those commitments bind-*

[9] Reply of the Commission to a question of Mr Battersby, *OJ* [1983], C 118/23. However, it is only after the settlements in important cases such as *IBM* or *Philip Morris* that the attention of lawyers was really drawn to the settlement practice of the Commission. (See D. Waelbroeck, "New forms of settlement of antitrust cases and procedural safeguards: is Regulation 17 falling into abeyance?", *E.L.R.*, Vol. 11, n° 4, August 1986). Even though EC Article 81 and 82 cases may be settled "*amicably*" with the Commission for various reasons, there is a genuine "*settlement*" with the parties only if the agreements or practices are modified by the latter so as to comply with competition rules and if an agreement is reached with the Commission in that respect. However, this does not exclude that the file may be closed for other reasons. For instance, it is possible that:

- the Commission, after examination, reaches the conclusion that the agreements involved are after all in compliance with the competition rules (so the Commission may decide not to take proceedings in the case as long as there are no changes in the undertaking's practice); or
- the practices or agreements are abandoned by the parties following the Commission's intervention (also in that case the Commission may decide not to take proceedings as long as there are no changes in the factual situation); or
- the practices have expired during the negotiation with the Commission (so it becomes pointless to take proceedings); or lastly
- the practices or agreements are modified by the parties so as to comply with competition rules (and an agreement is concluded with the Commission in that regard).

If at the beginning, the settlement procedure was entirely informal, it became soon clear that minimum guarantees were essential so as to protect the rights of both parties and third parties. The Commission accordingly decided in 1982:

(1) to publish the main contents of proposed settlements, so as to give interested third parties the opportunity to make their views known before taking a final decision (Notice published in the *OJ*, [1982], C 343/4 and *Eleventh Report on Competition Policy*); and

(2) to communicate to the undertakings concerned the views expressed by third parties and allow them, in their turn, to make comments before any settlement was agreed to (Reply of the Commission to a question of Mr Prout, *OJ* [1982], C 275/15. It should be noted that at the same time, the Commission decided to generalise its practice to cases under EC Article 85(3) [81(3)] and not anymore only to cases under EC Article 85(1) [81(1)], despite the fact that national Courts were not authorised at the time to apply EC Article 85(3) [81(3)]).

[10] Council Regulation N° 1/2003 of 16 December 2002 on the implementation of the rules on competition laid down in Articles 81 and 82 of the Treaty. See on the commitment procedure *inter alia* Pranvera Këllezi, "Les mesures correctives dans les cas de concentrations d'entreprises et d'abus de position dominante", PhD thesis at the University of Geneva, May 2007, from p. 361.

ing on the undertakings. Such a decision may be adopted for a specified period and shall conclude that there are no longer grounds for action by the Commission.

2. The Commission may, upon request or on its own initiative, reopen the proceedings :

(a) where there has been a material change in any of the facts on which the decision was based;

(b) where the undertakings concerned act contrary to their commitments; or

(c) where the decision was based on incomplete, incorrect or misleading information provided by the parties."

If the undertaking concerned does not honour the terms of the commitments, the Commission may "*upon request or on its own initiative, reopen the proceedings*". [11] Moreover, Article 23 (2)(c) of Regulation 1/2003 states that "*the Commission may by decision impose fines on undertakings and associations of undertakings where, either intentionally or negligently [...] they fail to comply with a commitment made binding by a decision pursuant to Article 9*". And Article 24 (1)(c) adds that "*The Commission may, by decision, impose on undertakings or associations of undertakings periodic penalty payments not exceeding 5% of the average daily turnover in the preceding business year per day and calculated from the date appointed by the decision, in order to compel them [...] to comply with a commitment made binding by a decision pursuant to Article 9*".

This system thus reflects to a certain extent the system of "*remedies*", already in existence when the merger control procedure was first implemented. However, non-compliance with the "*remedies*" accepted by the Commission in a merger decision entails in addition the retroactive inapplicability of the decision approving the concentration in question which is as a result null and void. [12]

Article 9 decisions resemble to a large extent also the former decisions granting negative clearance or conditional exemption, the main difference being that the "*condition*" (commitment) is henceforth – at least in theory – "*voluntary*" and not imposed by the authority, as a result of which it is normally not challengeable in court (see *infra* on this issue). Moreover, the respect of fewer pro-

[11] Article 9 (2)(b) of Regulation 1/2003.

[12] Regulation 139/2004 allows the clearance of a transaction following commitments by the undertakings meeting the concerns raised by the Commission. See Articles 6(2) and 8(2) of Regulation 139/2004 on the control of concentrations between undertakings, *OJ* [2004], L 24/1. See also Commission Notice on remedies acceptable under Council Regulation (EEC) No 4064/89 and under Commission Regulation (EC) No 447/98, *OJ* [2001], C 68/3 and the new Draft Notice, not yet published in the *OJ*.

cedural safeguards will be required than in the case of a "*conditional decision*".

In analysing judicial review of commitment decisions, it would seem helpful hereafter to assess successively :

- the legal nature and effect of "*commitment decisions*";
- the effect of Article 9 decisions on national courts; and
- the procedural safeguards for the main parties and third parties.

2. – *The legal nature of* "commitment decisions"

Before Regulation 1/2003, and in the absence of any legal basis in the procedural Regulation, "*negotiated solutions*" were initially assimilated to mere "*administrative*" or "*comfort*" letters, and were therefore not legally binding. Indeed, letters such as those "*... which were dispatched without publication as laid down in Article 19 (3) of Regulation N° 17 and which were not published pursuant to Article 21 (1) of that Regulation, constitute neither decisions granting negative clearance nor decisions in application of Article 85 [81] (3) within the meaning of Articles 2 and 6 of Regulation N° 17. As is stressed by the Commission itself, they are merely administrative letters informing the undertaking concerned of the Commission's opinion that there is no need for it to take action in respect of the contracts in question under the provisions of Article 85 [81] (1) of the treaty and that the file on the case may therefore by closed.*

Such letters, which are based only upon the facts in the Commission's possession, and which reflect the Commission's assessment and bring to an end the procedure of examination by the department of the Commission responsible for this, do not have the effect of preventing national courts, before which the agreements in question are alleged to be incompatible with Article 85 [81], from reaching a different finding as regards the agreements concerned on the basis of the information available to them. Whilst it does not bind the national courts, the opinion transmitted in such letters nevertheless constitutes a factor which the national courts may take into account in examining whether the agreements or conduct in question are in accordance with the provisions of Article 85 [81]." [13]

[13] ECJ, 10 July 1980, Case 253/78 and 1 to 3/79, *Procureur de la République and others v Bruno Giry and Guerlain SA a.o.*, ECR 2327, Para. 12-13; emphasis added.

The limited effect of "*settlements*" entered into with the Commission was generally reflected in their wording. For instance, the agreement in the *IBM* case provided expressly that it was not "*enforceable by any other natural or legal person or any authority or agency*".[14]

Moreover, even when the Commission decided in 1982 to formalise its practice by ensuring some publicity to its settlements, the latter remained nonetheless mere administrative acts – and not acts from the Commission itself – and had therefore no effect upon third parties[15], nor on national Courts. Nonetheless, plaintiffs were obviously always free to request a Commission decision in response to their complaint, and if the complaint was dismissed, an action by them before the European Court remained possible.

Henceforth however, the situation has been clarified in Article 9 of Regulation 1/2003 as:

- the settlement takes now the form no more of a simple letter from the *Administration* but of a *formal decision by the Commission* (as a college);
- this decision is moreover *binding*, at least on the parties (see the wording of Article 9 as well as Recital 13 of the Regulation; failure to respect a commitment entails fines and daily penalties); and finally
- contrary to a "*comfort letter*", a commitment decision is a challengeable act before the Court of First Instance of the European Communities (at least by some third parties; for the parties themselves this is more difficult – see *infra*).[16]

3. – *The effect of Article 9 decisions on national Courts*

In accordance with the general objective of decentralisation in the application of competition rules, it is normally for national

[14] In other cases, "*negotiated solutions*" had even less effects and consisted in reality only in a "*gentlemen's agreement*" stating that the Commission would, in the future, refer exclusively to the competition rules laid down in the Treaty and not take into consideration the commitments offered (see D. WAELBROECK, *op. cit.*).

[15] See D. WAELBROECK, "New forms of settlement of antitrust cases and procedural safeguards: is Regulation 17 falling into abbeyance?", *E.L.R.*, vol. 11, n° 4, August 1986.

[16] These acts are legally binding, definitive, produce legal effects and have been adopted by the Institution in the exercise of its powers. (See CFI, 11 July 2007, Case T-170/06, *Alrosa Company Ltd v. Commission*, not published. It is worth noting that the Commission decided to appeal the CFI judgment in that case before the Court of Justice).

courts to ensure compliance with Article 9 decisions.[17] Indeed, as much as possible, the Commission wishes to delegate to stakeholders themselves the responsibility to ensure the control of the correct implementation of the commitments.

Thus, in the initial draft Regulation 1/2003, the Commission even expressly stressed that "*where, in the course of proceedings which might lead to an agreement being prohibited, undertakings offer the Commission commitments such as to meet its objections, the Commission should be able to adopt decisions which make those commitments binding on the undertakings concerned, without settling the question of the applicability of Article 81 or Article 82, so that the commitments can be relied upon by third parties before national courts and failure to comply with them can be punished by the imposition of fines and periodic penalty payments.*"[18]

However, despite this system of decentralised enforcement, the effect of commitment decisions on national courts and national competition authorities is not entirely clear. Whilst the presence of a formal decision of the Commission making the commitments "*binding*" seems *a priori* to imply a binding effect not only on the parties but also on national courts and national competition authorities, the Regulation Preamble stresses, on the contrary, that there is no such effect :

- "*Commitment decisions should find that there are no longer grounds for action by the Commission without concluding whether or not there has been or still is an infringement. Commitment decisions are without prejudice to the powers of competition authorities and courts of the Member States to make such a finding and decide upon the case*".[19]
- "*Commitment decisions adopted by the Commission do not affect the power of the courts and the competition authorities of the Member States to apply Articles 81 and 82 of the Treaty*".[20]

[17] See e.g. MEMO/04/217 of 17 September 2007 on the procedure regarding the application of Article 9; Commission Notice on the co-operation between the Commission and the courts of the EU Member States in the application of Articles 81 and 82 EC, *OJ*, C 101, [2004], p. 54.

[18] Proposal for a Council Regulation on the implementation of the rules on competition laid down in Articles 81 and 82 of the Treaty and amending Regulation 1017/68, 2988/74, 4056/86 and 3975/87, *OJ*, C 365, [2000], p. 284. Emphasis added.

[19] Recital 13, emphasis added.

[20] Recital 22, emphasis added. For the same reason, the Commission does not consider that commitment decisions "*constitute precedents to establish recidivism*" (see MEMO 08/458 of 27 June 2008 on settlement procedure).

In this regard, one may however wonder whether these two recitals – in denying any binding effect to decisions taken under Article 9 upon national judges or authorities – are correct in law:

- First, according to the *Masterfoods* judgment, national Courts or authorities are bound by the decisions taken by the Commission.[21] Moreover, the recent *Alrosa-De Beers* judgment makes clear that a decision adopted under Article 9 is valid only if the "*measures made binding by the Decision were appropriate and necessary to bring to an end the abuse that had been identified in the Commission's preliminary assessment*"[22], i.e. there is clearly a formal "*decision*" by the Commission finding that the problems identified no longer exist. In other words, if the Commission considers that a commitment meets "*the concerns expressed*", it is clear that national Courts or authorities may not, in principle, prohibit such behaviour. The decision must be binding on national courts or administrations, at least regarding the points addressed by the Commission;
- Second, Article 10 of the EC Treaty should in any event prevent national courts or authorities from taking any action going against the "*effet utile*" of this decision;
- Third, the uniformity objective as expressed *inter alia* in Article 16 of Regulation 1/2003[23] might be seriously compromised if the decisions at stake did not bind national courts or authorities[24];
- Fourth – by virtue of Article 11 (3) of the Regulation – a decision by the Commission to open a procedure so as to adopt a decision under Article 9 deprives national competition authorities from their power to apply Articles 81 and 82 of the Treaty and it would be paradoxical if these authorities continued to be prevented to act when Article 7 or 10 decisions are taken, but regained suddenly their full powers in case of a commitment decision; and

[21] ECJ, 14 December 2000, Case C-344/98, *Masterfoods*, ECR I-11369. See also ECJ, 22 October 1987, Case 314/85, *Foto-Frost*, ECR 4199. See also on that issue W. WILS, "Settlements of EU Antitrust Investigations: commitment decisions under Article 9 of Regulation N° 1/2003", *World Competition*, 2006, p. 345.

[22] Point 111 of the judgment, emphasis added.

[23] Which expressly prohibits national Courts or authorities from "*giving decisions which would conflict with a decision contemplated by the Commission in proceedings it has initiated*".

[24] See also R. WHISH, *Competition Law*, 5th Edition, Butterworths, p. 257 who also raises questions on that issue.

– Finally, under *TWD* case-law third party complainants are in principle not allowed to challenge before a national court the conclusions reached by the Commission in a decision adopted under Article 9 if they could have challenged the decision before the Court of First Instance and have not done so. The case-law indeed prohibits a party from questioning the validity of a Community act when it did not challenge it within the time-limit before EU Courts, although it had a right to do so. [25]

It seems therefore to us that the above Recitals in the Preamble of the Regulation should not be taken too literally. In practice, the binding effect of Article 9 decisions will presumably depend on the wording of each decision. Thus, if the Commission considers in its decision that the commitments bring the infringement to an end, national courts or authorities may clearly not – irrespectively of the wording of the recitals in the Regulation – prohibit the agreements or practices at stake [26]. If however the decision does not specify whether or not "*there still is an infringement*", national courts and authorities will have more flexibility to adopt a negative decision regarding the practices at stake, at least *on the issues not decided on by the Commission*. This will be so for instance if the Commission considers that there is no "*Community interest*" to proceed further in its decision (which then leaves the door open to stricter decisions at national level), or if the decision does not assess certain aspects of the practice, or still if the preliminary assessment did not permit the detection of all anticompetitive effects. [27] In each case, national courts and authorities will therefore be strictly bound by the content of the Commission decision. [28]

In the same vein, the wording of the decision will be decisive for a national court when it has to decide whether a practice was initially problematic under competition rules before the commitment

[25] ECJ, 15 May 1997, C-335/95 P, *Textilwerke Deggendorf GmbH (TWD)*, ECR I-2549.

[26] It is worth noting that Recital 13 of the Regulation seems to exclude this possibility since it indicates that Article 9 decisions should not conclude whether or not "*there still is an infringement*".

[27] It should be remembered, however, that Article 3 of Regulation 1/2003 does not preclude Member States from adopting stricter national laws than Articles 81 or 82 "*which prohibit or sanction unilateral conduct engaged in by undertakings*".

[28] Moreover, and in any event, the existence of a decision under Article 9 will in practice presumably tend to dissuade national Courts or authorities from challenging the behaviour in question (See for instance, in the *Coca-Cola* Case (Commission decision of 22 June 2005, *Coca-Cola*, *OJ*, N° C 289/10, [2004]), where the Spanish Competition Authority closed the procedure).

was given (as the existence of an Article 9 decision necessarily assumes that there has been technically an infringement justifying the Commitment).[29]

In this regard, as far as we can see, the Commission tends to use in practice the conditional tense when it refers to the identified infringement[30]. In those cases, national courts would presumably be free to decide that after all, the said practice was not infringing

---

[29] This is important as the fact that an Article 9 decision was adopted does not mean that the "*concerns*" expressed by the Commission which the commitments were supposed to remedy were necessarily justified, nor that the decision does not go beyond what is necessary to comply with competition rules (see *Alrosa* judgment quoted above), nor even that the decision will always provide clear indications on the potential existence of an infringement from the start.

[30] See for instance decision of the Commission of 22 February 2006, Case COMP/B-2/38.381, *De Beers*, at paragraph 30 : "*In its preliminary assessment, the Commission took the view that De Beers' continuous purchase relationship with Alrosa constituted a recourse to methods different from those consistent with normal competition and had the effect of hindering the maintenance of the degree of competition existing in the market or the growth of that competition and of maintaining De Beers' control over the rough diamonds market*". In Paragraph 31, the Commission adds that "*As a consequence, De Beers would eliminate an alternative and independent source of supply for potential customers*". See also the decision of the Commission of 22 June 2005, *Coca-Cola*, *OJ*, C 289, 26 November 2004, at paragraph 29 : "*The Commission took the preliminary view that financing agreements are likely to give rise to foreclosure of competing suppliers if concluded for long periods, if exit conditions are overly burdensome for the customers and if the TCCC branded beverages, with which the loan is repaid, are bundled together*". At Paragraph 32 : "*The Commission took the preliminary view that growth and target provisions increase customer's switching costs and bind them to TCCC and its bottlers to the detriment of competitors and final consumers by reducing variety of choice and the downward pressure on prices*". Also :

- In the *Bundesliga* Case (Case COMP/C2/37.214, *Bundesliga*, *OJ*, C 229, [2004], p. 13), the Commission simply "*assumes*" the relevant market and notes that the practice "*would raise competition concerns*";
- A similar expression is used in the *Cannes extension agreement* Case (*OJ*, L 296, [2007], p. 27);
- In the *Repsol* Case (Case COMP/38.348, *Repsol CPP SA*, *OJ*, C 258, [2004], p. 7), the Commission considers that the problematic clauses "*could*" contribute to significant foreclosing effects;
- In the *FA Premier League* Case (Case COMP/C-2/38.173, *FA Premier League*, *OJ*, C 115, [2004], p. 3), the Commission considers in its decision that the restrictions on the upstream market will probably affect the downstream markets and adds that the common sales of TV rights may limit the production and create foreclosure effects on the markets;
- In the *Distrigaz* Case (Case COMP/B-1/37.966, *Distrigaz*, *OJ*, C 77, [2007], p. 48; see also the Commission Decision, not yet published), the Commission expresses concerns that long-term gas supply contracts would limit the scope for other gas suppliers to conclude contracts with customers;
- In the cases involving several car manufacturers regarding the refusal to give independent garages access to repair information (Case COMP/39.140, COMP/39.141, COMP/39.142, COMP/39.143, *DaimlerChrysler, Toyota, Opel and Fiat*), the Commission raises concerns regarding possible negative effects;
- In the *SkyTeam* Case (Case COMP/37.984, *SkyTeam*, *OJ*, C 245, [2007], p. 46), the Commission also raises concerns and concludes that "*this enhanced cooperation would be likely to have anti-competitive effects in view of the strong market position of the SkyTeam members involved coupled with the existence of significant barriers to* entry".

In all these cases, it can already be inferred from the decisions themselves that the Commission does not take a firm conclusion as to whether or not there has been an infringement in the past (which is consistent with Recital 13 of the Regulation).

competition rules. And indeed, Recital 13 of the Regulation explicitly states that "*commitment decisions should find that there are no longer grounds for action by the Commission without concluding whether or not there has been or still is an infringement*".[31]

However, in cases where Article 9 decisions are more affirmative,[32] the *Masterfoods* case-law implies that such decision must have a binding effect on national judges (and in case of doubts regarding the legality of this decision, a preliminary ruling in validity should then be referred to the ECJ as to the validity of the decision[33]).

4. – *The procedural safeguards for the main parties and third parties*

(a) *The procedural safeguards for the main parties*

Due to the informal nature of the procedure, the procedural rights of the parties are relatively limited. They are normally entitled to a "*preliminary assessment*" by the Commission before the negotiation starts. But very few other rights are given to them. This calls for the following comments:

- regarding the identification of the infringement itself, the parties should in our view obtain from the Commission in all circumstances a relatively detailed clarification of the objections before conceding commitments, as it is very difficult otherwise to devise the proper remedies.[34] As stated in in this respect in the *Alrosa/*

[31] This recital was presumably intended to make it easier for undertakings to accept commitment decisions without any admission of guilt which could be used for damages actions.

[32] See for instance the Commission Notice in the *BUMA/SABAM* Case (*OJ*, C 200, [2005], p. 11): at Paragraph 11 of the Notice, the Commission notes the existence of an absolute territorial exclusivity and that "*the multi-lateralisation of this limitation throughout the network of bilateral agreements, supported on a multilateral reassurance that all other collecting societies will be subject to the same territorial limitation, leads to a standardisation of the licensing terms throughout the EEA, preventing the market from evolving in different directions and crystallising the exclusivity enjoyed by each of the participating societies*". See also the decision in the *Coca-Cola* Case mentioned above at Paragraph 31 regarding fountain dispensers: "*[...] these fountain dispenser exclusivity provisions unduly hinder the outlets from turning to rival suppliers and thus reduce the competitive pressure on the incumbent if their duration is excessive, because it extends beyond the amortisation period for such equipment*".

[33] *Masterfoods* Case, see *supra*.

[34] True, if a commitment appears retrospectively to be unjustified and excessive, a party may theoretically request from the Commission its modification – but this may often be hard to obtain. Meanwhile, a party who has accepted a commitment may not depart from it without incurring the risk of fines or daily penalties.

De Beers judgment at paragraph 100, "*the Commission is not required formally to establish the existence of an infringement [...] but it must nonetheless establish the reality of the competition concerns which justified its envisaging the adoption of a decision under Articles 81 EC and 82 EC and which allow it to require the undertaking concerned to comply with certain commitments. This presupposes an analysis of the market and an identification of the infringement envisaged which are less definitive than those which are required for the application of Article 7(1) of Regulation No 1/2003, although they should be sufficient to allow a review of the appropriateness of the commitment*".[35]

In this regard, it is questionable whether the "*preliminary assessment*" – as required by Article 9 – today always meet these requirements.[36] This is particularly so where they are sent out after the commitment have been offered, a practice which does not seem compatible with Article 9 of Regulation 1/2003 which – by imposing a "*preliminary assessment*" – seems to require their adoption not only before the adoption of the decision itself but also before the start of the "*negotiation*". The very submission of commitments before any "*preliminary assessment*" is received features – as we have said – the risk of unjustified concessions[37]. The "*preliminary assessment*" moreover should be sufficiently detailed so as to set out the substance and the nature of the problems identified commitments[38];

---

[35] Emphasis added.

[36] In some cases, as the *Alrosa/De Beers Case*, the preliminary assessment can however be long and even take the form of a Statement of Objections. In the *Coca-Cola* Case (*OJ*, C 289, [2004], p. 10), the commitments were offered before the statement of objections was issued and before the preliminary assessment (O. ARMENGOL and A. PASCUAL, "*Some reflexions on Article 9 commitment decisions in the light of the Coca-Cola Case*", *E.C.L.R.* [2006], v. 27, n° 3, March, pp. 124-129).

[37] See on this issue J. DAVIES and A. DE BROUSSE, "*Le point de vue de praticiens du droit de la concurrence*", *RDLC*, n° 1, 2005, p. 13.

[38] In its judgement of 16 October 2007 in *Bijourma v. Festina France* regarding a procedure similar to the procedure laid down in Article 9 of Regulation 1/2003, the Court of Appeal of Paris considered that "*the Conseil de la concurrence has rightly considered that the commitment procedure featured some peculiarities, and in particular lightened inquiry measures compared to the regular procedure, consisting of a mere 'preliminary assessment' of the practices concerned so as to identify the competition concerns, without qualifying the practices in legal terms [...], nor* a fortiori *evidencing an infringement [...], and did not therefore require the definition of the exact relevant market; the Conseil, following the whole data provided by the professional organisations of the clockmaking sector as well as the detailed studies on this market, found that, whichever the relevant market of the product was chosen [...], Festina did not have more than a 30% market share*" (translated from the French), and that therefore, the group exemption Regulation 2790/1999 exempting vertical agreements was applicable to selective distribution system implemented by Festina.

- second, faced with the threat of fines, the pressure can be big for companies to give in to the *wishes* of the Institution, even where the latter are unfounded. This may explain why under Recital 13 of Regulation 1/2003, "*commitment decisions are not appropriate in cases where the Commission intends to impose a fine*". Given the great discretion of the Commission as to which cases are suitable for a fine or not, it is however difficult to see how this recital should be applied in practice.[39] The fact that the Commission itself recognises that the procedure in itself is not suited for cases where fines are considered nevertheless points to a basic conceptual problem in applying the procedure and shows that it may in practice not be always of a "*voluntary*" nature as claimed;
- finally, it is clearly difficult for the parties to challenge in court a decision to which they gave – at least seemingly – their "*consent*"[40] (to be compared with the old system of conditional clear-

[39] There are numerous commitment decisions where a fine could arguably have been justified. See for instance the *Alrosa/De Beers* case. Also when one compares the *Coca-cola* case with the fines imposed on *Michelin* (CFI, 30 September 2003, Case T-203/01, *Michelin*, ECR II-4071) or *British Airways* (ECJ, 15 March 2007, Case C-95/04 P, *British Airways*, ECR I-2331) for exclusive rebates, the latter were arguably less restrictive than those at stake in the *Coca-cola* case. Where there is a possibility of fines, it is questionable whether a system of negotiations and commitments is at all acceptable if the decisional power to impose sanctions relating to the practice under investigation, in the absence of an agreement, is not granted to a third party i.e. an independent judge (see in this regard *infra*, section C (g) with respect to settlements). In France for instance, commitments are negotiated with the *Rapporteur* but confirmed afterwards by the Council. Similarly, in the absence of settlements, it is the Council and not the *Rapporteur* who has the power to make a decision regarding the infringement. It is worth noting that in its judgement of 6 November 2007 in *Canal 9 v. GIE Les Indépendants*, an argument was even made before the Paris Court of Appeal according to which the modification of the commitments negotiated with the *Rapporteur* could not be discussed before the Council by application of the principle of separation of the prosecuting and judging powers. The Court however did not go that far and stated in this regard that "*the Conseil de la concurrence [...] provoked a debate between the parties regarding the proposed commitments and the comments submitted by [...] concerned third parties, at the end of the exchanges, took act of the new commitments offered by the concerned undertaking, which meet, in its view, the competition concerns previously identified; the fact that the Council took an active part to the debates, due to the consensual character of this phase of the procedure and the fact that it evaluates, at the end, the relevance of the commitments and give it a binding effect, does not mean that it interfered in the inquiry; [...] therefore, the argument relating to a violation of Article 6 (1) of the European Convention on human rights is unfounded*" (translated from the French) (emphasis added). Since the *Conseil de la concurrence* only "*invited*" the parties – following the comments made by third parties – to discuss the commitments without intervening itself, in any way, in the determination of their content, this does not constitute, according to the Court of Appeal, an "*inquiry*" and therefore not an interference in a power which does not belong to the Council.

[40] Contrary to a third party who can always challenge such decision, as in the *Alrosa* Case. The case-law admits the existence of an "*estoppel*" principle which prohibits a party to go back on a point that it admitted ("*venire contra factum proprium*"); see H. SCHERMERS and D. WAELBROECK, *Judicial Protection in the European Union*, Kluwer, 2001, 6th Edition, pp. 104-108. It is worth noting that the case-law admits that where there is unevenness between the parties or

ance where appeals were always possible). Thus, in the context at least of the Merger Control Regulation, commitments are in principle not challengeable by the parties because they are assumed to have been offered voluntarily.[41] The parties may only challenge a commitment decision if they can prove that they offered the commitment "*under the arbitrary constraint of the Commission*".[42] Within the context of Article 9, and taking into account the criminal nature of the procedure as well as the real risk of sanctions, may this idea be generalised? A particular interpretation of the *Alrosa* case could support this argument. Thus, at paragraph 87 of the judgment, the CFI underlines that a decision adopted under Article 9 "*cannot be considered as being a mere acceptance on the Commission's part of a proposal that has been freely put forward by a negotiating partner, but constitutes a binding measure which puts an end to an infringement or a potential infringement, as regards which the Commission exercises all the prerogatives conferred on it by Articles 81 EC and 82 EC*".[43] If the proposal cannot be regarded as "*freely consented to*" – which arguably is the case whenever fines could be imposed –, the argument could be made that the party who consented to the commitment cannot be prevented from challenging the decision.[44] Therefore it

---

if one party acts under "*constraint*", the principle does not apply (ECJ, 20 September 2001, Case C-453/99, *Crehan v. Courage* Ltd, ECR I-6297). It should also be noted that if the Commission rejects a proposed commitment and takes a negative decision, the Court may ensure that the Commission was right to do so (see e.g. ECJ, 18 December 2007, Case C-202/68, *Cementbouw, not yet published*).

[41] In the *Cementbouw Handel & Industry BV v. Commission* Case (CFI, 23 February 2006, Case T-282/02, *Cementbouw Handel & Industry BV v. Commission*, ECR II-319, para 301), the applicant contested the commitments offered on the ground of principle of proportionality and of the necessity to restore the situation preceding the concentration. However, the CFI recalls that (Paragraph 308), "*the notifying parties are not required to confine themselves to proposing commitments aimed strictly at restoring the competitive situation existing before the concentration in order to allow the Commission to declare that transaction compatible with the common market*" and "*the Commission is authorised to accept all commitments by the parties which allow it to adopt a decision declaring the concentration compatible with the common market*". Therefore, a notifying party "*cannot plead failure to respect the principle of proportionality*".

[42] *Cementbouw Handel & Industry BV v. Commission* Case, Paragraphs 313-319.

[43] See also Paragraph 101 and 140 of the judgement which shows that the CFI wants to control the proportionality of the commitments.

[44] This approach has as consequence largely the assimilation of a commitment decision to a conditional clearance decision (see in this respect Paragraph 102 of the *Alrosa/De Beers* Case and the reference at paragraph 106 of this case to the *Ahlström* Case where the Court assimilated commitments to an injunction to put an end to the infringement). In other words, if the Commission has originally removed from Regulation 1/2003 the concept of conditional exemption decision and replaced it by commitment decisions, the case-law seems to provide some openings to assimilate the two kinds of decisions and therefore restore the right to a judge. In the same vein, the ECJ ruled in its *Cementbouw* case that (Paragraph 54) "*when reviewing the proportion-*

is questionable whether it is really possible under such circumstances to rule out *a priori* an action from the parties against the commitment decision.[45] This is so in particular since the right to a judge is a fundamental right, particularly in an area of intrinsic criminal nature such as competition law.[46]

(b) *The procedural safeguards for third parties*

With the adoption of Regulation 1/2003, the procedural safeguards for third parties have been both formalised and reinforced. Thus, as in the past[47]:

- third parties are informed of any Article 9 decision prior to its adoption through publication in the *Official Journal* and are given the opportunity of submitting their observations[48];

---

ality of conditions or obligations which the Commission may, by virtue of Article 8(2) of Regulation No 4064/89, impose on the parties to a concentration", it is necessary "*to be satisfied that those conditions and those obligations are proportionate to and would entirely eliminate the competition problem that has been identified*".

[45] In this regard, see in particular J. TEMPLE LANG, *op. cit.*

[46] Even if appeals are possible, the Commission would presumably continue to have an interest in accepting negotiated solutions even if these could be challenged afterwards before a Court. Indeed, even though legally speaking, a legal action is conceivable, it is doubtful that the parties will in practice often challenge decisions to which they had given their consent, voluntarily or under pressure. The same issue arises with respect to "*settlements*" in cartel cases and it seems that the Commission will have to accept that its settlement decisions will be, to a certain extent, challengeable by the parties (see *infra* Section C (g)).

[47] See as regards the previous regime D. WAELBROECK, "New forms of Settlement of antitrust case and procedural safeguards : is Regulation 17 falling into abeyance?", *E.L.R.*, Vol. 11, n° 4, August 1986. At that time, there was no legal requirement to send a copy of the statement of objections or the comments of interested undertakings to the complainants or that they be invited to the oral hearings (although the Commission has always done so).

[48] Recital 32 of Regulation 1/2003 states that the Commission should give third parties whose interests may be affected by a decision the opportunity of submitting their observations. This right is now formally established by Article 27 (4) of the Regulation. The Commission should publish a *concise summary of the case* and the main content of the commitments and allow for one month for replies to be submitted. Third parties, whether interested or not, may submit their observations regarding the scope of the commitments offered. In practice, observations made by third parties are often taken into account, as for instance in the *FA Premier League* Case, where third parties pointed out that the commitments were not sufficient to ensure that the rights will effectively be put on the market. Following these observations, the Commission required the *FA Premier League* to modify its commitments (see also the influence of third parties observations in the *Alrosa/De Beers* Case). In its judgement of 6 November 2006, *Canal 9 v. GIE Les Indépendants*, the Paris Court of Appeal considered – that the procedure applicable in France (which is similar to the procedure under Article 9) – protects adequately the rights of third parties in allowing complainants to make their comments known, both in writing, as soon as the commitments have been presented, and orally, during the hearing where the latter are assessed by the *Conseil de la concurrence*, and finally in writing again before the commitments are made binding by the *Conseil*.

- the complainants are informed of the reasons for rejecting their complaint and given a time-limit within which to make their views known in writing before a final decision is adopted[49];
- the complainants have as in the past a right to challenge the decision rejecting their complaint before EU Courts (or any decision addressed to the undertakings concerned affecting their interests); and
- the complainants may still introduce an action before national courts to protect their rights[50].

In addition, it is now clear that:

- third parties have the possibility to challenge the commitment decision before EU Courts via an action for annulment (for example the *Alrosa/De Beers* Case[51]), and not only the decision rejecting their complaint as in the past (where the settlement itself was not a challengeable act);
- the Commission, irrespective of its margin of appreciation in the application of Article 9, must respect the principle of proportionality when it decides to adopt a binding commitment decision under this provision[52], and this even if the commitment was in theory "*voluntarily*" offered.[53]

---

[49] See Article 7 of Commission Regulation 773/2004 relating to the conduct of proceedings by the Commission pursuant to Articles 81 and 82 of the EC Treaty, *OJ*, L 123, [2004], p. 18.

[50] With the double advantage that Article 81(3) has henceforth a direct effect since May 2004 and that the right to launch an action before national Courts has been clarified further to the *Courage/Crehan* and *Manfredi* cases. ECJ, 20 September 2001, Case C-453/99, *Courage Ltd v. Bernard Crehan*, ECR I-6297 and ECJ, 13 July 2006, Cases C-295/04 and C-298/04, *Manfredi*, ECR I-6619. See also the efforts of the Commission to encourage damages actions before national Courts and in particular the Green Paper of 19 December 2005, Doc COM(2005) 672 final.

[51] See above. Indeed, the commitment decision henceforth constitutes a binding decision of the Institution itself and not merely an administrative arrangement as in the past.

[52] Paragraph 97 of the *Alrosa/De Beers* case mentioned above. Note however that in the *Energías de Portugal* Case the Court of First Instance found on the contrary in the context of merger control that the Commission, may only assess a concentration "*as modified by the commitments validly proposed by the parties to the concentration*" (CFI, 21 September 2005, Case T-87/05, *Energías de Portugal*, ECR II-3745, para 63). The EC Court confirmed that it is the parties, and not the Commission, which decide whether or not to submit commitments. The Draft on remedies acceptable under Council Regulation (EEC) No 139/2004 and under Commission Regulation (EC) No 802/2004 (http://ec.europa.eu/comm/competition/mergers/legislation/draft_remedies_notice.pdf) confirms accordingly that the Commission Decision concerns only the concentration as amended following the commitments offered by the parties. Paragraph 7 of the Draft Notice on remedies underlines also that the Commission may not refuse the commitments offered by the parties even though they go beyond what is necessary to maintain the competition *statu quo ante*. Thus, the parties cannot challenge commitments offered (see ECJ, 18 December 2007, Case C-202/68, *Cementbouw*, not yet published). However, third parties have this right, even in the context of merger control, if the commitments are excessive, as set out in the *Kali*

Third parties are thus fairly well protected and it is difficult to see that they should be given more rights than is currently the case. The possibility of settlements during the administrative stage, as expressly encouraged by the Court [54], necessarily requires some administrative flexibility which might not be achievable if the complainant were involved throughout the discussion "*on equal terms*" with the accused party.

B. – The leniency program and non-contestation of the facts

1. – *The leniency program – control by the judge*

Under the leniency policy introduced in 1996 and amended since, [55] the collaboration with the Commission obliges the undertakings to cooperate throughout the proceedings "*fully, on a continuous basis and expeditiously*" [56]. The undertaking can neither go back on its decision, nor on its statements; otherwise, it would face the risk of losing the benefit of the leniency application. Irrespective of the quality of the decision adopted by the Commission, the undertaking benefiting from immunity or reduction of fine is generally estopped from challenging it before the EU Courts on the substance. [57] In addition, the existence of a full confession by a

& Salz Case (ECJ, 31 March 1998, Case C-68/94, *France v. Commission*, and C-30/93, *SPCA v. Commission*, ECR I-1453).

[53] The situation is similar for conditional decisions in merger cases. See ECJ, 31 March 1998, Case C-68/94, *France v. Commission* and C-30/93, *SPCA v. Commission*, ECR I-1453 where commitments affecting third parties were challenged.

[54] See e.g. ECJ, 8 November 1983, Joined Cases 96/82 to 102/82, 104/82, 105/82, 108/82 and 110/82, *ANSEAU v Commission*, ECR 3369 which stresses that one of the main role of preliminary administrative proceedings is to "*provide the undertakings concerned with an opportunity to bring the practices complained of into line with the rules of the Treaty*".

[55] See the latest Commission Notice on immunity from fines and reduction of fines in cartel cases, *OJ*, C 298, [2006], p. 17. See on the leniency Notice and its success, J.S. Sandhu, *E.C.L.R.* [2007], v. 3, n. 3, pp. 148-157.

[56] Paragraph 12 of the Notice mentioned above.

[57] See footnote 50 on the principle *venire contra factum proprium*. The undertakings may however challenge the discount obtained for cooperation and sometimes did it successfully (See e.g. CFI, 20 March 2002, Case T-31/99, *ABB v. Commission*, ECR II-1181 where *ABB*, the only multinational company in a cartel of small and medium sized family undertakings, and "*leader*" of the cartel was the only undertaking for which the CFI granted a reduction of the fine because the non-contesting of the facts and the absence of exercise of its rights of defence deserved to be better rewarded – even though the seriousness of the fines led in fact to the elimination from the market of the number 2 and number 3 in the market – than reinforcing ABB's position as a leader).

party makes the contestation of the facts by the other parties often rather difficult.

However the extent to which the allegations of "*repenting*" undertakings are always credible is another question. These undertakings denounce not only their practices but also those of competitors which were part of the cartel. Certain to obtain immunity or at least a significant reduction of the fine, the undertaking denouncing the agreement may be tempted to exaggerate the reality of the facts. The Commission – and subsequently the Court – have therefore in our opinion the obligation to verify scrupulously the statements made by the undertakings before using them against competitors. Confessions constitute only a starting point in the procedure and should be followed up by an in-depth inquiry. The EC Courts should ensure that the sentencing of an undertaking is not based only on the subjective confession of a competitor directly concerned.

2. – *The non-contestation of the facts – control by the judge*

In the initial 1996 Notice on leniency,[58] an undertaking could benefit from a reduction *in fine* if it disclosed the existence of an agreement but also if it did not contest the facts alleged in the statement of objections. Thus, a "*significant reduction*" was originally granted where "*an enterprise informs the Commission that it does not substantially contest the facts on which the Commission bases its allegations*". However, this practice was rapidly abandoned due *inter alia* to its lack of transparency, and its potentially discriminatory application. Moreover, arguably, the system could be perceived as infringing the rights of defence of undertakings,[59] in so far as it penalised undertakings for exercising their rights of defence.

In the *Cartonboard cartel* case,[60] the Commission accepted for instance to reduce the amount of the fines for some undertakings "*owing to the fact that in their replies to the statement of objections they had not contested the essential factual allegations on which the*

[58] Commission Notice on the non-imposition or reduction of fines in cartel cases, *OJ*, C 207, [1996], p. 4.

[59] CFI, 5 April 2006, Case T-279/02, *Degussa v. Commission*, ECR II-563; CFI, 14 May 1998, Case T-304/94, *Europa Carton AG v. Commission*, ECR II-869.

[60] CFI, 14 May 1998, Case T-347/94, *Mayr-Melnohf Kartongesellschaft mbH*, ECR II-1751.

Commission based its objections".[61] The CFI acknowledged in its judgment that the Commission should not in so doing breach "*the rights of the defence, a fundamental principle of the Community legal order (...), by exercising allegedly unlawful pressure on the applicant during the administrative procedure so as to induce it to acknowledge the factual allegations in the statement of objections*".[62] However, the CFI held that "*the fact that, without specifying the size of a reduction, the Commission indicates, during the administrative procedure, to an undertaking involved in the investigation that it would be possible to reduce the fine to be imposed if it were to admit most or all of the factual allegations, cannot of itself constitute pressure on that undertaking*".[63]

C. – The introduction of a settlement procedure in EC law

1. – *Origins of the system*

On 1st July 2008, the Commission published its new Regulation n° 622/2008 and Notice on the conduct of settlement procedures in cartel cases.[64] In these provisions, the Commission offers the possibility in certain cases to reduce the amount of fines by 10 % for undertakings which acknowledge their participation in a cartel, together with their liability and therefore accept "*expedited and simplified proceedings*". Contrary to the leniency program, what is rewarded here is not the fact that an undertaking discloses the existence of an infringement to the Commission, but the fact that the undertaking significantly renounces a number of procedural rights, and thus "*facilitates the life of the Commission*". As reported in the press, the purpose of this reform for the Commission is that its civil servants "*do not have to worry about details, the risk of judi-*

[61] See Paragraph 307 of the judgement mentioned above.

[62] See Paragraph 313 of the judgement mentioned above.

[63] See Paragraph 314 of the judgement mentioned above. Interestingly, the Commission at the time limited the "*bonus*" for cooperation to the absence of "*contestation of the facts*", the argument being then made that extending this "*bonus*" to those undertakings which renounce their legal arguments and not only purely factual arguments would violate the rights of the defence. This is a reservation which the Commission does not seem anymore to have as it decided to extend this policy to any undertaking which not only acknowledges its responsibility but also renounces its essential procedural rights in the context of a "*settlement*" (see below Section C).

[64] See the drafts in *OJ*, C 255, [2007], p. 48 and the definitive text in *OJ*, L 171, [2008], p. 3.

cial proceedings disappears", as does the necessity to enter into discussions with "*highly paid lawyers*".[65]

It should be noted that at this stage, the Commission does not envisage applying this procedure to cases other than cartels.

The implementation of a "*settlement*" procedure in the EU constitutes an additional means for the Commission to shorten the time period necessary for the assessment of the cases by concentrating its resources essentially on contested infringements. Thus, 35 to 40 % of the Commission's workload is devoted to anti-cartel enforcement today and proceedings take generally several years.[66] The "*settlement*" procedure, less formal, is supposed to enable the Commission to deal with the cases brought before it in more timely fashion. It allows the Commission to simplify the procedure for access to file (which often requires scrutinizing hundreds and thousands of pages and handling numerous and complex requests for confidentiality), as well as with holding oral hearings, to dispense with drafting detailed statements of objections and decisions, to avoid the translation of thousands of pages in a number of languages and finally to avoid lengthy judicial proceedings (with the risk of judicial disavowal).

This new "*settlement*" procedure is apparently inspired *inter alia* by various similar systems in a number of Member States as well as by the "*plea bargaining*" procedure frequently used by the "US *Department of Justice, Antitrust Division*" in the United States. This procedure – since its legality was confirmed by US Courts[67] – allows for a fast settlement of the dispute if the defendant does not contest the raised objections and accepts to cooperate in return for reduction of fine to an amount negotiated and agreed with the authority. Today, over 90 % of cartel cases in the United States are said to be settled through the "*plea bargaining*" procedure.

German competition law has a similar procedure ("*einvernehmlicher Bußgeldbescheid*") in which the German competition authority ("*Bundeskartellamt*") conducts discussions with the parties before

---

[65] See *Frankfurter Allgemeine Zeitung*, 13 November 2007, p. 22.

[66] M.J. Reynolds, D.G. Anderson, "Immunity and leniency in EU cartel cases : current issues", *E.C.L.R.*, [2006], vol. 27, n° 2, p. 82.

[67] See *Santobello v. New York*, 404 *US* 357, 260 (1971); *Blackledge v. Allison*, 431 *US* 63, 76 (1977). See also the "*Plea Agreement Guidelines*" of the "*US Department of Justice*" : "*Antitrust Grand Jury Practice Manual*", Chapter 9 (1st Edition 1991), available at http://usdoj.gov/atr/public/guidelines/207144.htm.

the statement of objections is sent so as to set the amount of the fine.[68] Further to the negotiations, the "*Bundeskartellamt*" adopts a draft decision. There is no undertaking not to appeal the decision.[69]

In French competition law, the Commercial Code[70] contains a similar procedure ("*non-contestation des griefs*"). In order to benefit from negotiated solutions, two conditions must be fulfilled : on the one hand, the undertaking under investigation should not contest the facts (but legal arguments can still be made) and, on the other hand, it undertakes to modify its behaviour in the future. This procedure may allow undertakings to benefit from a significant reduction of the fine. The commitments are negotiated with the *Rapporteur général* and then monitored and, if necessary confirmed by the *Conseil de la concurrence*. The *Conseil de la concurrence* has often imposed lower fines than those agreed with the *Rapporteur général.*[71] The French *Conseil de la concurrence* confirmed recently that this procedure was applicable to cartel cases – which has been discussed at lengths previously.[72]

Although inspired by the US "*plea bargaining*", the French and German procedures differ from it in the fact that the parties do not waive (at least legally speaking) their right to initiate legal actions.[73]

---

[68] See J. BURRICHTER and D.J. ZIMMER, "Reflections on the implementation of a 'plea bargaining'/'Direct settlement' system in EC competition law", in CD. See also EHLERMANN and ATANASIU, *European Competition Law Annual 2006 : enforcement of prohibition of cartels*, Hart Publishing Oxford, Portland, Oregon.

[69] However, where an appeal is nevertheless filed, the "*Bundeskartellamt*" withdraws its initial decision (which would be too short and would therefore not survive judicial scrutiny upon appeal) and adopts a new decision with more legal and factual details.

[70] Article L. 4642 III and R. 4674-4 of the French Commercial Code.

[71] However, in one case, the Council did not follow the proposals of the *Rapporteur général* and set higher fines, which seriously undermined the industry's confidence in this procedure. (See Decision 03-D-45 of 25 September 2003 of the *Conseil de la concurrence*, regarding practices in the school calculators sector, upheld by the judgement of the Paris Court of Appeal of 21 September 2004).

[72] See Decision 07-D-21 of 26 June 2007 of the *Conseil de la concurrence, Rental sector, clothing maintenance*.

[73] Finally, it is worth noting that, in our experience, the Commission has in the past occasionally used in practice – and outside any legal framework – similar negotiated solutions, for instance by committing not to impose fines if the undertaking commits itself not to challenge the decision before a Court. We had this experience in the *Bayer Dental* Case (Commission Decision of 28 November 1990, *Bayer Dental*, *OJ*, L 351, [1990], p. 46.) as well as in the alleged Belgian banks cartel, where the Commission accepted – after the statement of objections had been sent and after the oral hearings – not to take a formal decision nor *a fortiori* to impose a fine if the parties committed themselves to ensure the free change of Belgian Francs into Euros to consumers. Similar approaches were taken in the alleged German banks cartel.

Also in the United Kingdom, the OFT uses in practice a settlement procedure. This procedure is not regulated. In practice however, settlements tend to take place after the statement of objections.

The Commission underlines in its draft Notice that it would not be the only one to benefit from a "*settlement*". It is generally in the undertaking's best interest – the Commission argues – that the case be settled as quickly as possible with reduced procedural costs. And the interest will be even greater – still according to the Commission – if a speedy procedure is combined with a reduction of the fine. The negative publicity would be more limited. Furthermore, the infringement decisions will be shorter and the reasoning more concise. All the parties will – *dixit* the Commission – potentially take advantage of the procedure. In particular, it is clear that when an illicit agreement involving a company is discovered, it is easier for its corporate executive to spread the message that the problem has been "*sorted out*" through a supposed "*settlement*" with the Commission rather than having to make important contingencies and face continuous questions on proceedings that could last many years. [74]

2. – *The procedural safeguards for the main parties and third parties*

(a) *The procedural safeguards for the main parties*

(i) *The safeguards envisaged by the Commission*

In order to protect the parties' rights, some procedural safeguards are envisaged by the Commission. First, the main "*facts*

---

[74] Finally, since it is unlikely that a party will accept a "*settlement*" if it is not sure that it will not be prosecuted for the same facts in the different Member States, it is important here that, as in the case of a leniency application, the principle described in Article 11 (6) of Regulation 1/2003 applies and that the initiation of proceedings in order to conclude a "*settlement*" relieves national Courts or competition authorities of their competence. Therefore, according to the new amendment to Article 2 (1) of Regulation 773/2004, when the Commission considers it suitable to explore the parties' interest in engaging in settlement discussions, it will initiate proceedings no later than the date on which it either issues a statement of objections or requests the parties to express in writing their interest to engage in settlement discussions, whichever is the earlier. This constitutes a guarantee for the parties that only the Commission will be competent to apply Article 81 of the EC Treaty in the given case. (See Paragraphs 8 and 9 of the new Commission Notice on settlement proceedings).

alleged" as well as "*evidence used to establish the potential objections*" will be disclosed to the parties.[75]

The parties will however only "*be informed of the essential elements taken into consideration*",[76] and thus will be asked to settle before any statement of objection is issued. This goes further than initially envisaged by the Commission. Indeed, the Commission originally indicated that such a procedure could not take place before the notification of the statement of objections.[77]

Thus, contrary to the French procedure of "*non-contestation of objections*" for instance, the parties do not have unlimited access to the file, nor will they receive a proper statement of objections before "*settling*".[78]

A "*streamlined*" statement of objections will only be sent *after* the settlement. As to the file, no full access will be given, but only those documents chosen by the Commission. The parties will further renounce their right to a hearing, and the decision itself will also be in a short form.

As to the amount of fine to be imposed, the Commission indicates in a new Article 10*a* of Regulation 773/2004 that the parties willing to present proposals for "*settlement*" will be informed of the range of "*potential fines*".[79] The reduction rate for undertakings accepting a "*settlement*"[80] is of 10 %.

---

[75] The parties may also request the disclosure of certain specific documents in so far as the request is justified and reasonable. Nevertheless, it is for the Commission ultimately to decide whether or not it will grant access to the documents.

[76] See para 16 of the new Commission Notice.

[77] See the speech of Neelie KROES on 13 October 2006, SPEECH/06/595.

[78] As indicated below in Section 3, it is not clear that this approach is at all compatible with Article 27 of Regulation 1/2003.

[79] Similarily, in the United States, in the "*plea bargaining*" system, the discussions concern the maximum amount of the fine that cannot be exceeded in the final decision. (See Ted. R. Crim. Proc. Rule 11 (b) (1) (H) provinding that the Court should inform the defendant "*of any maximum possible penalty, including imprisonment fine and term of supervised release*" before it accepts to plead guilty) An undertaking will therefore be in a position to consider, regarding the incurred punishment, whether it is worth waiving its procedural rights. The French and German procedures are similar in this respect.

[80] Under French law, the *Conseil de la concurrence* draws a distinction concerning the reduction rate of the fine. If the underlying purpose is to reward procedural efficiencies, the rebates should not exceed 10 %. However, if the undertaking offers important commitments so as to remedy the infringement, the reduction may reach 25-30 % (see Decision of the French *Conseil de la concurrence*, n° 07-D-33 of 15 October 2007, *France Telecom*; n° 07-D-21 of 26 June 2007, *Rental sector, clothing maintenance*). It is worth noting that when a party decides not to contest the objections, the maximal amount of the fine is divided by two (5 % of the worldwide turnover instead of 10 %). Since the *France Télécom* case mentioned above, it seems that the Rapporteur general will offer a maximum amount of the fine rather than a reduction range in the future. If

In order to avoid the difficulties that arose from the concept of "*non-contestation of the facts*" set out in the first Leniency Notice, an offer of the same reduction to all the undertakings which accept to "*settle*" with the Commission is foreseen. Thereby, the Commission believes that it will avoid any criticism of possible discrimination.

In this regard, it is worth noting moreover that the reductions of fines resulting from the "*Notice on leniency*" could apply simultaneously with those of the "*Notice on settlements.*"

As mentioned by the Commission in its Draft Notice, "*reference to the 'potential fine' gives 'the Commission services the possibility to inform the parties concerned by settlement discussions of an estimate of their potential fine in view of the guidance contained in the Guidelines on fines, the provisions of this Notice and the Leniency Notice, where applicable'*".

Finally, it should be noted that the Draft Notice does not contain any provision with respect to the information of undertakings on the *wording of the decision* before "*settling*" with the Commission.

If the undertaking accepts the "*settlement*", it will be required to sign a statement with :

a) an "*acknowledgement in unequivocal terms*" of liability as regards "*the main facts, their legal qualification, and the duration of [its] participation in the infringement*";

b) a "*confirmation*" that it does not request further information regarding the "*objections*" raised against it;

c) a confirmation that it has been given "*sufficient opportunity to make [its] views known to the Commission*";

d) a "*confirmation*" that it does not contemplate "*requesting access to the file*"; and

e) a "*confirmation*" that it is not "*requesting to be heard again in an oral hearing*".[81]

---

the Council wants to exceed this amount, it will probably have to indicate it to the parties to allow them to decide if they maintain their request to benefit from the procedure of non-contestation of objections.

[81] See Paragraph 20 of the Commission Notice on settlements. Moreover, any party accepting a "*settlement*" is required to accept a succinct decision "*in an agreed official language of the European Community*" and to have a single representation (if there are several companies from the same group) (See Paragraphs 12 and 20 of the Commission Notice on settlements).

However, the Notice states that judicial review remains possible (although this is probably more theoretical than real, see below).[82]

(ii) *The compatibility of the system with the rights of defence*

When looking at the legitimacy of the proposed new settlement system, it is worthwhile recalling that it is generally accepted that in *criminal law*, only the offences expressly provided by the law, of relatively limited gravity and where the primary victim is the "*Administration*" may be subject to a "*settlement*".[83] The other offences in criminal law are excluded from the scope of "*settlements*" in criminal proceedings.[84] In addition, it should always remain possible to challenge the agreement before criminal or administrative Courts.[85] Finally, it appears that a "*settlement*" in criminal proceedings is subject to increasingly strict conditions and procedural guarantees, the Administration's margin for manœuvre to negotiate the terms of the agreement being more controlled and the right to appeal more extensive.[86]

Reference can in this context be made in particular to the Opinion of Advocate General Ruiz-Jarabo Colomer of 19 September 2002 in Case C-187/01, *Gözütok*. Following an extensive comparative law analysis of settlement procedures in criminal law cases in 14 Member States, the Advocate general notes that settlements are in all systems only possible for minor offences "*which do not require the imposition of heavy sentences*". He stresses also that the procedure "*is characterised by the fact that the State authorities act from a position of superiority*", i.e. it is not a negotiation among equals, and that there is therefore a need for strict guarantees for the protection of the rights of the parties concerned. He also makes the point that "*the freedom to accept or reject the settlement is fundamental*" and that these should be no undue pressure to sign.

Mutatis mutandis, one may wonder whether similar principles should not apply in competition law cases where significant fines are imposed.

[82] See para. 41 of the Notice according to which decisions are "*subject to judicial review*" under EC Articles 229-230.

[83] J.F. DUPRÉ, *La transaction en matière pénale*, Ed. Litec Droit, 1977.

[84] *Ibidem*.

[85] *Ibidem*.

[86] *Ibidem*.

The fundamental question is, in our view, whether such a "*settlement*" procedure where undertakings are asked to renounce their essential procedural rights – with the risk otherwise that heavier fines will be imposed – is at all compatible with the rights of the defence.

In practice, as indicated the undertaking will be succinctly informed of the alleged objections, of the existence of a few documents which underpin the accusation and will be promised a maximum fine if it accepts:

– to plead guilty;

– to renounce access to the file;

– to renounce the right to a proper statement of objections,[87] and

– to renounce the right to an oral hearing.

If it refuses, it cannot be excluded that it will incur a much heavier sentence (not yet defined). Thus, the pressure on parties to "*settle*" might be in practice high. Or, to use the words of President Badinter regarding the implementation in France of a "*guilty plea*" procedure for minor criminal offences: "*which accused will resist? Which lawyer will advise his client to refuse the proposal and risk a more severe sentence than the one proposed? In this procedure, the 'level playing field' and equality is actually 'the weak against the strong'. As for the judge, his/her only remaining task will be to endorse the agreement or reject it, without being able to propose any amendment. An almighty Prosecutor, a begging lawyer and a controlling judge, this is what we qualify, in tens of thousands cases, as French 'guilty plea'. The heart of the criminal procedure is the oral hearing. It is the place where the extent of evidence, liability, and finally of the sentence and of damages for the victim is decided. During the oral hearing, the Prosecutor is not a privileged party. The hearings are public. Since the Revolution, this publicity is a guarantee for the accused and for the people that justice is neither manipulated nor confiscated. With the 'guilty plea' procedure, we skip the oral hearing, we fall into administrated repression and raise suspicions as to a fair trial*".[88]

[87] The statement of objections is sent only after the commitment by the undertaking, in order, it is assumed, to respect the requirements set out in Article 27 of Regulation 1/2003 and the Commission should effectively take it into account (see Paragraphs 23-27 of the Notice). However, since the "*settlement*" actually took place before the statement of objections was issued, this becomes somewhat artificial.

[88] See R. Badinter, "On tombe dans la répression administrée et on ouvre la voie à tous les soupçons", *Le Monde*, 27.1.2004. Translated from French.

(iii) *The difficulty to accept "settlements" without minimal procedural guarantees*

As indicated above, very few procedural safeguards will be applicable before settlements are signed. Settlements should take place before any Statement of Objections are sent, the parties being only "*informed of the essential elements taken into consideration*" by the Commission.[89] Parties will not be given access to the file but only to a few selected pieces of evidence at the discretion of the Commission. They are supposed on this basis to plead guilty "*in unequivocal terms*", both as regards "*the main facts, their legal qualification, and the duration of [their] participation in the infringement*". They will also have to renounce their right to a hearing, and the decision itself will be "*streamlined*".

Thus, the system is significantly less transparent than initially envisaged (where settlements were only considered possible after a proper statement of objections – see above). It is also less transparent than in other systems – such as France or the United Kingdom– where a settlement normally only takes place after a normal statement of objections is sent (see above).

Thus, the reward is not for "*some procedural efficiency*" but for effectively giving up in practice most procedural rights.

Clearly the system inherently implies that there must be some "*trade off*" between procedural economies for the Commission, but also sufficient procedural guarantees to ensure proper decision-making. But it is unclear in our view that a proper balance has been found in this regard by the Commission :

- First, it is clearly difficult for a party to settle if objections are not defined properly (see above about the difficulties sometimes encountered for Article 9 decisions if the "*preliminary assessment*" is not clear). Past experience shows that there are numerous instances where the Commission dropped even cartel cases altogether after the statement of objections,[90] or at least dropped it against certain companies,[91] or reduced the scope or duration of the alleged infringement. Therefore, it would seem to us necessary

[89] See para. 16 of the Notice.

[90] See for instance the alleged bank cartel cases at the time the Euro was introduced.

[91] This has been very frequent, often for minor players, or where it was not clear which entity in a group was liable.

for the Commission first to set out its objections fully in a statement of objections *before* settlements are considered;

- Second, also without access to the file, the risk to reach wrong conclusions is much greater (it is difficult in big companies to keep accurate track record of everything that may happened; employers may leave the company or have died; documents may disappear, etc.)[92];
- Third, even where full adversarial procedures were followed, respecting all the rights of the parties, the court occasionally found that the Commission had been wrong to find the existence of a cartel.[93] The risk of error or of "*sloppy*" work appears however to us to be much higher if none of the usual procedural requirements apply and if ultimately judicial control is more theoretical than real.

In conclusion, it seems to us therefore that at least some basic procedural safeguards should be introduced before a settlement is agreed to (in particular a proper statement of objections as initially envisaged).

(iv) *The particular problem arising from the fact that the applicable fine, should the undertaking defend itself is unknown and unforeseeable*

In addition to the fact that procedural rights are extremely limited in the current draft notice, it should be noted that for such a "*settlement*" to be admissible, it is essential that the undertakings are aware not only of the amount of "*potential fines*" they could face if they enter a "*settlement*" but also the amount of the fines that would be imposed in the absence of one.[94] If undertakings do not know the maximum amount of the potential fine incurred in the absence of a "*settlement*" the pressure to sign is great.

Thus, in the United States, the "*Antitrust Division*" of the "*Department of Justice*" considers that the procedure for setting the

[92] And indeed the Commission may itself not present the facts accurately. See e.g. for an extreme example the *SIV case* where the CFI found in its judgment that some documents had even been "*manipulated*" by the Commission; CFI, 10 March 1992, *SIV v. Commission*, cases T-68/89, T-77/89 and T-78/89, [1992] ECR II-1546.

[93] See e.g. the *Woodpulp* and *Italian Flat Glass Cartel* cases.

[94] K. Gardiner, B. Calhoun, M. Scarlato, V. Soyez, "Exchanging glances", *Global Competition Review*, August-September 2007, p. 37.

fines should be transparent and foreseeable for the undertakings. Consequently, the fines are set in compliance with the "*US Sentencing Guidelines*" [95] which are said to set out precisely the elements that should be taken into account for the calculation of the fine in the context of a "*plea bargaining*" procedure. [96]

In this regard, and without expressing any view as to how clear the US sentencing guidelines are, we certainly do not believe that the new Commission Guidelines on the method of setting fines [97] are sufficiently precise to allow the undertaking to know the amount of the fine normally incurred in the absence of "*settlement*". First, as regards the basic amount of the fine, the Commission may take into account the relevant market "*in the relevant geographic area within the EEA*" but also beyond this territory if necessary. The basic amount of the fine may go as far as 30 % of this amount, and generally "*at the higher end of that scale*" for the most serious infringement like cartels. Aggravating or mitigating circumstances may result in the increase or decrease of the basic amount. For instance, in the case of repeat offences, the basic amount will be increased by "*up to 100% for each such infringement established*". The Commission may also "*increase the fine to be imposed on undertakings which have a particularly large turnover beyond the sales of goods or services to which the infringement relates*", but a reduction could be granted "*in a specific social and economic context*". We are clearly far from a precise mathematical formula and considering the amount of the fines imposed to this date as well as the margin left to the Commission, it can double, triple or quadruple.

It is common knowledge that the Commission is traditionally opposed to any transparency in this matter. According to the Commission, too much foreseeablity in the setting of fines would enable

[95] See *US Sentencing guidelines manual*, 1 November 2004, §2R1.1., p. 286.

[96] Part R of the *US Sentencing guidelines manual* entitled "*Antitrust offenses*" provides precise figures concerning the amount of the fines. The amount is set depending on the entity responsible for the infringement to competition law (legal person or individuals). Moreover, an "*offense level*" is attributed to each type of infringement which will determine the basic amount of the fine. This basic amount will be adjusted depending on several factors such as the undertaking's volume of commerce or the benefits or losses due to the infringement. It should be noted that stricter criteria apply to some infringements considered as particularly serious (for instance "*bid rigging*"). The "*Antitrust Division*" of the "*Department of Justice*" should thereafter refer to a table which recapitulates the basic amount of the fine depending on the seriousness of the infringement (Part C of the US sentencing guidelines).

[97] Guidelines on the method of setting fines imposed pursuant to Article 23(2)(a) of Regulation n° 1/2003, *OJ*, [2006], C 210, p. 2.

undertakings to calculate the likely "*cost/benefit ratio*" and assess from the beginning whether it is worth infringing competition rules.[98] Apart from the difficulties it raises in a system of "*settlements*", the position of the Commission on this point seems questionable in its principle. It seems indeed natural in the legal order of things, that a person subject to trial should know what he/she risks if he/she behaves in a given manner (as it is the case in criminal law).[99]

In those circumstances, is such a "*bonus*" for a party which does not defend itself – i.e. in reality a "*penalty*" of a unknown amount for the one which chooses to exercise its rights of defence – at all compatible with the rights of the defence and non-self-incrimination[100]?

– Reference must here be made to the case-law of the European Court of Human Rights' ("*ECHR*"). In the *Deweer* Case[101] for instance, the ECHR condemned a system of criminal "*settlements*" implemented in Belgium. The applicant, a butcher by profession, violated a ministerial order regarding the sale price of meat to consumers. The Royal Prosecutor proposed that the case be settled and that the applicant pay 10 000 Belgian francs. Otherwise, the applicant would face temporary closure of his shop as well prosecution and risk from one month to five years of imprisonment and a fine ranging from a minimum amount of 3000 Belgian francs to a maximum amount of 30 000 000 Belgian francs, as well as the potential definitive closure of his butchery. In its judgment, the ECHR acknowledges that the "*right to a judge*" is sub-

---

[98] See Neelie KROES's speech, "The first hundred days", 7 April 2005, SPEECH/05/205; See also the speech given by M.G. ROCCA on 4 February 2003 in *Les Mardis de la concurrence*, at the Institute for European Studies, Free University of Brussels.

[99] Moreover and in any event, an undertaking can never be aware of the final cost of a conviction it would incur, since in addition to the fine, there is a risk of private damages actions by individuals and competitors in different Member States or elsewhere.

[100] Whilst the CFI seems to have accepted in the *Mayr Melnhof Case* mentioned above the legality of a system where, "without specifying the size of a reduction, the Commission indicates, during the administrative procedure, to an undertaking involved in the investigation that it would be possible to reduce the fine to be imposed if it were to admit most or all of the factual allegations" (CFI, 14 May 1998, Case T-347/94, *Mayr-Melnhof Kartongesellschaft mbH*, ECR II-1751, para 314), it should be noted that the CFI ruled only on a system of non-contestation of "facts" and and not one where they renounce their legal arguments and in particular their rights of defence. The rights of the defence – as well as the right to a judge – are undoubtedly public policy provisions; moreover, the statement of the CFI has not been confirmed, to our knowledge, by the ECJ. More importantly, we note that it is questionable whether it is compatible with ECHR case-law.

[101] ECHR, 27 February 1980, *Deweer v. Belgium*, Case n° 6903/75.

ject to implied limitations, even in criminal proceedings, such as a decision not to prosecute and an order for discontinuance of the proceedings. The ECHR also admits that *"fines paid by way of composition"* are frequently encountered and have *"undeniable advantages for the individual concerned as well as for the administration of justice"*. According to the ECHR, such a concept *"does not constitute in principle a violation of the Convention"*.[102] The ECHR also notes[103] that *"while the prospect of having to appear in court is certainly liable to prompt a willingness to compromise on the part of many persons 'charged with a criminal offence', the pressure thereby brought to bear is in no way incompatible with the Convention."* However, what the ECHR considers unacceptable is the *"combined use of the two procedures"* i.e. the settlement and the temporary closure of the shop. It is indeed essential that a *"settlement"* takes place without *"constraint"*. But in the given case, *"there was a 'flagrant disproportion' between the two alternatives facing the applicant. The 'relative moderation' of the sum demanded [...] added to the pressure brought to bear by the closure order. The moderation rendered the pressure so compelling that it is not surprising that Mr. Deweer yielded"*.[104] The ECHR concludes that *"Mr. Deweer's waiver of a fair trial attended by all the guarantees which are required in the matter by the Convention was tainted by constraint. There has accordingly been breach of Article 6, Para 1"*[105];

- similarly, in a recent judgement, the German *Bundesgerichtshof* expressed its reservations regarding the settlement procedure as against the constitutional principle of the separation of powers; the *Bundesgerichtshof* also underlined the urgency of a legislative reform in this area.[106] According to the Court, any *"settlement"* should be subject to careful judicial review to see if the parties faced undue pressure but also to ensure that the facts have been correctly established and that the sentence is appropriate. In one case for instance, a confession was obtained under the threat of

[102] See Paragraph 49 of the judgment mentioned above. We assume that what the ECHR meant by *"fines paid by way of composition"* are classic settlements for minor offenses, such as parking fines.

[103] Paragraph 51 (b) of the judgment.

[104] See Paragraph 51 *in fine* of the judgment mentioned above.

[105] See Paragraph 54 of the judgment mentioned above.

[106] BGH, Case GSST 1/04, *BGHST* 50, 40; *NJW*, 2005, 1440, 1443.

immediate arrest.[107] In another case, the accused was offered a two year suspended prison sentence if he confessed and waived his rights, or a six year prison sentence otherwise.[108] According to the *Bundesgerichtshof*, such methods are incompatible with a "*Rule of law*";

- finally, in France, several decisions of the *Conseil constitutionnel* on settlements in criminal proceedings confirmed that a sentence should necessarily be delivered by a judge. (Note that this excludes *de facto* the possibility of settlement in an institutional context as in the Community where the Commission is both judge and prosecutor). In that respect, reference can be made to Decision N° 95360 DC of 2 February 1995 of the *Conseil constitutionnel* condemning the criminal injunction procedure.[109] The *Conseil constitutionnel* considered that the Prosecution cannot pronounce criminal sanctions in violation of individual freedoms. These measures *require a decision by a judicial authority*. In support of its decision, the *Conseil constitutionnel* invoked successively i) the presumption of innocence, ii) the role of the judicial authority as guardian of individual freedoms, iii) the rights of the defence, and iv) separation of the prosecution and judgment authorities, which principle derives from the right to a fair trial and contributes to the protection of individual freedoms. Reference may also be made to Decision N° 2004-492 of 2 March 2004 regarding the French procedure of the "*appearance (before the Court) after preliminary acknowledgement of liability*".[110] The *Conseil constitutionnel* admitted the principle of this procedure with some reservations concerning the right to a fair trial in general, and more precisely the principle of separation of prosecution and judgment authorities. In this regard, the *Conseil constitutionnel* stressed that the judge should maintain a significant power of appraisal at the stage of acceptance or refusal of the homologation (legal qualification of facts, taking into account the victim's statements, public interest, etc.).

[107] See *Paderborn* Case, *BGH, NSt Z*, 2005, 279 : *St V*, 2004, 636.

[108] BGH, *St V*, 2004, 470 (471).

[109] Article 35 of the Draft Act regarding the organisation of tribunals and civil, criminal and administrative procedures which became Act n° 95-125 of 8 February 1995.

[110] "*Comparution préalable sur reconnaissance de culpabilité*" or "*CRPC*". Article 137 of the "*Perben II*" Act of 9 March 2004.

(v) *The additional problem that the judge is not involved in controlling the settlement*

A final problem with the new settlement system introduced by the Commission is that the Community judge is not involved in the settlement procedure.

In most systems, the accused party is informed of the objections raised against it as well as the maximum sentence incurred if it pleads guilty but it is the judge who sets the fine. For instance in the United States, although the plea agreement is negotiated by the "*Antitrust Division*" in the absence of a judge [111] who can only accept or reject the agreement, the agreement is still subject to judicial approval afterwards. The US judge thus controls, in accordance with Article 11(b)(2) of the *Federal Rules of Criminal Procedure* whether the "*settlement*" "*did not result from force, threats or promises*", whether the undertaking has effectively renounced its rights voluntarily, knowingly and whether it was assisted by a lawyer. [112] Moreover, the intervention of a judge is a guarantee that the "*Antitrust Division*" will be more careful. [113]

Similarly in France, it is the *Conseil de la concurrence* – as an independent third party – that adopts a decision on the "*settlement*" proposed by the Rapporteur général. [114] The case-law of the *Conseil*

[111] Under Article 11(c)(1) of the Federal Rules of Criminal Procedure, the judge is expressly prohibited from participating in the negotiations.

[112] See Scott D. HAMMOND, "The US model of negotiated plea agreement : a good deal with benefits for all", *OECD Competition Committee working party,* n° 3, http://www.usdoj.gov/atr/public/speeches/219332.htm.

[113] *Ibidem.*

[114] French criminal law has since an Act of 9 March 2004 (now Articles 495-7 and 495-16 of the Code de procédure pénale) a procedure of "*appearance after preliminary acknowledgement of culpability*" ("*Plaider coupable*") for minor offences. This procedure applies to persons who have committed an offence punished with a fine or jail sentence of maximum 5 years. The accused is summoned before the Prosecutor and must be assisted by his/her lawyer. The procedure allows the Prosecutor to propose a determined punishment directly and without trial under the condition that the person acknowledges the alleged facts. The Prosecutor will propose to issue a jail sentence of maximum one year or a fine which cannot exceed the amount of the maximum fine incurred. Following the proposal by the Prosecutor, the accused has three options :

- either he/she refuses the proposal;
- or he/she requests a reflexion time-period;
- or he/she accepts the proposal.

If he/she accepts the Prosecutor's proposal, a minute is drafted. Hereafter, the homologation phase before the judge starts. The defendant is heard by the President of the Tribunal of First Instance. The Tribunal should verify the acknowledgement of the facts, whether these are substantiated together with their legal qualification. The judge will then decide whether or not he/she will accept the Prosecutor's proposal but cannot amend it. The homologation of the punishment is carried out through an Order which is immediately applicable and should be notified

Constitutionnel requires – as mentioned – such a system for "*settlements*" in criminal proceedings.

Under EC law, the situation is obviously different since it is not the judge but the Administration which imposes the fines. No need however to stress the fact that Article 6 of the European Convention for Human Rights provides that "*in the determination of his civil rights and obligations or of any criminal charge against him, everyone is entitled to a fair and public hearing within a reasonable time by an independent and impartial tribunal established by law*".[115] As we know, there are strong reasons to consider that the fines imposed in competition law are of a criminal nature in spite of the wording of Article 23(5) of Regulation 1/2003.[116] Since the Commission is under the obligation to respect fundamental rights when setting a fine, the question of the legality of the "*settlement*" procedure will therefore inevitably be raised in a system where the fine is imposed by the Commission and not by a judge.

Fully aware of this, the Commission has indicated in its Notice that nothing would prevent an undertaking from challenging the final decision before a Court. As is the case in Germany, the Commission indicates that there will be a right to appeal. In this respect, we observe however that such actions will have limited chances of success since the undertaking has "*acknowledged the infringement.*" Therefore, it is unclear whether the undertaking may at all challenge a decision that it has negotiated and accepted, except when the parties offered it "*under the arbitrary constraint of the Commission*" (*Cementbouw* case-law mentioned above) – which will raise some difficulties for the undertakings in terms of evidence. The Commission would then be able to adopt a much less detailed

to the defendant who may challenge it within 10 days (see the reservations of R. Badinter in Section C(d) (b) above).

[115] Emphasis added.

[116] See for more details in this regard *inter alia* D. Waelbroeck and D. Fosselard, *op. cit.* See also CEDH, *Deweer v. Belgium*, n° 6903/75; Cases *Société Stenuit v. France*, n° 11598/55; and *Lilly France SA v. France*, n° 58892/00. AG Mayras also stressed the criminal nature of fines long before their amount became very significant (Opinion of AG Mayras, 29 October 1975, Case 26/75, *General Motors v. Commission*, ECR 1367). In any event, even if fines were not of a criminal nature Recital 37 of Regulation 1/2003 compels the Community to respect "*the fundamental rights and [observe] the principle recognised in particular by the Charter of Fundamental Rights of the European Union*". Article 47 of the Charter provides that "*everyone is entitled to a fair and public hearing within a reasonable time by an independent and impartial tribunal previously established by law*".

decision similar to those adopted under Article 9 of Regulation 1/2003 [117].

It seems to us therefore that the possibilities of challenges in court for the parties will be *de facto* almost inexistent. As for the other parties that refused to settle, the case-law provides that a party cannot complain about the illegality in the setting of the fine of another party which is party to the same infringement. [118] Thus, the Commission could well have developed a system which *de facto* falls outside all judicial review, i.e. which is outside any proper system of "*checks and balances*".

For all the reasons mentioned above, it seems to us that the solution which is most compatible with our legal traditions would be to leave, as in most States, the final decision to the judge. Any proposed settlement would have to be officialised by a judge so as to make it binding (this would also be published). Although the intervention of a judge might slow down the proceedings, somewhat, it would ensure ultimately better procedural safeguards and be more compatible with our general system of law.

Indeed in such a system, the judge setting the fine, would be automatically involved in the final decision. The automatic involvement of the judge allows for not only the control of the legality of the procedure but also for the respect of the public interest in the final decision. It would also present the advantage that where the final decision lies with the judge and not with the prosecuting Administration, the pressure to "*settle*" is less significant.

In this regard, reference can be made to the case-law of the German *Bundesgerichtshof* quoted above according to which the obligation for courts to investigate the material truth of the case is not open to discussion between the parties, as it raises "*public policiy*" interests.

(vi) *Conclusions*

We conclude that the system introduced by the Commission raises a number of serious problems both as regards insufficient pro-

---

[117] However, it is clear that if an action is launched, the Commission will probably have to withdraw its decision and replace it with a new decision with a longer reasoning (a decision with concise reasoning will not survive judicial review). This possibility could be expressly provided in the "*settlement*" decision.

[118] CFI, 14 May 1998, Case T-327/94, *SCA Holding*, ECR II-1373, para 160; CFI, 29 April 2004, Case T-236/01, *Tokai Carbon*, ECR II-1181, para 316.

cedural safeguards, risks of undue pressure and non-involvement of the judge in the procedure.

(b) *The procedural safeguards for third parties*

It is difficult to see how third parties and particularly complainants would be able to participate in the proceedings. Contrary to the Commission's practice in the context of Article 9 of Regulation 1/2003, it is hardly conceivable that a draft settlement be published in order to gather the comments of third parties.[119] The Commission itself indeed even insists in paragraph 7 of the Notice that "*the parties to the proceedings may not disclose to any third party in any jurisdiction the contents of the discussions or of the documents which they have had access to in view of settlement*". More generally, the Commission is inclined to limit the rights of third parties in other respects. Thus, paragraph 40 of the Notice, according to the Commission, states that "*public disclosure of documents and written or recorded statements (including settlement submissions) received in the context of this Notice would undermine certain public or private interests, for example the protection of the purpose of inspections and investigations*", which presumably justifies the absence of public disclosure.

Also the situation of third parties is therefore less favourable than in normal procedures.

3. – *The legal basis issue*

Finally, it is striking that no amendment to Regulation 1/2003 was proposed by the Commission. The decisions will still be adopted under Articles 7 and 23 of Regulation 1/2003, but the procedural Regulation 773/2004 has been amended to adapt the procedures accordingly. This allowed the adoption procedure to occur rapidly since the assent of the Community legislator was not necessary.

However, given the strict requirements set out in Article 27 of Regulation 1/2003 regarding the rights of the defence via a statement of objections, access to file, oral hearings, etc., it is unclear whether the Commission has at all the power to adopt rules inter-

[119] The latter would only be able to make comments on the amount of the fine and not on the commitments or other remedies.

fering as fundamentally with these rights on its own initiative without amending Regulation 1/2003 itself. Indeed, Regulation 773/2004 is merely an implementing Regulation adopted on the basis of Article 33 of Regulation 1/2003 which only authorizes the Commission to take measures concerning "*the practical arrangements for the hearings provided for in Article 27*".[120] The formal settlement procedure in Regulation 1/2003 – i.e. Article 9 – besides expressly provides that it is not applicable in cartel cases (or in cases where a fine is envisaged – see Recital 13 – presumably because a "*settlement*" under the threat of a fine is not a genuine "*settlement*"; see *supra* Section A (5)).

D. – Conclusions

In the present contribution, we have tried to discuss the increasing use by the Commission of "*negotiated solutions*". In particular, three major points have been made hereabove :

- first, especially when fines are at stake, but also when important remedies or commitments are required from the undertakings, acting outside certain procedural safeguards, which alone are able to provide justice as well as quality of decisions, raises a number of problems. Therefore, it seems to us that a more transparent procedure respecting some basic rights of the parties would be warranted (and in particular a true statement of objections as was initially envisaged by the Commission when it first considered introducing a settlement procedure, or a proper "*preliminary assessment*" – similar to a statement of objections – for Article 9 decisions);
- second, to avoid any undue pressure on the parties to agree to settlements, it seems to us that there is a need for more clarity on the fine level if no settlement is agreed than is currently the case;
- finally, as we have tried to show, it is essential that the EC judge controls in all circumstances the final decision particularly where settlements with fines are at stake. In our view, the fundamental requirements of our legal system can indeed only be respected if

[120] The Commission tries to avoid this obstacle at Paragraphs 23-27 of its Notice by providing an *ex post* statement of objections after the undertaking has renounced to its rights which – as indicated – hardly resolves the problem.

a distinct authority, independent from the Commission, plays the role of a "*judge*" following the inquiry of the Commission services. A system where the Administration is not subject to any control is fundamentally problematic under the Rule of law.

CONTENTS

PART I.

PRIVATE ENFORCEMENT

PART II.

SETTLEMENTS AND COMMITMENTS

PART III.

TRANSVERSAL ISSUES

IMPRIMÉ EN BELGIQUE

ETABLISSEMENTS EMILE BRUYLANT, société anonyme, Bruxelles
Prés.-Dir. gén. : JEAN VANDEVELD, av. W. Churchill, 221, 1180 Bruxelles